Educating
the Infant
and Toddler

———

Educating the Infant and Toddler

Burton L. White, Ph.D.

Center for Parent Education

Lexington Books

D.C. Heath and Company/Lexington, Massachusetts/Toronto

Library of Congress Cataloging-in-Publication Data

White, Burton L., 1929–
Educating the infant and toddler.

Bibliography: p.
Includes index.
1. Education, Preschool—United States—Parent
participation.   2. Child development—United States.
3. Education, Preschool—Missouri—Parent participation—
Case studies.   I. Title.
LB1140.35.P37W44   1988   372'.21   86-45293
ISBN 0-669-13137-7 (alk. paper)
ISBN 0-669-13136-9 (pbk. : alk. paper)

Published simultaneously in Canada
Printed in the United States of America
Casebound International Standard Book Number: 0-669-13137-7
Paperbound International Standard Book Number: 0-669-13136-9
Library of Congress Catalog Card Number: 86-45293

The paper used in this publication meets
the minimum requirements of American National Standard
for Information Sciences—Permanence of Paper
for Printed Library Materials, ANSI Z39.48-1984.

88 89 90 8 7 6 5 4 3 2 1

This book is dedicated to Barbara Finberg of the
Carnegie Corporation of New York and Jane
Paine of the Danforth Foundation of St. Louis.
These women have been program officers for
their respective foundations for many years.
Because of the nature of their jobs, they rarely
receive either attention or due credit for their
work. I believe each of these women is
extraordinary in her dedication, her talent, and
her vision. Without them, my work—and indeed
a good deal of other work of special significance
performed over the past twenty years—would
probably not have been done.

Contents

Figures and Tables

Figures

Tables

Preface and Acknowledgments

Have you ever wondered why children first go to school when they are five or six years old? This is generally true in all countries with national educational systems. Some countries don't begin the process until the child is seven years old, and, on occasion, there is talk of lowering the school admission age to four years. Nevertheless, five or six years has been the starting point ever since public education became common during the last century.

Certain events since 1965, however, seem to be leading to dramatic changes in that policy. Research associated with the Head Start project has focused attention on learning in the first years of life. It seems clear that if a child of three years of age is advanced in respect to language and intellectual skills, he is very likely to be well prepared for formal education when he turns five or six. Equally important is the fact that a child who is nine months or more behind in language and intelligence at three years of age rarely achieves above average or even average levels of later educational success.

Such powerful findings have led to numerous attempts to help parents become more effective teachers, starting with the very first days of their children's lives. These efforts are called *education for parenthood*. A wonderfully successful education for parenthood program has just been completed in the state of Missouri. That program and the recent research discoveries upon which it was based are the focal points of this book.

This book has two central purposes: (1) to provide the professional or professional-in-training with reliable, practical information on what is known and what is not known about the learning process and about how to work with parents of infants and toddlers; and (2) to tell the story of the Missouri project—its origins, goals, methods, and results.

Although my colleagues and I have always tried to maintain a strict focus on education, our definition of education is broad. I never have been interested only in the academic aspects of early development. I always have embraced a "whole child" orientation, with a primary emphasis on the interpersonal qualities of the child. In other words, my goal has been the production of children who are not merely bright but are also emotionally secure and a pleasure to live with.

This focus does have limitations, in that it does not address special needs situations, nor does it fully address full-time day care of infants and toddlers. I have concentrated on children who are free from serious mental and physical handicaps (for example, prematurity, Down's syndrome, deafness), who are being raised mainly in their own homes by their own families, and whose parents are not suffering from debilitating problems themselves (such as abject poverty or alcoholism). I believe that most of the information provided here will be applicable to approximately 85 percent of the children and family situations one could encounter, and much of it will be applicable to any child under any circumstances.

One of the more striking features of this book is its background. It is based on an unusually extensive history of sustained research on the role of experience in the development of young children. That research began at Brandeis University in 1957 with a small-scale study of young infants. It expanded dramatically in 1965 with the creation of the Harvard Preschool Project, which existed for thirteen years. Our early findings were tested in large-scale, school-based research performed for several years in the Brookline, Massachusetts, public schools and, from 1981 to 1985, in Missouri's New Parents as Teachers project. In all, the research has spanned about twenty-eight years. The recently announced results of the Missouri project constitute some of the most powerful evidence to date for the value of parent education.

This book presumes the reader's acquaintance with basic information about the development of infants and toddlers. Part I presents my views of what I call "the knowledge base," discussing what I believe is currently known and not known about all major developments in the first three years of life (e.g., the development of language, motor abilities, social skills). Part II presents a wide variety of issues of practical importance to professionals and parents (e.g., the effects of sibling spacing, a consideration of bonding), and part III discusses specific educational issues. Finally, part IV provides an extensive treatment of the Missouri project and concludes with some brief final comments. Appendixes list and discuss resources for professionals and parents.

The book is designed to help practitioners and students of early education. It is aimed at professionals working in the field with parents and at undergraduate and graduate students preparing for careers in education for parenthood in particular and in early childhood development in general.

Acknowledgments

I owe gratitude to a very long list of individuals. Support for my research efforts over the years was provided by key individuals at Brandeis, MIT, and Harvard—most conspicuously, Peter Wolff, Richard Held, and Gerald Lesser. The type of research that I have been engaged in costs a great deal of money. Two especially helpful supporters over the years have been Barbara Finberg of the Carnegie Corporation and Jane Paine of the Danforth Foundation.

Numerous personnel in the Missouri project made major contributions. Two that should be singled out are Mildred Winter, the project director, and Arthur Mallory, the state's commissioner of education.

For ten years now, I have worked closely with Dr. Michael K. Meyerhoff. His efforts in connection with the operations of the Harvard Preschool Project, the Center for Parent Education, and Missouri's New Parents as Teachers project have been consistently valuable and very much appreciated.

Finally, the single greatest source of information in my research over the years has been families of many kinds. Without the cooperation of literally thousands of young parents, this book could never have been written.

Introduction

The information in this book about how children learn in their first years and the information about how professionals can assist families in connection with that learning have a common source—my long-standing interest in how well-developed adults get to be that way. It was that interest, first clearly perceived in the 1950s, that led to my sustained career involvement in research on human development. It was a happy accident that soon after the beginning of that work, the civil rights movement began to gather strength; that strength, in turn, led to the creation of the Head Start project in 1965, which ushered in a twenty-year period of focused study on development in the first years of life unlike anything else in history.

The initial focus of my interest was not on babies but on adults. My work in psychology soon led to the conclusion that to understand how a well-developed adult got to be that way, one had to pay particular attention to the experiences of the early years of life. My specific research on the development of early abilities, which began in 1957 at Brandeis University under the direction of Richard Held, focused on the first six months of life and involved vision and the infant's acquisition of the ability to reach for objects under the guidance of the eyes. That research effort was quite small, generally involving only two people at a time. The results focused on the details of the development of vision skills and on the effects of attempts to help those skills develop better—most commonly the design of crib environments for new babies.

That work probably could have gone on for many years except for an accident in history. In 1965, Project Head Start was announced. It received enormous publicity, and a great deal of money was made available for research on the general topic of learning during the preschool years. Along with several other institutions, the School of Education at Harvard was granted a very large amount of money to establish a research center in education, a part of which was to focus on preschool learning. Harvard engaged my services in 1965 as a result of my suggestions about how to approach the subject of early learning. A very substantial amount of research money was made available, and the Harvard Preschool Project was born. Its purpose was to explore the question of how *any* child could be helped to make the most of his or her innate potential through the provision of the most beneficial experiences throughout the first six years of life. The Preschool Project, which employed some seventeen full-time researchers, concentrated heavily on observations of many different kinds of children as they went about their daily activities in their own homes.

The project's first target was the question of the definition of a well-developed six-year-old. Its second target was determining when in the early years signs of very good development first surfaced. Only two or three years after its inception, the project personnel concluded, as a group, that all the distinguishing characteristics of wonderful six-year-olds were sometimes present by the third birthday. At about the same time, Head Start research was coming to similar conclusions about the importance of development in the first three years of life. Reports that were being published in the late 1960s made it increasingly clear that reversing the poor pattern of development after the third birthday was a surprisingly difficult enterprise. There was, indeed, a strong trend in experimental programs focused on children from low-income families toward intervening well before the third birthday.

In addition to the findings of the Preschool Project and Head Start research programs, early important work in the field of child development research reinforced the notion that the first years of life were of special importance. Maternal deprivation studies that began in the mid-1940s had convinced most mental health specialists that the first years were critical for building important social and emotional foundations in a child. Piaget's work on the development of intelligence was coming into its own in the United States during the 1960s, and it, too, turned the attention of research workers to the first years of life. By the late 1960s, because of all these factors, a goodly number of child development research workers had become especially concerned with the subject of learning during the first three years of life.

My next major enterprise in the study of the young child, created in the late 1960s, was the Brookline Early Education Project, otherwise known as BEEP. BEEP was an attempt to see if, by providing parents with the best available information on optimal conditions for learning during the first years, the public schools could help children off to a better start educationally. As big as the Preschool Project was, BEEP was approximately three times larger. About fifty people worked under my direction in an attempt to apply the university-based notions of the Preschool Project to the real world. I left the BEEP project a few years after its inception to concentrate on the work of the Preschool Project.

The research of the Preschool Project continued throughout most of the 1970s. It went from attempts to define the special qualities of the well-developed six-year-old to a concentration on the development of the outstanding three-year-old through analyses of childrearing styles, both effective and ineffective. Observations of naturally successful and less successful families were followed by training programs for other parents in an attempt to test ideas about effective childrearing practices.

In 1978, the work of the Preschool Project came to an end and, with the help of Dr. Michael K. Meyerhoff, I established the Center for Parent Education as a free-standing, nonprofit agency. The Center for Parent Education was, and remains, an attempt at further application of all that had been learned in the preceding twenty-one years. It has two goals: (1) to lobby for better services for new parents in their important task of helping their children to a good start in life, and (2) to provide services of various kinds to professionals working in the field. The latter work involves regular reviews of the results of new basic and applied research and examinations and evaluations of new assessment procedures, books, magazines, and audiovisual materials for use in the newly developing field of education for parenthood.

Perhaps the most important work of the Center for Parent Education was initiated in 1981, when representatives of the State Department of Education in Missouri asked for our help in creating a series of experimental programs designed, like BEEP, to test the question of whether the public schools should provide assistance in helping with the educational process from birth through the first three years of life, rather than waiting until the children entered kindergarten. The Missouri project, which came to be known as New Parents as Teachers (NPAT), delivered services to families from the beginning of 1981 through September 1985. It was evaluated by an independent agency, and the results were made public in October 1985. The NPAT project, its results, and their significance are dealt with in detail in the final portion of this book.

Finally, a note is necessary to those who are interested in the emotionally charged issue of full-time day care for infants and toddlers. This book presents an extensive treatment of my views on this subject. However, because some people have especially intense feelings on the matter, and because my public position on the subject is strongly opposed by some, I feel called upon to comment before I begin the text of the book.

I am on public record as consistently expressing opposition to the widespread use of full-time day care for infants and toddlers. It is said that I am just not facing up to reality. Statements are made such as "This practice is here to stay," "There are young parents for whom there is no choice but to use this kind of service," and so on. I would like the reader to understand that my principal concern is to describe what I and others have learned about the best kind of early experience for babies. This is a subject I am uniquely qualified to teach. It is because I believe that it is rare that full-time day care is better for babies than being cared for by their own parents or grandparents, and for no other reason, that I continue to maintain my position. Further, I would ask any new parents who maintain that they both *have* to work (1) to think carefully about whether what is really meant is that they both *want* to work—whether for a continued high level of income or to meet existing bills or to pursue careers—and (2) to consult at least two other books: "Of Cradles and Careers," by Kaye Loman, and "The Heart Has Its Own Reasons," by Mary Ann Cahill.

The bottom line is that you, the reader—no matter what your opinions are—and I, the author, both have one goal in mind: the best possible introduction to life for every new child.

Part I
Basic
Developmental
Processes

———

1
The Knowledge Base

The child's discovery of the anatomical sex difference . . . takes place
sometime during the 16th to 17th month or even earlier, but more often
in the 20th or 21st month. . . . The girl's discovery of the penis confronts
her with something she is lacking. This usually brings on a range of
behaviors that clearly demonstrate her anxiety, anger, and defiance. In
girls, masturbation takes on a desperate and aggression-saturated quality more often than in boys and at an earlier age.
> —From a best-selling book (more than 300,000 copies sold)

While diapering the [three- to four-month-old] infant, be sure you occasionally stroke his thighs. Tactile stimulation is important during the
first months of life.
> —From a federally sponsored curriculum on raising babies

You feel both the tranquil and dynamic waiting of the egg and the com-
pelling race, the fundamental need of the sperm. . . . By consciously experiencing the moment of conception, women may bring about an evolutionary leap as momentous as the transformation which took place
when we grew from four-legged to erect posture.
> —From a brochure advertising a conference on
> childrearing cosponsored by the United Nations

The foregoing quotations are admittedly on the outlandish side,
but only slightly so. For several years now, about three dozen
new books on raising babies have been published annually. Statements such as these on what babies are like and what they need to
develop well are the stuff of these books. Is it any wonder that parents are confused? But parents are not the only ones; professionals
are confused as well. It is not uncommon for incorrect information
to come from authorities with the very best credentials.

This peculiar state of affairs has existed for quite some time,
and helping parents and professionals cope with it is one of the

primary reasons for establishing the Center for Parent Education. In this part, I will be describing what I call the *knowledge base*—simply, what we actually know about babies and what we know about how to help them develop well.

Much reliable knowledge about babies has come from research. Piaget's work on the development of intelligence is one example. Another source of useful knowledge is experience. For example, the knowledge a mother acquires about her own children is valid and useful. Moreover, although the knowledge that *metapelets* (trained teachers) acquire by working with babies in Israeli kibbutzim may not be accumulated with such research tools as standardized tests, it is no less true. However, in attempting to understand the knowledge base, it is important to note the source from which a particular piece of information has been derived.

It is also useful to distinguish between information about what babies are like at any point in their development and information about what influences their development. The former is infinitely easier to accumulate than the latter. With relatively little difficulty, one can determine when babies typically begin to walk or to talk as well as the variability in the onset of such achievements among different children. Learning *why* one child begins to walk or talk much earlier or later than another is a problem of much greater complexity.

One might assume that our knowledge of *what* happens *when* is more plentiful and trustworthy than our knowledge of *how* that development takes place; to a certain extent, that assumption is correct. Unfortunately, the knowledge base has significant weaknesses in both areas. Although I believe that the knowledge base contains a great deal that is useful and reliable, I also feel that it has many huge and embarrassing gaps.

For example, thanks to Piaget, we have a great deal of information about the growth of intelligence in babies—information that anyone interested in babies can profit from. However, the information provided by Piaget comes mainly from his studies of his own three children; to this day, no one has taken the required step of studying a substantial number of children to see how accurate his research was. In any other branch of science, such an omission over a fifty-year span would be unforgivable. Furthermore, Piaget concentrated on what intelligence is (and is not) as it takes shape in the new human; he never displayed much interest in the question of how to help a child develop a high level of intelligence.

The immaturity of the science of early human development is probably due to several factors. One is that human development is very complicated. Studying the causes of development, to some degree, is beyond our current scientific capabilities. The problem is magnified by the strict limits inevitably imposed on experimentation with babies. Another factor is the inaccessibility of babies in their natural environments. The sanctity of the home and the inconvenience of traveling to study one baby at a time, with the mother looking on, constitute serious obstacles to research. One more factor is that because babies are everywhere, people automatically assume that we *must* be very knowledgeable about them.

When dealing with very young children and their families, the stakes are too high for us to be careless about what we know and don't know, so professionals must proceed with utmost caution when it comes to these issues. This book is intended to serve as a resource in this area. I have been involved in the creation and evaluation of information on early development for thirty years. However, I do not pretend to be infallible, nor do I suggest that mine is the best approach to the problem. For a long time, I have tried to get sponsorship for a blue-ribbon national commission to review information on early development as an ongoing function. I am still trying, but in the meantime, I hope the discussions in this part will represent a modest contribution toward filling the need.

2
The Development of Intelligence

High on most people's priority list of human attributes is the capacity for intelligent behavior. Indeed, improvement in the development of intelligence probably has been the single most popular topic in the incredible activities of early education since 1965. Although there is virtually unanimous agreement about the desirability of attending to the development of intelligence in young children, there is by no means equal agreement on how that goal is to be achieved.

I believe that our understanding of the evolution of intellectual abilities is considerably more valid and detailed than our understanding of most other areas of early development, such as the emergence of creativity, the child's concept of self, and many other important subjects. The reason that we are better off in this area is surprisingly simple. It is because of the work of one man: Jean Piaget of Switzerland. Because of the work of this genius, we have a reasonably workable understanding of the changing forms of intelligence in the first years of human life.

Varying Definitions of Intelligence

What most laypeople and professionals mean by intelligence is some form of higher mental ability—that is, some capacity to deal with abstractions, to consider ideas, and to produce insightful solutions to problems. However, this is not the only conception of intelligence in use. If a dog figures out how to open a gate by fumbling around with his mouth or paws, we consider him "intelligent." We do not consider him as intelligent as someone who plays a first-rate game of chess; nevertheless, most people consider that any form of problem solving implies the existence of some degree of intelligence. According to J. McVicker Hunt (1961) of the University of Illinois, the first form of problem solving seen in human development occurs at about the seventh month of life, when a baby becomes capable of moving an obstacle aside in order to procure an object—a procedure very much like the canine behavior described above.

In the history of measurement of intelligence, the third year of life traditionally has been considered a transition period. People who have developed tests of intelligence have been reluctant to consider problem-solving ability prior to the third birthday an indication of higher mental skill. A good example of this distinction is Arnold Gesell's use of the term *developmental quotient* (DQ) for very young children, in preference to the traditional term, *intelligence quotient* (IQ).

If you are not impressed with Gesell's views, you might consider that Piaget described the intelligence of the first two years in an equally distinct manner by referring to it as "sensorimotor intelligence." What Piaget was referring to was the fact that so much of the problem solving of the first two years takes place out in the open and involves, for example, the hands operating under the guidance of the eyes. In Piaget's system, mental activity does not become dominant in problem solving until sometime between eighteen and twenty-four months.

Then there is the question of "learning" as it relates to the development of intelligence. Learning has been an extremely popular topic in the field of psychology during this century. Perhaps more studies of learning have taken place than of just about any other topic. It should be noted that learning is a *process*, whereas intelligence is a *capacity*. The learning process, as traditionally studied in the field of psychology, involves the acquisition of simple habits— sometimes called reflexes, sometimes called conditioned responses, and other times referred to as instrumental responses.

The roots of such studies are in the work of such people as Pavlov, Thorndike, and Skinner. They feature concepts such as stimuli, responses, reinforcements, and the like. Much first-rate experimental research of this type has been performed, and although most of this work has been done on other animal species—such as mice, dogs, pigeons, and infrahuman primates—the findings have frequently been applied to humans. In fact, until about 1965, graduate students taking courses in learning theory in preparation for careers in teaching often were exposed to principles of learning derived primarily from basic studies of the acquisition of conditioned responses in other animal species. Competing ideas, such as those of the Gestalt psychologists (who studied so-called insightful problem solving) and Piaget, were not popular in those days.

In brief, it appears that there have been three major conceptual approaches to the study of the development of intelligence. The first is the idea of intelligence as the capacity for complex mental behavior, including memory, causality, object permanence, and so on. The second focuses on the simplest type of problem-solving behaviors seen in the first two years of human life and in the behavior of many other animal species. The third is the conditioned response approach to problem solving, which, though rooted in the behavior of simpler animal species, has been considered by many researchers to be the *only* scientifically valid approach to the study of problem-solving abilities for any creature at any age level.

This book is not the place to engage in a full-blown debate on this matter. I will simply say that I believe that the third approach drastically oversimplifies the problem. Conditioning explanations may work well for simpler animal species, and they may be useful for testing sensory abilities in young babies. They also may be useful in treating disturbed young children through behavior modification practices. However, I do not believe that they take us very far in explaining the full complexity and power of the human mind as it begins to develop once a child goes beyond six or seven months of age. Studies of the sensorimotor stages of intelligence (as well as those of the learning theorists) seem to be especially appropriate for understanding the development of children in the first months of life. But beyond the first seven or eight months, the capacity for abstract mental activity surfaces and grows with such dramatic speed that such restricted approaches to the topic of intelligence become inadequate. From seven or eight months on, an understanding of Piaget's views is indispensable.

Basic Piagetian Principles

According to Piaget, babies are born with virtually no ability to "think" at all. Moreover, they are unable to distinguish themselves from the world around them, because they know nothing about it.

They have no conception of time or space, and they are not even familiar with their own hands and feet, much less their mothers and fathers.

What they *do* have at birth is what Piaget called the "ready-made schemata" or reflexes, which include sucking, swallowing, grasping, crying, responding to sounds, looking at sources of light, and gazing at human faces (especially the eyes). These behaviors are primitive and uncoordinated, but they are the building blocks of intelligence. They allow babies to begin the process of adapting to their environments, and adaptation to the environment is what intelligence is all about in Piaget's system.

As Piaget saw it, the ability to adapt grows through the continuous interaction of two major functions: *assimilation* and *accommodation*. On the one hand, babies are constantly taking in, or assimilating, various elements of their environments through their existing mental structures. On the other hand, they are constantly adjusting, or accommodating, those structures so as to improve their capacity to assimilate.

Piaget called the first two years of life the *sensorimotor* period because intellectual and physical growth are so closely interrelated in the beginning. Babies begin to learn about the world through their senses and the motor activities of their bodies. Gradually, they achieve greater control and mastery of their bodies, and they gain greater experience with more aspects of their surroundings through exploration and experimentation.

Eventually, they come to the realization that they are only a small part of a much larger world. The practical intelligence they acquire, which is limited to getting direct information and results from their immediate surroundings, slowly but surely forms the foundations for the distinctly "intellectual" functions of memory, language, and imagination. By age two, they have moved into the period of *representation* and can deal with things through strictly mental manipulations, even if those things are not present to their senses.

The Stages of Sensorimotor Development

Piaget claimed that all children develop this early intelligence through an invariant series of stages, with each level of mental functioning building upon the preceding one.

Stage 1

During Stage 1, which occupies the first month of life, babies simply exercise their ready-made schemata—the basic structures they were born with. This enables them to take in what is necessary for their survival. For example, the sucking reflex allows an infant to assimilate nourishment from the mother's breast.

At the same time, as the infant gains experience, those basic structures evolve into more effective and efficient forms. Whereas a newborn often has difficulty finding the nipple—sometimes sucking the skin of his mother's breast in the wrong place—once he is a few days old, he has learned to adjust his body, head, and lips in ways that will best accommodate the size and shape of the mother's breast and her position during nursing.

At this point, however, the infant's behaviors remain essentially reflexive in nature. He will suck not only on his mother's breast but also on anything else that happens to come into contact with his mouth, such as his father's little finger. Moreover, his various behaviors remain largely independent of one another. For instance, he will look at a rattle that is placed in his field of vision, and he will grasp a rattle that is placed in his hand, but he will not grasp a rattle that he sees, nor will he look at a rattle that he is grasping.

Stage 2

During Stage 2, which goes roughly from one to four months of age, babies begin to coordinate basic motor activities and sensory experiences to form simple skills and perceptions. As they exercise their bodies, they gain greater control over their movements, and they gain more and more information about the results of those movements. Eventually, their activities become more varied, they start to discriminate among different aspects of their environments, and they learn to combine previously unrelated activities in ways that produce more beneficial results.

It is during this period of life that a baby will make the remarkable discovery that she is connected to her own hand. Previously, the soothing (if not nourishing) activity of sucking on her hand when it happened to reach her mouth—as well as the interesting spectacle of seeing her hand when it happened to pass through her field of vision—were merely the results of lucky accidents. Having experienced these fortuitous events, she now moves around in an effort to make them happen again. Gradually, she learns to control her hand and her head so that the act of bringing one into visual or tactile contact with the other becomes a smooth, regular pattern of behavior.

The crowning achievement in the coordination of these basic behaviors is the development of *prehension,* or visually directed reaching. Now, for example, when a baby hears a rattle, she will look at it as well. Having seen it, she will move her hand toward it and grasp it. Having grasped it, she may bring it to her mouth and suck on it. This indicates that she has become reasonably familiar with the limits of her own body and therefore is ready to start exploring the world of things "out there."

Stage 3

During Stage 3, which goes from four to approximately eight months of age, babies start applying the simple strategies they have developed to a whole new world of objects. At first, they simply take a more active interest in their immediate surroundings. Eventually, as they achieve the ability to crawl around, they develop a seemingly insatiable appetite for exploring every area they have access to and thoroughly investigating everything they encounter.

As they go about their activities, they discover that they can create rather interesting events, and they continually strive to make those events last longer and/or happen again. Early on, they merely apply their simple skills at random. For instance, a baby will first suck on anything he finds, then shake it, then throw it. Later, as his various actions produce different results or different degrees of the same result, he begins to develop a crude classification system.

By hearing a toy make a rattling sound, watching a ball roll, and feeling the soothing effect of a teething ring, he learns that some objects are "things to be shaken," others are "things to be thrown," and still others are "things to be sucked." He also learns some basic principles about the relationship between actions and things, such as harder, faster, louder, and so on.

However, the baby still has no real understanding of cause and effect. He just knows that his behavior seems to have some magical power. Thus, for instance, he may notice that banging on his crib rails will make a mobile suspended above him move about. Then, when he sees a window curtain fluttering in the breeze, he may bang his crib rails in the expectation that the curtain will move again.

Stage 4

During Stage 4, which occupies the balance of the first year of life, children develop a better sense of the relationship between means and ends. For the first time, they begin to exhibit truly intentional behavior. As a result of the many experiences they have had in using their simple strategies on different objects in different situations, they have learned a great deal that now enables them to coordinate these strategies in order to cope with more complex challenges.

For instance, during Stage 3, if a child saw an interesting toy on a table but couldn't reach it, she would have been stymied. She might have waved her arms or kicked her feet, but all to no avail. Now, in Stage 4, she knows that if she pulls the tablecloth, everything on the table will tumble down to the floor, where she can get to it. By using one object to reach another, or by moving one object aside to reach another, she shows not only that she is capable of purposeful, goal-directed actions but also that she is abandoning "magical" repetitive strategies in favor of realistic behaviors adapted to specific situations.

Unfortunately, her ability to keep a goal in mind as she works to achieve it remains at a rudimentary level during this period. The child still cannot perceive of things existing independent of her actions upon them. In other words, so long as she can see the object of her desire, she can pursue it. But for the most part, once it is out of sight, it also is out of mind.

Stage 5

During Stage 5, which goes roughly from twelve to eighteen months of age, children become much more adept at getting around, using their hands, and various other activities. They continue to explore and investigate, but now experimentation becomes a strong interest as well. Previously, they had used their skills only to learn about specific things they encountered and to get specific things they wanted. At this point, they also use those ever-improving skills to find out what will happen "if."

Whereas their behavior was primarily repetitive during Stage 3 and mainly purposeful during Stage 4, during this period, it can best be described as *systematic*. For instance, a toddler may take his rubber duck out of the bathtub and drop it in the toilet. Enjoying the splash this makes, he will reach in, take it out, and drop it in again—but this time from a greater height. Soon, he will take a bar of soap and drop that in to see what kind of splash it will make. Eventually, he will manage to drop anything and everything he can get his hands on into the toilet as well.

By bringing new objects into the game and creating new events, the child has demonstrated that he is beginning to understand the distinction between himself and the world around him. He now knows that things exist even though he can't see them, and he realizes that they have properties that are independent of his actions upon them. However, he is still largely tied to the "here and now," so his explorations and investigations of possibilities remain on the level of "groping" or trial and error.

Stage 6

During Stage 6, which occupies the remainder of the second year, children finally achieve *representation*—the capacity to retain mental images and to work out new strategies through strictly internal mechanisms. When presented with a novel problem, they now can take all they have learned from their experiences with different things in different situations, test the possibilities mentally, and then pursue a directly appropriate course of action.

For instance, a child may want to move a pile of blocks from one room to another. She collects the blocks and walks to the door. Since she needs her hands to open the door, she puts the blocks down in a neat stack on the floor. However, as she starts to open the door, she realizes that the stack of blocks will be in its path, so she stops and carefully moves the blocks aside. In other words, she now can create a picture in her mind of what will happen and then use this picture to readily figure out a new and better way to achieve her goal.

Having achieved the ability to "use her head" at last, it is clear that the child has come a long way. Nevertheless, the growth of intelligence is far from finished at this point. Although she is now capable of true "thinking," that thinking is still rather crude. In much the same way that she learned how to use her body and her senses in an increasingly appropriate fashion, she will spend the next several years learning how to use her head more efficiently and effectively.

Assessing Early Intelligence

As noted earlier, most test makers have concluded that children possess very little intelligence prior to their third birthday. Among currently popular tests, the Bayley Scales probably are the most commonly used to assess "mental" ability during the first thirty months of life. The Bayley Scales are technically excellent, and they are therefore probably the best test of early abilities. They do not, however, provide a sophisticated measure of intelligence during the first years of life.

The items on the Bayley Scales are very similar to those on the "adaptive" scale of the earlier Gesell Schedules. Their emphasis, naturally enough, is on sensorimotor skills. Except for chronically low scores (less than 85), there is no predictive power from scores obtained during the first eighteen months to performance on mental tests such as the Stanford-Binet or Wechsler at three years or later. One has to conclude that either the intelligence level of the child (as measured by the Bayley Scales) changes dramatically between the first and third birthdays or that something other than intelligence is being measured during those early months. Most specialists hold the latter view.

In my opinion, the Bayley Scales should be used only as a screening tool. Infants scoring repeatedly below 85 are likely to have significant developmental problems. Infants scoring over 85— even as high as 150—during the first eighteen months of life should be considered "normal." It should be noted that the infant who scores 150 is no more likely to score above average on a Stanford-Binet test at three years of age than an infant who scores 95. By twenty-four months of age, scores on the Bayley Scales do begin to correlate well with Stanford-Binet scores that follow one or two years later. Attempts to measure skills by using clusters of Bayley items should be regarded as experimental, however, since none have as yet been validated.

Attempts to use the Bayley Scales to measure early mental development are seriously hampered by the simple fact that no clear picture of early mental development underlies the individual test items. As was the case with the Gesell and earlier scales, items were selected on the basis of common sense and a generally vague appreciation of early development. In contrast, the Hunt-Uzgiris Scales of Sensorimotor Intelligence have been constructed directly from Piaget's sophisticated description of the origins of intelligence (Uzgiris and Hunt, 1975).

With the growth of interest in Piaget's ideas during the 1960s, many of us were hopeful that more powerful tests of infant skills would be developed. Those developed by Hunt and Uzgiris, Escalona and Corman, and a few others are, indeed, more powerful, but they do not have the technical strengths of the Bayley Scales or the Stanford-Binet test, and there is no extensive normative data for any of them as yet. The best of these tests, the Hunt-Uzgiris Scales, must be regarded as an experimental instrument, but I believe it can provide an accurate and reliable measure of sensorimotor intelligence.

There is reason to believe that, like the Bayley Scales, the Hunt-Uzgiris Scales are useful only as a screening device for identifying serious delays in development. The highest levels of sensorimotor development are attained by most children between eighteen and twenty-four months of age, and the test is inappropriate beyond that age. On the basis of my research and the research of others, it appears that children who are falling behind on early language development, for example, often seem to be developing normally in sensorimotor intelligence. My interpretation is that both the Hunt-Uzgiris Scales and the Bayley Scales (during the first eighteen months) measure basic *pre*intellectual abilities so fundamental to human function that, like basic perceptual/motor and motor abilities, they are much less likely to develop poorly than language or higher mental abilities. Since language and higher mental abilities begin their development during the second half of the first year of life, deviations of significance are not easy to identify much before the second birthday.

If this judgment is correct, early identification of any but major delays in the development of intelligence is not feasible until at least the second birthday. I believe that there is a possibility of such early identification by age fourteen months through tests of receptive language development; however, practically speaking, I feel that the first reliable testing for moderate delays in the development of higher mental abilities must wait until the child is at least two and a half years of age.

For such children, testers may use either the Kaufman Assessment Battery for Children (ABC), the McCarthy Scales of Intelligence, the Stanford-Binet, the Bayley Mental Scale, or the Palmer Concept Familiarity Scale. (The order reflects my preferences.) Although all of these instruments are of high quality, I have learned that testing two-and-a-half-year-old children is a very chancy affair. Cooperation is nowhere near as likely as it is at later ages. Many two-and-a-half-year-old children I have tested scored lower than they could have because of this factor.

Scores become much more reliable by three years of age. Since deviations from average performance become more stable during the third year, it is clear that the test results procured by the third birthday will be more accurate than earlier ones. On the other hand, given the results of recent compensatory education programs for children over three years of age, it is equally clear that three years is too late to begin to monitor the growth of intelligence.

Influences on the Development of Intelligence

It is most unfortunate that Piaget showed so little interest in optimizing early intellectual development—having the power of his splendid mind addressing the problem would have been quite a plus. Nor have many others studied optimal early intellectual development extensively. Terman's studies of gifted children were superbly executed, but they provided no detailed information on the effects of early experiences on development.

My own research with the Harvard Preschool Project, though not specifically focused on intellectual development, did gather much data on children who were developing very high levels of intelligence by their third birthdays. We also studied others who looked similar at the first birthday but developed only average levels of intelligence over the following two years. We even developed some ideas about how to help intelligence develop optimally, and we put them to test with fairly impressive results.

Putting together our results with a handful of other findings, including some on the relation of early language learning to early intellectual development, I can sketch a crude picture of how to help a child develop a high level of intelligence by her third birthday. I must emphasize that all I can provide is a crude sketch, and I should point out that other writers are less modest. Numerous books for parents promise high levels of intellectual development if their advice is followed. *I do not believe that any of them are rooted in a reliable knowledge base.* It is my judgment that none of them has as much to go on as I do, and I have no more than a minimal science.

Both parents and professionals should proceed with caution in this area. The biggest hazard lies in accepting as reliable any of the extensive extrapolations and personal guesses contained in both the lay and professional literature. Please note that even if recommendations come with Piaget's theory attached, they will concern only sensorimotor intelligence during the first years, and sensorimotor intelligence apparently does not need a great deal of encouragement. For example, object permanence seems to develop nicely even when parents do not play much peek-a-boo or hide-and-seek with their babies.

The Harvard Preschool Project recommendations for helping to develop intelligence are too lengthy to include here in detail. In brief, they emphasize the importance of learning conditions during the eight- to thirty-six-month period. Newly crawling infants should be allowed to practice their climbing and other emerging motor skills. *For most of their waking hours, they should have easy access to people who have a very special love for them.* Those people should talk to them about what they are focusing on at the moment, using ordinary language to expand ideas and introduce new ideas. They should lavish affection, encouragement, and enthusiasm on the babies, thereby intensifying their interest and excitement in learning. They need not make use of elaborate educational toys or programs.

These simple prescriptions are a distillation of what we have seen repeatedly in homes where children move well above national averages in the development of higher mental abilities between their first and third birthdays. Other chapters of this book will be providing additional details.

3
The Development of Language

Like many other very important functions, language undergoes its major development during a child's first three years. Average three-year-olds can understand most commonly used words and grammatical forms. Although they certainly cannot express their thoughts in very complicated or sophisticated ways, they usually can make themselves understood.

The fact that most children learn so much language during the first years of life frequently has been marveled at by professionals as well as parents. It is interesting that no special effort seems to be necessary to teach language adequately to most children. However, when this "natural process" does not produce adequate language skills by the third birthday, the result is a significant educational problem. Language delays have been found to be a common source of educational difficulty during the school years.

The relationship between early language learning and early intellectual development has confused educators and psychologists for many years. When language ability is seen as distinct from intellectual ability, questions of their relatedness are posed. No adequate answers have ever been found as to whether one precedes the other in development or how they interact. Nevertheless, all agree that language skill contributes substantially to performance on tests of intelligence and that intelligence suffers if language ability is below par.

Especially during the eight- to thirty-six-month period, children become socialized. They enter into the world of other people, and they must learn how to ask for help, how to cooperate, how to deal with prohibitions, and so on. Adults teach these and other basic social skills precisely during the period when language is developing most rapidly. Furthermore, social skills are taught by adults through the medium of language. Therefore, poor language ability directly hinders the acquisition of social skills.

Some important differences between *receptive* language abilities and *expressive* language abilities during the first years of life merit attention. The variability of the onset of expressive language is much greater than that of receptive language. As is the case with the ability to walk, within a normal population, the first spoken words can appear at any time during the eight- to eighteen-month period. In contrast, the first few words usually are understood between eight and ten months of age. Once started, the acquisition of receptive language proceeds steadily. That means that, for the purposes of early detection, receptive language is a far more appropriate process to monitor than speech. However, the early development of speech has been well studied and documented, whereas the early development of receptive language has not. A search of the literature reveals that references to studies of the acquisition of receptive language are very scarce and usually very old. (Indeed, the best work was done in the 1920s and 1930s.) Figure 3–1 presents our best estimates of what is known regarding the language development processes.

Assessing Early Language Ability

Probably the most common tools used for assessing language ability during the first years have been the Gesell Schedules and the Bayley Scales. The primary purpose of both tests is to provide a broad picture of a child's abilities. Therefore, there is little emphasis on the details of early language acquisition, although significant delays can be detected using these tests.

The Ammons Full Range Picture Vocabulary Test can be used with children as young as two years of age, and the Peabody Picture Vocabulary Test has a floor of two and a half years. Although neither test goes beyond receptive vocabulary, both are considerably better constructed and studied than most tests of language for children under three years of age. On the surface, the Receptive and Expressive Language (REEL) Scale would appear to be an exception to this statement. However, in my opinion its reliance on maternal reports for what appear to be technical data makes it unsuitable for general use.

The Harvard Preschool Project research required a tool to monitor language growth from its beginning to the third birthday. We created our own test, which deals with receptive vocabulary, the ability to follow instructions, and the understanding of grammatical elements such as prepositions and reflexives. This test can be used with children as young as eight months of age. Unfortunately, however, it is only an experimental instrument and provides no substantial normative, reliability, or validity data.

Recently, I have become aware of the Reynell Developmental Language Scales (RDLS) from England. I consider this device to be the equal of the Harvard Preschool Project test in terms of coverage, ease of administration, interest to children, and reliability. It is somewhat superior in that there is a body of normative data associated with it, although the data are based on studies of British children. Unfortunately, obtaining a copy of the RDLS involves a long and complicated procedure—designed to ensure that the instrument will be used properly—so it is not always a practical alternative.

Influences on Language Development

How babies learn language is not yet fully understood. Studies on alternative teaching styles used with infants and toddlers are virtually nonexistent, although nearly all infant education research since the 1960s has included language development as a major goal. Typical curricula advise adults to talk to children a great deal from birth on. The advice usually includes the suggestion that stories be read to the child regularly, although the stage at which children would profit from stories is generally not clearly indicated. It probably is fair to say, however, that any normal baby who receives a great deal of language from birth on, including stories from the first birthday on, would learn language well.

From my own research on well-developing children, I have tried to isolate the main features of the language teaching styles of parents whose children acquired language especially well during the first three years:

1. The child (between nine and twenty-four months of age) usually initiated about ten interchanges an hour with her parents during typical daytime activities. The parents usually initi-

Birth	3 mos.	6 mos.	9 mos.	1 yr.	15 mos.	18 mos.	21 mos.	2 yrs.	27 mos.	30 mos.	33 mos.	3 yrs.

Startles to sharp noises

Interest in sounds, plays with saliva, responds to voices

First words understood
(3) (12) (50) (100) (>300) (>750) (>1000)

Growth of receptive vocabulary (average no. of words understood)

First instructions understood ("wave bye bye," etc.)

First words spoken
(0–5) (10–15) (20–25) (200–275) (400–450) (800–900)

Growth of spoken vocabulary (average no. of words)
(1) (2) (3)

Length of spoken sentences (average no. of words)

Typical Language Achievements

At Two Years of Age	At Three Years of Age
Repeats two consecutive numbers	Uses pronouns *his* and *my* and prepositions *in front of*, *toward*, and *behind*
Understands a few prepositions—*out, in, on*	Uses *what* and one or two other "question words"
Understands some common pronouns, e.g., *me, mine, you*	Forms negative sentences
Uses the word *no*	Uses present and past tense of verbs
Produces the sounds *p, m, n, b, w,* and *h* at the beginning of words	Pronounces the letters *p, b, w, m, n, h, t, d, –ng, k+g*
Uses words to make requests	Repeats three numbers
	Understands most adult sentences
	Understands reflexives (touches herself), possessives ("daddy's boy")

Figure 3–1. *A Chronology of Language Development*

ated a similar or smaller number of interchanges. (With first-born children, parents initiated more interchanges than were evident when later-born children were involved.)

2. The parents took the time to identify the interest of the child.

3. Words and appropriate actions, focused on the child's interest, usually followed.

4. The words used were at or slightly above the child's apparent level of comprehension.

5. Full sentences, rather than single words or brief phrases, were the norm.

6. Related ideas were introduced often.

7. Most interchanges lasted between twenty and thirty seconds. Lengthy teaching sessions were rare.

8. Stories were read often, but the child's attention did not become sustained until well into the second year. For a few months after the child's first birthday, picture books were used habitually for "labeling" sessions.

Language development during the first three years of life is of central importance to the overall educational development of the child. As noted earlier, our understanding of the development of expressive abilities is well advanced, but the more basic development of receptive language has not yet received enough attention, so many details of the process are not yet clear. How to help a child avoid very poor language learning seems to be reasonably well understood. How to help a child acquire language most effectively has rarely been studied, although some clues may be found in the work of the Harvard Preschool Project.

Monitoring of early language acquisition should emphasize the growth of the first receptive language skills. Although the field is somewhat handicapped by the scarcity of well-developed tests, with the increased interest in the developments of the first years, we can look for better assessment tools soon. In the meantime, we are obliged to recognize our limitations and work with what we have.

4
Social Development

Although a great deal of emphasis has been placed on intellectual and linguistic development in very young children (especially since 1965), it is clear to many professionals—and perhaps to an even larger proportion of parents—that such treatment of early development is not complete. Among people specializing in early education, such a narrow view has led to considerable dissatisfaction. For example, in the early 1970s, when the early evaluations of Project Head Start seemed to indicate disappointing results, Dr. Edward Zigler of Yale, who was then the director of the federal Office of Child Development, went to great lengths to point out the unfairness of depending exclusively on measures of intellectual and linguistic development in evaluating the effectiveness of Head Start programs.

The common expression used by those interested in employing a broader conception is the "whole child" orientation. This approach emphasizes the social development of children as much as, if not more than, intellectual and linguistic development. Unfortunately, social development covers more diverse topics than other major headings used in child development research. It includes, but is not limited to, the development of social skills, the evolution of social interests, the development of attachment between child and adult, the acquisition of social attitudes, the acquisition of self-concept, and the assumption of sex-role identity. As a result, people often fail to communicate well when dealing with the topic of social development.

Perhaps the most serious example of this confusion concerns the use of the term *social competence*. To some, competence means ability or skill; therefore, social competence means skill in social situations. To others, social competence has come to mean the entire collection of abilities needed to function as a member of society—including sensorimotor, intellectual, and linguistic skills along with a host of others. In my work, although I have taken the broad approach to early education in general, I have taken the narrow road with respect to social development in particular. However, as will soon become evident, taking the narrow road in this area is still a rather complicated affair.

The Stages of Social Development

In my judgment, children need to achieve two primary social goals during the first three years of life. First, and most basic, is the development of a healthy emotional bond or attachment to one or more older people, usually members of their own family. The result is a sense of personal security, which involves both an absence of chronic fear or anxiety and a presence of comfort and confidence in dealing with other people. The second goal is the acquisition of a collection of interpersonal skills for interacting successfully with adults and peers.

As children move toward these goals, they reveal an evolution in social interests, beginning with virtually no sociability at birth, moving to an initial awareness of the primary caretaker, then to an intensification of that interest, and finally to an interest in their agemates. They start out with a few important but rudimentary means of forming and regulating interpersonal interactions and gradually add to these social capacities as their mental and physical growth proceeds. The following is a brief picture of the process.

Birth to Six Weeks

At birth, there is no commonsense manner in which a baby can be considered sociable. Although it is true that the process of attachment to another member of the species begins immediately after birth, to call the behavior of the newborn "sociable" would be inappropriate. Most newborns sleep more than 90 percent of the time, and when they are awake, they are more inclined to be fussy or drowsy than alert and interested in other people. It would appear that the first weeks of life are devoted to getting over the tiring effects of the birth process and that attention to other people is minimal during this period.

There is clear evidence of infants showing eye contact during the first few weeks of life, and there are some suggestions in research results that there may be modest interaction patterns in eye contact behavior. Nevertheless, by any reasonable standards, in the first five or six weeks of life, babies show little that could be defined as social behavior. After all, looking at someone's eyes, though likely to be sociable in an adult, need not be sociable at all in babies. Eyes, noses, ears, and plants are all targets to be looked at. The fact that a baby may look at your eyes when he is in your arms really does not mean that he is doing anything social. If that analysis seems a bit strained, perhaps the later discussion regarding first smiles will help elaborate the matter.

One last comment about the first six weeks is necessary before moving on. Certain qualities of the baby are of fundamental importance in determining the beginnings of social development. The baby's helplessness and her cry are two characteristics that usually lead to social interchanges, and they are both extremely important. Also, the baby who breast-feeds contributes to certain very rewarding feelings on the part of the mother, both because the breast-feeding mother knows that she is doing something important for her child, and because the experience is pleasurable to successful nursing mothers.

Six Weeks to Four Months

Between six and ten weeks of age, the first easily elicited smiles surface. Although there are occasional smile patterns prior to this age, from this point on there is absolutely no doubt that you will see full-blown smiling in normal children. There is a strong and reasonable tendency to label such behavior as social. However, in the work of Piaget and other researchers, there is clear reason to be uncertain of such a label. Ten- to twelve-week-old babies will smile at their own hands, at bits of cloth that hang over the crib, at familiar toys, at pen-and-ink sketches of the upper half of the human face, and at many other things. Either one has to expand the definition of *social* quite a bit, or one has to reexamine the idea that the first smiles are simply social behavior. In Piaget's system, the first smiles are linked to the development of familiarity with what the baby is looking at. Therefore, it seems that the first smiles are better viewed as a sign of recognition than as exclusively social.

It also seems useful to keep in mind the survival function of early social behavior. After all, we are creatures who have evolved over millions of years, and we are born helpless. The first smiles seem to be a built-in guarantee that nearby adults will fall in love with the infant. It is a rare adult who does not melt at the sight of these early, drooly grins. These factors relate to questions about early social development in an important way. Without such an evolutionary perspective, it is more difficult to grasp the significance of some early behaviors.

By the time the baby reaches four months of age, genuine sociability is clearly present. Several studies have indicated an acquired preference for the faces, voices, scents, and other qualities of the parents as compared to those of others to whom a child is exposed. A child's parents are better able than others to get the child to smile and continue to smile during the fourth month, and it does not seem merely a matter of familiarity anymore. The fourth month is also a time when children begin to be vocal and giggly. This is a time of great attractiveness; as a result, the social activities of children with their parents accelerate dramatically during this period.

Four to Eight Months

The four- to eight-month-old child ordinarily is not yet a mobile creature; yet she is capable of seeing and hearing quite well. This period, then, is the beginning of the concentration on nuclear family members and the assimilation of their responses to the child's behavior. This also is the time when the child can begin to show the first signs of spoiling. By this time, the primary behavior a baby displays when uncomfortable from the very beginning of life— crying—has produced many experiences of reduced stress upon the arrival of the adult. Through a basic conditioning process, the baby has learned that the cry is followed by events that lead to feeling better. By five or six months of age, children begin to use the cry intentionally in order to be picked up and held. This behavior can increase for the balance of the first year to the point where it becomes burdensome on parents. This can be the first sign of spoiling, but it also is a sure sign that the child has received a great deal of attention during the first six months of life.

Eight to Fifteen Months

This is a particularly exciting and dramatic period of life with respect to social development. It is a time when many major competencies of lifelong value in interactions with other people develop through interactions with parents or other adults. During this time, the child learns a variety of ways of getting and holding attention and learns how to use an adult as a resource, to express affection or annoyance to other people, to show pride in achievement, and to adopt imaginary roles. In addition to these interpersonal behaviors, the child moves from a totally naive creature with virtually no self-consciousness to one who begins to have a sense of self as separate from others, to manipulate older people, and to resist authority in order to determine just how much control he has and how restricted he might be.

This also is a very interesting and important period in the life of a young child if there is a slightly older sibling in the home. Children a year or two older than an eight-month-old child begin to show displeasure at the presence of a competitor when the younger child begins to crawl about the home (thus requiring additional attention from the parents). In such cases, the younger child must learn to defend against increasingly serious expressions of jealousy from the older child. This requirement, of course, will color his social development at this stage of the game. By twelve to fifteen months of age, a stand-off situation usually emerges, wherein the baby has learned to cope with the older one. Nevertheless, tension remains, and so do hard feelings in the older child.

Fifteen to Twenty-Four Months

This stage of the game is also quite remarkable in that it frequently features the completion of the early attachment process and the repeated testing of the power of the older person around whom the day revolves. This is a stage at which most children are so concerned with their growing awareness of social circumstances that life outside the home becomes intimidating. This is not true of all children; an occasional child will be quite comfortable in strange surroundings even during this stage of life, but that is not the norm.

The growth of personal power manifests itself in another interesting and important way at this time, when younger siblings begin to turn on the slightly older family members who had been hostile to them for several months now. Indeed, many younger children learn to intimidate their older siblings at this point. It should be noted that toward the end of the second year, it is not uncommon for the younger child to have to look back over his shoulder at another, still younger child who is now beginning to crawl about and take his place. The dynamics of this process for the middle child are unquestionably different from those for the first child, although such differences have not been adequately researched to date.

Also developing during this fascinating period are some modest sexual differences, although similarities in interests, behaviors, and preferences continue to overwhelm the differences. Finally, the end of this period is signaled by a growth of interest in agemates and by the return to rationality within family activities.

Twenty-Four to Thirty-Six Months

What is most striking about this age range is that it signals the beginning of a long-term trend toward increasing interest in agemates. Of course, that will not happen unless there are opportunities for interaction with other children, but there usually are such opportunities. The abilities to lead and follow peers, to compete with them, and to express emotions freely to them all surface during the third year. There is a continued divergence of sexual behavior and interests, and if there is a closely spaced sibling, this is the time of continued tension between siblings, often occupying a good percentage of the day.

The end of the process, when all goes well, is a three-year-old who is a sophisticated social being and who probably could get by quite nicely in a classroom with twenty other children if a school situation were attempted. Alternatively, a three-year-old child may have already acquired harmful social patterns, which may be class-ified by specialists as behavior disorders and which may not be easy to treat.

I offer these six stages as a framework within which to examine various aspects of social development. It is surely not the only way to analyze this aspect of early development, but until someone comes along with a conceptualization of social development that is the equal of Piaget's conceptualization of early intellectual devel-opment, it should be useful.

Assessing Early Social Development

No measurement procedure can be any better than the preceding effort to identify what is worth measuring. For example, the pow-erful approach to measuring the emergence of intelligence during the first years of life represented in the Hunt-Uzgiris Scales of Sen-sorimotor Intelligence is based on the brilliant work of Piaget, which describes the emergence of intellectual structures and abili-ties. As noted earlier, however, social development is considerably more diverse than the development of intelligence and in many ways is not as well researched.

With regard to the two primary goals of early social develop-ment mentioned earlier in this chapter—the development of a strong emotional bond or attachment to another human being and the acquisition of social skills—we probably are a little stronger when it comes to assessing the former as compared to the latter. As a result of the outstanding work of Mary Ainsworth, a standard procedure for measuring the strength of a baby's attachment to an-other person has become very popular (Ainsworth et al., 1972).

The Strange Situation Procedure involves observation of a baby while he is in the presence of his primary caretaker, then upon the caretaker's departure, and finally in the presence of someone not previously known to the baby. Most of the work involving this pro-cedure has been done on two-year-olds; more recently, however, a good deal has been done on one-year-olds as well. The great major-ity of the work has been done in laboratory situations, which have the virtue of being controlled and standardized. By now, it is fair to say that this procedure for gauging the quality and strength of attachment relationships has become the most accepted method of its kind.

Measuring social skills or social competence is far more complicated. First, definitions seem to present a serious problem in this area. Given the origins of the interest in social competence, there should not be too much difficulty with definitions; unfortunately, however, such is not the case.

Bear in mind that preschool educators and parents, when referring to an interest in social development, traditionally have done so because of dissatisfaction with an excessive concentration on the development of intelligence and language. It follows, then, that the label *social competence* should address factors that differ from intelligence and language or, at the very least, do not overlap with them any more than is necessary.

In the area of the assessment of social abilities, it has long been recognized that the field of developmental psychology has failed to provide a wealth of useful procedures. As a result, a number of programs over the past twenty years have employed the Vineland Social Maturity Scale as a measure of social development in young children. The Vineland Social Maturity Scale was designed many years ago to assess the degree to which *retarded children* were capable of taking care of themselves. Its use of the term *social competence* rests upon the concept of socialization as *the general capacity to function in a society.*

This is the sense in which socialization is assessed by anthropologists and sociologists. If one looks closely at the Vineland instrument, it is immediately obvious that the emphasis is on self-help skills: Can the child take care of himself in the most fundamental ways? Can he feed himself? Is he toilet-trained? Can he tie his shoelaces? And so on. The scale provides very little coverage, however, with respect to social skill development.

This does not take away from its use as originally intended. It may very well be a good test for determining the degree to which a retarded child can function under normal societal conditions, whether the child needs to be institutionalized, and so on. For the field of early human development, however, it has served as a distraction and often has been misused as an index of social skill development.

In addition to the Vineland instrument, many programs have employed portions of the Bayley Scales, the Gesell Schedules, the Denver Developmental Screening Test, or the Griffiths Scales to measure early social development. Once again, however, each of these instruments labels a collection of items "personal-social," and most of those items address social maturity in the Vineland sense.

For example, in the Gesell Schedules, a twenty-four-month-old child is supposed to stay dry at night, be able to pull on a simple garment, and hand someone a cup full of cubes. At six months, the Denver Test likewise suggests that the normal child can feed himself crackers and play peek-a-boo at six months, play patty-cake at eight months, and drink from a cup at eleven months. In the Griffiths Scales, at the twentieth month, the child is supposed to have complete control of her bowels, use a spoon well, and be able to control her bladder by day.

In all fairness, a few other items on these instruments more closely resemble social behavior narrowly defined, such as "tries to tell experiences" in the twenty-first month and "asks for things at the table" in the twenty-second month. But the general use of the term *personal-social* in these devices is similar to the concept that underlies the Vineland Social Maturity Scale.

During the late 1960s, the federal Office of Child Development (OCD) commissioned the Rand Corporation to study the issue of social competence, with a special emphasis on assessment. I was among the many people interviewed in connection with that work, and I was somewhat surprised to find that in addition to the issue of social skills, the interviewers were very much interested in intellectual and linguistic skills. When I asked why their domain was so broad, they responded that they had been handed a definition of social competence by the people at OCD and that it was to include these areas because it was clear that social competence rested upon intellectual and linguistic skills. At the time, I thought this position was loaded with potential hazards; what happened subsequently only served to confirm my fears.

In 1973, Dr. Zigler defined *social competence* as "an individual's everyday effectiveness in dealing with his environment." This laid the foundation for the work of Anderson and Messick (1974) at the Educational Testing Service in Princeton, New Jersey. Using OCD funds, they mounted yet another analysis of social competence in young children. They brought together a panel of experts in 1973 and proceeded to discuss—at length—just what social competence was. Their conclusion was that it contained the following twenty-nine components:

Differentiated self-concept and consolidation of identity

Concept of self as an initiating and controlling agent

Habits of personal maintenance and care

Realistic appraisals of self

Differentiations of feelings and appreciation of their manifestations and implications

Sensitivity and understanding in social relationships

Positive and affectionate personal relationships

Role perception and appreciation

Appropriate regulation of antisocial behavior

Morality and prosocial tendencies

Curiosity and exploratory behavior

Control of attention

Perceptual skills

Fine motor dexterity

Gross motor skills

Perceptual/motor skills

Language skills

Categorizing skills

Memory skills

Critical thinking skills

Creative thinking skills

Problem-solving skills

Flexibility and the application of information processing

Quantitative and relational concepts

General knowledge

Competence and motivation

Facility and the use of resources for learning and problem solving

Positive attitudes in school experiences

Enjoyment of humor, play, and fantasy

I submit that such a list is as effective a way of destroying a definition as one could create. The idea that the field of developmental psychology and early education could develop usable assessment techniques for all twenty-nine of these components in less than twenty or thirty years is absolutely out of the question. The possibility that functioning programs for young children could implement such a huge collection of assessment techniques and concepts is even more far-fetched.

Nevertheless, that work did not end there. In the mid-1970s, the OCD, now called the Administration for Children, Youth, and Families (ACYF), sponsored a substantial research effort by the Mediax Corporation of Connecticut in a further attempt at analysis and action in the area of social competence (Mediax Associates, 1980). Once again, along with many other people in the field, I was asked for my views. I replied by asking how broad a definition of social competence was being pursued. It soon became clear that the orientation of the Mediax group was much the same as that of the earlier groups. I told them that their chances of mastering the problem were not good if they chose to follow this course; a few years later, the Mediax group disbanded without ever coming close to achieving their goal.

What can be done to measure the development of social skills during the first years of life? Unfortunately, not very much. The Harvard Preschool Project created two assessment devices based on our studies of preschool children who were developing beautifully and the social abilities that appeared to distinguish them from their peers. One device is a rating scale; the other is a behavior checklist. Neither is a particularly good instrument. The checklist is more powerful, but it requires lengthy, repeated observations, and it is most difficult to train people to use it reliably. To aggravate the situation, there are no national norms, so it cannot be called a standardized test.

I believe that it is important to be able to measure social development accurately and that interpersonal skills are of especially great importance. At this point, the apparently most powerful conceptual approach is the one we developed at the Harvard Preschool Project, but the procedures for measuring just how well a child is doing in this regard are admittedly primitive and inadequate.

What is needed first and foremost is a sane research effort. Work parallel to that of Piaget and similar to what the Harvard Preschool Project has begun has to be done before the fields of psychology and education can really be considered competent to deal with this issue. It is hoped that with the expanded interest in research on the first years of life, better procedures will come along in the near future. In the meantime, in examining claims that someone has a good way of measuring early social development, the professional should first examine the definition of *social development* that is being used and then should take a close look at whatever assessment procedure is being recommended.

Influences on Social Development

The topic of influences on social development is every bit as broad as the main topic itself. For a variety of reasons, especially the limitations in respect to measurement, we have a dramatically incomplete understanding of the subject.

Starting with the work of Spitz in the 1940s, we began to acquire information on the subject of disturbances in the early parent-child relationship. Many studies—generally lumped together under the title "maternal deprivation"—have been done since the mid-1940s. Summarizing their findings is not very difficult: A child who does not have the opportunity for the establishment of a good parent-child relationship during the first three years of life, or who has that relationship interrupted for three or more months (after the first six months of life), suffers rather serious negative consequences. No relationship at all leads to an emotional cripple who will never be socially normal throughout his life. An interrupted relationship of three months or longer once the child is six months old leads to emotional distress whose intensity and longevity is linked directly to such factors as the length of the separation.

The early studies were performed with children being reared in orphanages. It is not likely that their findings tell us much about the impact of modern child care practices, such as full-time day care; indeed, the modest amount of research that has been done on the impact of day care shows nothing like the devastating results of maternal deprivation situations. That is not to say that mental health experts are unconcerned about the social consequences of full-time day care during the first years of life; rather, it would be improper to apply the results of studies of maternal deprivation to the modern day care controversy.

Many studies of the adult–child relationship have come to be called studies of the "attachment" process. A good deal of work on the subject has focused on other animal species as well as on young children. Several studies have provided suggestions regarding how early childhood experiences and parenting tactics can affect the strength and quality of the attachment. At present, however, not a great deal can be said with confidence about the subject that goes beyond the obvious. That is, lots of affection seems to be required for a healthy attachment to develop in the first two years of life. Affection accompanied by too much control may sometimes lead to overattachment. Too much coldness by the adult can perhaps lead to underattachment. The main focus of the attachment studies has been on the development of a measurement procedure and on the assessment of variations in the strength and quality of the attachment, rather than on the relationship between various childrearing procedures and the attachment results.

The acquisition of social attitudes, self-concept, and sex-role identity are all subjects about which we remain largely in the dark. Attitudes, self-concepts, and sex-role identity are all notoriously difficult to measure, and without being able to apply reliable measurement techniques—or, for that matter, good definitions—it is most difficult to accumulate useful information about a subject.

On the matters of social interests and social skills, my own research has provided a good deal of suggestive data over the years, but not much that is definitive. For example, because I have invested so much time in naturalistic observations of children from birth to the sixth birthday, I have naturally generated information about the evolution of social interests. However, I have never directly addressed the question of influences on those developments. Common sense suggests certain notions—for example, that a good deal of affection displayed by parents toward children should produce children who enjoy people, and so forth. Such suggestions, however, do not a science make.

The situation with respect to social skills is slightly better. In identifying social skills that distinguish the outstanding three-year-old from other children, and in plotting their emergence during the first years, reasonably useful ideas about influences on the development of these skills seem to have surfaced. For example, if a ten-month-old child shows, for the first time in his life, a developing tendency to ask for assistance, observations of different childrearing patterns, along with common sense, suggest that human influences do indeed make a great difference in the destiny of such early important developments. A child who spends very little time in direct interchanges with older people will not get the same reinforcement and encouragement to ask for help and to develop skills in that direction as a child who spends a great deal of time most days in the presence of an interested and caring adult.

Likewise, a child whose emerging tendencies toward role play and make-believe behavior are not enjoyed, commented upon, and nurtured by significant other humans is less likely to expand her tendencies in that direction as she moves through the second and third years of life than a child who regularly receives such responses. A child who spends most of those months confined to a crib or a small playroom or a playpen—or, for that matter, a child in a group care situation that features large numbers of children and very few adults—is very probably not going to develop as well in that regard.

This, then, is where we currently stand on influences on interpersonal skill development. By virtue of the nature of the skills, and also on the basis of extensive research *close* to the subject, we have some pretty good hypotheses. Once again, however, because of fundamental weaknesses in our capacity for the measurement of interpersonal skills, we are some distance away from impressive, solid knowledge in this area.

5

The Development of Personality

W ebster defines *personality* as "individuality, or habitual patterns and qualities of behaviors, or the sum of such qualities likely to impress others: as, 'she has personality.' " A psychological dictionary defines it as "the integrated organization of all the cognitive, affective, conative, and physical characteristics of an individual as it manifests itself in focal distinctiveness to others, or the general pattern of an individual's total behavior." Clearly, personality is a more complex and more difficult subject to talk about than height or weight.

Historically, psychologists have combined the term with others, such as *motivation* or *social,* as in "Motivation and Personality" as a course title or *Journal of Personality and Social Psychology*—further testifying to its peculiar identity. Of the major figures in the study of personality—including Freud, Adler, Sullivan, Erikson, Sheldon, and Maslow—very few have attempted to study the personality of infants and toddlers, although any observer can attest to its presence, particularly during the second and third years of life. Instead, partly because of the general neglect of this period of life, and partly because the measurement of personality is very complicated, people have turned to the concept of *temperament.*

The dictionary definition of *temperament* is equivalent to the definition of *disposition;* it has to do with characteristic mood rather than the broader realms of personality. Indeed, a psychological dictionary defines *temperament* as "the general affective nature of an individual." Thus, temperament is midway between personality and very simple approaches to individuality, such as "activity level" or "soothability."

The work of Fries in the 1930s (see Fries and Woolf, 1953), commonly cited through the 1960s in books and courses on personality, established the fact that from the first months on, the sheer amount of motor activity varied from child to child. This "activity level" variability was advanced as evidence of important innate differences (that is, evidence of individuality) among infants. However, evidence on the persistence of early differences was never clear nor vigorously emphasized.

Little attention was paid to the subject during the 1940s and early 1950s, as most developmental research shifted toward a heightened interest in behaviors that could be measured with precision—notably, visual/motor activities such as visual attention, visually directed reaching, and so on. Although activity level was measurable and new mechanisms for objective measurement, such as the stabilimeter, were being explored, not much else was being addressed in respect to more complex approaches to personality.

The major exception was the work of Birch, Chess, and Thomas. Herbert Birch was widely regarded as a brilliant developmental researcher. His team launched a major longitudinal study of the origins of personality during the 1950s. In an important book, *Behavioral Individuality in Early Childhood* (1963), they derided what they saw as the extreme environmentalism of the early longitudinal studies of personality growth, described their view of the necessary approach, and then reported on the early stages of their own study. Their work intended to document the existence of multifaceted patterns of innate behavior and then explore the evolution of interactions among innate child qualities, particular parenting activities, and universal factors such as the infant's attachment requirements.

Unfortunately, Birch died, and the project—though very substantial—has never reported on the interaction processes it initially claimed to be essential. Later, the team produced a popular and influential paperback book, *Your Child Is a Person* (Chess, Thomas, and Birch, 1965), which reflected a combination of psychiatric, ethological, and comparative psychological traditions. To date, the team's findings indicate that a baby's temperament can be reliably assessed during the first months of life on a nine-dimension scale (which includes activity level as well as persistence, level of sensory threshold, characteristic mood, and so on) but that long-term stability is present in only two of the nine dimensions.

The same sort of finding was also reported in a major study by

Escalona and Heider (1959). Extensive descriptions of individuals were used as the basis for identifying personalities in later life. However, no capacity for such predictions was found. The search for powerful identifiers of innate personality or temperamental patterns is an expensive undertaking, and the past thirty years has been a period of ever-shrinking research funds.

The only study of size that has emerged in recent years is the work of T. Berry Brazelton, a psychiatrically oriented pediatrician. At the heart of his work throughout the years has been the goal of reducing the anxiety level of new parents. This anxiety often has been increased by writings that seem to indicate that any and all failings of young children are the result of the childrearing tactics of their mothers. Brazelton has pursued the subject of innate temperamental characteristics—partly, at least—to be able to demonstrate to new parents that they are only partially responsible for the behavior and development of their young children.

Brazelton (1973) has produced a scale that is designed to provide a reliable profile of individuality in infants as young as newborns. It has been employed in numerous studies and in several countries. (Promising medical research often gets wide currency.) Reliability has been established, but predictive validity has not. As with previous studies, the Brazelton patterns do not persist over the first years of life. Indeed, they do not persist over the typical four-day lying-in period. Nevertheless, many have found the Brazelton procedure quite useful for the purpose of discussing the behavior of babies with new parents.

Recently, Brazelton has been deemphasizing the importance of long-term stability of personality patterns, looking instead to a combination of innate temperamental and environmental circumstances as a more powerful approach to the predictive requirement. In this initiative, Brazelton is retracing the footsteps of Birch. The search for predictability of later personality from neonatal behavior is parallel to the search for the predictability of later intelligence from very early behavior. It rests on the assumption of the insignificance of learning and experience in general. Such an anti-environmental position is not popular with many people.

In my work, for example, I have been enormously impressed with the impact of experiences during the six- to twenty-four-month period, especially when there are no siblings who are closely spaced. The blossoming of individuality and power that often takes place during the second year of life leaves the experienced observer convinced that an understanding of the learning process must be combined with information on infant and parent characteristics for a complete analysis of the development of personality.

Either the procedures of the Birch team or those of Brazelton can be used for reliable assessment of individuality throughout the first years, although neither fully describes personality because they were built to describe the newborn, and the newborn does not have many of the personality qualities of the three-year-old. The work of Schacter et al. is an attempt at dealing with the latter. Their Q-Sort approach includes dimensions that encompass every aspect of personality one could possibly desire (there are no fewer than 113 items to utilize) (Schacter, Cooper, and Gordet, 1968). Unfortunately, the instrument has yet to be fully developed, validated, and put into general usage. However, the Q-Sort is well worth a closer look.

In summary, the study of personality during the first years of life needs considerable attention. Starting with a resolution of the substantial difficulties of definition, what is needed is much more basic plotting of the emergence of individuality, the creation of assessment procedures, the identification of salient experiential factors and ways of measuring them, and experimental work on the developmental process.

6
The Development of Curiosity

T he dictionary definition of *curiosity* is "a desire to learn or know" or, simply, "inquisitiveness." Given such a definition, it is obvious that curiosity and education are intimately related. Although there are other reasons why people learn—for example, to avoid pain—parents and professionals alike generally agree that a strong desire to learn or know is of fundamental importance to the process of education.

Helping a child to acquire a high level of intrinsic interest in learning requires certain basic knowledge, parallel to the knowledge base needed to help a child become intelligent or proficient in language. What is needed is an understanding of what curiosity is, how it develops as a child grows, and what helps or hinders its growth. Unfortunately, although it may be hard to believe, no one has yet attempted to trace the development of curiosity during infancy and toddlerhood.

The closest work involves studies of "visual interest" and of "expectancies" or "surprises." A modest number of studies performed since 1960 have explored the topic of stimulus complexity and "faceness"; others have examined the responses of infants to unexpected visual events. We need at least a hundred times such efforts—or one study by someone with the genius of Piaget—to provide a reliable picture of the origins of curiosity. However, my own extensive observations of infants and toddlers, combined with the work of others—especially Piaget—may provide some useful information on this topic.

The very first signs of curiosity are the "looking" behaviors of the neonate. Though not a sophisticated looker, the newborn can see some things and, indeed, will try to see when conditions are appropriate. Slow movement of large, nearby (about eight to twenty inches from the eyes), intensely colored objects will sometimes produce glances by a newborn baby. Steady staring with close examination of detail is lacking at first. However, during the first eight weeks or so of life, the tendency to look steadily at another person's eyes emerges and grows. The initial signs of visual interest in humans are followed slowly between eight and twelve weeks of age by hand regard and obvious examination of fine detail as visual capacity improves.

A possible, more subtle form of curiosity may be involved from the first days of life in the sucking activities of babies, especially as they suck their fists and thumbs. From eight weeks on, it becomes more reasonable to talk about *tactual curiosity* because so much finger and mouth activity begins to take place.

During the period between the third and eighth month, given the opportunity, infants will show much interest in looking at, mouthing, and fingering small objects, in looking at human faces or similar patterns, and in looking all about themselves. Also during this period, apparent curiosity about sounds is prominent in their behavior.

Perhaps the most impressive evidence of early curiosity is in the virtually universal tendency of new crawlers to explore their environments. In this respect, eight-month-old humans resemble puppies, kittens, and colts who have just learned to move about on their own.

Until the age of eight months or so, there is a remarkable consistency of behavior among infants with regard to curiosity. Most healthy three-month-olds stare at their hands for long periods each day, most six-month-olds reach for and explore any small nearby object, and most new crawlers will explore if allowed to do so.

From eight months on, however, divergence of curiosity behavior becomes considerably broader. Some one-year-olds show far more curiosity than others. The same is true of two- and three-year-olds. The one-year-old who is routinely kept in a playpen will show far less interest in exploration than the free-roaming one-year-old. After all, there is only so much to do in a four-foot by five-foot space. Turned loose, the penned one-year-old child will explore. It is interesting, and sad, that this is not as true for two- and three-year-olds. Although the evidence is hardly solid, I have seen many two- and three-year-olds whose interest in learning seems to have been severely depressed.

For the child whose curiosity level remains very high throughout the first three years, there is, of course, an evolution of interests. Between six and twenty-four months, for example, much curiosity is focused on small objects and their paths of motion. Between eight and thirty-six months, children show much interest in hand—eye activities and in simple mechanisms (e.g., light switches). During the second year, much interest is shown in the behavior of other people and in language. Whereas visual interest remains high throughout the early years, exploration with the fingers and mouth declines steadily after the first year.

These are some of the indicators of curiosity or the desire to learn during the first years. A truly useful knowledge base would require a complete inventory of such indicators, a workable definition of a sign of curiosity as distinct from other forms of attention (such as attention due to fear or command), a reliable way of measuring how much curiosity a child has at any point in time, normative data for the population, and an understanding of the factors that influence the growth of curiosity (e.g., physical features of the environment, childrearing practices, etc.). We have a modest collection of ideas about nurturing the growth of curiosity—derived from our research on good development—but it is clear that the field of child development research has a long way to go on this basic topic.

Given this situation, what should we do as educators? First, conservatism is called for. If parents ask for guidance in nurturing their child's curiosity, the professional must reply that all we have are educated guesses. If someone publishes an infant stimulation curriculum or markets a toy with the promise that it will stimulate curiosity, the informed professional has to point out that such promises cannot be made in good faith. These points are made not to discourage the nurturing of curiosity but rather to help keep professional efforts operating at a responsible level.

7

Physical Development

Newborn children have very little control over their bodies. They can't sit up, climb, or walk. They can't use their hands to procure nearby objects. They can't even keep their heads erect when they are being held in an upright position. Their bodies are simply too much for them. Most three-year-olds walk, run, and climb with considerable skill and some grace. They use their hands, under the guidance of their eyes, to perform numerous fine-muscle tasks successfully. This capacity to use all or part of the body with accuracy and control is what we mean by *physical abilities*.

Comparatively little attention has been paid to the development of physical abilities during infancy and toddlerhood in recent years. Although research, especially in the medical field, has built an impressive body of knowledge on the topic, most studies have indicated that poor development of physical abilities is not nearly so widespread as poor development of the intellectual, linguistic, and social abilities. Unless there are clear indications of central nervous system damage, most underachieving preschoolers seem to acquire normal physical abilities. As a result, very few early education programs even include the development of such abilities among their goals.

However, a few early childhood specialists are very concerned with physical development. They range from fitness advocates, such as Bonnie Pruden and Betty Perkins, to people such as Emme Pikler of Hungary, Magda Gerber of California, and Jaroslav Koch of Czechoslovakia, who see a much deeper significance in the subject. For example, Pikler has a well-developed curriculum for infants and toddlers that focuses mainly on physical development. Her claim is that a child who is helped to perfect each new motor skill, such as crawling, will move forward more slowly but with much more self-confidence and personal security, provided that there is no pressure to accelerate the pace of development. Her movies of her students are very impressive.

Although such views are held by a very small minority of specialists in the field, educators should be knowledgeable about the development of physical abilities. Figure 7–1 illustrates the basic pattern of motor development during the first three years of life. The average age of onset for each ability is indicated by a short vertical bar; the horizontal bars indicate the approximate variability in the age of onset.

Testing for most motor skills can be done rather easily, using

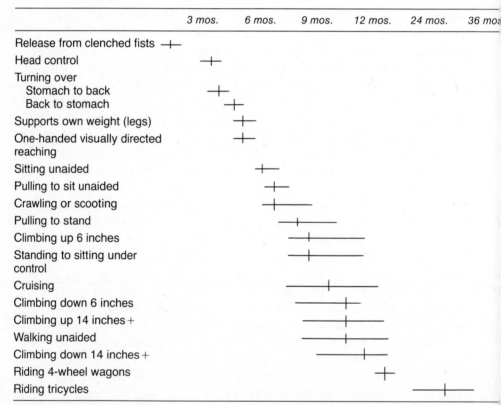

Vertical bars indicate average age of onset; horizontal bars indicate approximate variability in age of onset.

Figure 7–1. *A Chronology of Physical Development*

one of several well-developed instruments, such as the Gesell, Bayley, Griffiths, or Denver tests. I prefer the Bayley test.

There are certainly important environmental and experiential influences on the development of physical abilities. There are indications that you can impede development if you try hard enough; that the average environment is adequate to sustain normal progress; and that you can accelerate or otherwise significantly influence at least some motor skill development if you provide special materials and/or learning experiences.

Twenty-four hour swaddling undoubtedly would delay the development of motor skills, especially the development of visually directed reaching. This point is academic, however, since the practice is virtually unheard of. Special crib toys can increase early visual exploration and accelerate mastery of the hands as reaching tools, and specially designed gymnastic equipment and/or training can lead to more graceful behavior in two- and three-year-olds.

Although encouraging motor skill development can lead to earlier acquisition of some skills, I would not recommend that motor development be viewed as a central goal of early education. However, I do believe that there are important reasons why some encouragement makes sense. Infants whose motor development is assisted by appropriate environmental conditions have the opportunity to engage in experiences that are intriguing, challenging, and satisfying for them. Success, particularly in the presence of people who care very deeply for the children, leads to repeated praise for genuine achievement and, in turn, a solid sense of pride in self. For these reasons—supported by extensive observations of the quality and quantity of the time infants devote to mastery of their bodies—I believe that the acquisition of physical abilities is an important element in the education of infants and toddlers.

8
The Development of Perceptual Abilities

Perceptual development is the acquisition of awareness of external objects, qualities, or relations on the basis of sensory information. It is clear that the newborn, though neither blind nor deaf, does not see or hear with the precision of the normal three-year-old. Of all the sensory systems, the early development of only one—vision—has been studied extensively. However, we do have some extremely valuable information regarding the growth of hearing abilities. We also know that the tactual, vestibular, and kinesthetic systems are the most mature at birth. We have very little information on the acquisition of taste, pain, and smell, but, in all, the information that we *do* have has important practical value.

The fact that the sensory systems are activated when a baby is picked up, cuddled, and rocked—along with related information on the significance of such experiences—supports recommendations that parents should lavish gentle physical affection on their very young infants. The fact that normal infants will react routinely to abrupt, loud noises allows us to identify profound hearing losses as soon as a child is born, if not earlier. The fact that the normal infant of four to five months of age will turn accurately to the source of a soft sound enables us to identify mild to moderate hearing losses several weeks before the first words can be learned.

Profound hearing losses during infancy constitute a most serious development hazard for a child. Mercifully, indications are that their frequency is very low. Also, early detection is very likely and first-rate treatment is widely available. Mild to moderate losses are a different story, however. They are considerably more common; they are likely to hinder development in significant ways; and they are very often overlooked.

Practically speaking, the most important facts to know are the following. From birth, infants should respond immediately (when not in a deep sleep) to any nearby abrupt, loud noise. The responses can take several forms. Newborns may interrupt their sucking or smooth breathing rhythm or, indeed, anything they are doing. During the initial two or three months, they are very likely to startle to such a noise. Increasingly, toward the fifth month, they should be more attentive to ordinary sounds, although they do not usually startle them. By the fifth month, babies with normal hearing should turn accurately to the source of a nearby whisper (six to twelve feet away) in a quiet room.

Our modest knowledge suggests that significant visual problems are rare during the first few years of life. Nevertheless, it is important to understand and monitor visual development for effective early identification of problems, for design of materials for the baby's use, and to enable parents and others to understand a baby's visual abilities and limitations.

At birth, babies spend little time looking at anything. For the first month or so, they seem uncomfortable with their eyes open in bright light; looking is most likely to occur under conditions of dim illumination. Newborns are capable of focusing only in the rare moments when they are alert (less than thirty minutes per day). During the first month of life, focusing is limited to a very narrow range of an inch or so, usually seven to nine inches from the eyes. Until they are eight to ten weeks of age, infants' eyes do not turn in (visual convergence) to maintain a single image as objects come close to them.

The absence of visual convergence, along with limited focusing ability, means that during the first two months of life, babies are not suited to visual examination of objects closer than seven or eight inches away. Estimates are that the normal newborn has about 20/200 vision. Overall, newborns tend not to look much at small, nearby, detailed objects. A newborn's attention can be captured, at times, by a slowly moving, fairly large (more than five or six inches) object near the line of sight and about twelve inches from the eyes. All one should expect, however, is momentary attention in such a situation.

Toward the end of the second month, rapid changes begin. First, the baby starts to spend much more time looking about. Thirty-minute periods of alertness are now common during the day. Second, there is a rather abrupt appearance of the capabilities for and interest in examining nearby objects. There are two dramatic signs of this shift: hand regard and smiling at faces. Underlying these behavior changes is the emergence of visual convergence and flexibility in focusing ability.

Also at this time, tracking of nearby objects becomes reliable; in the weeks to follow, it becomes smooth, in contrast to the jerky style of the six-week-old. By three and a half or four months of age, focusing ability develops fully, and acuity approaches its final stages of development. The third and fourth months of life are a time for

Birth	1 mo.	2 mos.	3½ mos.	8 mos.
Fixed focus between 7 and 9 in. (only when alert and inactive—a few minutes per hour)	Focusing range begins to expand (from less than 1 in. during first mo.)	Focusing range now approx. 5 to 12 in.	Development of flexible focusing now complete	
Acuity: 20/200 (estimate)		Acuity: adequate to support sustained examination of details within focusing range (e.g., faces)	Acuity: 20/30 (estimate)	Acuity: 20/20 (estimate)
Visual motor pursuit: occasional brief regard of large nearby objects moving slowly near the line of sight	Visual motor pursuit: reliable, but must be evoked repeatedly; target leads the infant	Visual motor pursuit: smooth, anticipates object; visual convergence functional (eyes turn in as object becomes closer, maintaining a single image); sustained hand regard begins; marked increase in periods of visual alertness	Visually alert more than one-third of the day	Intense interest in small particles (e.g., bread crumbs)

Figure 8–1. *A Chronology of Visual Abilities*

many hours of close visual examination of anything within three feet of the baby. The last development of note occurs at about eight months, when infants show a fascination with looking at tiny particles, such as bread crumbs. To some extent, this short-lived interest may be due to newly acquired hand–eye skills, but it also probably reflects the attainment of 20/20 vision.

Pediatric ophthalmologists and optometrists are often, but not always, knowledgeable about these details of early visual function. Most do a good job of screening vision, and the incidence of difficulty seems low. The design and selection of toys for babies under six months of age should be based, in part, on such information. Test procedures for each of the developing skills are available, but they usually require extensive training for their use. Therefore, in contrast to hearing screening, vision screening is best done by a specially trained person. Figure 8–1 provides a general outline of what to expect in this area during the first months of life.

9

The Development of Interests

O ne of the several benefits of doing longitudinal observational research with babies is that we acquire a degree of understanding of their rapidly changing interests. We know that what excites a two-month-old is quite different from what excites an eleven- or twenty-two-month-old. This chapter outlines that evolution from birth to the third birthday.

During the first six weeks of life, most babies are totally uninterested in explorations of the external world, except for occasional brief glances at human faces. Sometime around the middle of the second month, most children exhibit a rather abrupt increase in wakefulness during the daytime hours and, at the same time, begin to show what seems to be a parallel increase in curiosity about the appearance of their surroundings.

Recently, several reports have led people to conclude that from the very first months of postnatal life, children are actively and vigorously exploring the world and interacting in what might be considered a sophisticated style. The point to be made here is that there is a vital difference between what babies *can* do and what they *do* do. Given carefully arranged conditions, a neonate *can* turn toward the source of sound. However, such conditions almost never occur naturally, so infants almost never orient to sounds during typical day-to-day living until they are two to four months old. What they *do* do most of the time during the first four to six weeks of life is sleep. The primary interest of children during this period seems to be comfort.

Between six and nine weeks of age, children begin to spend much more time—from about 15 to 30 percent of the day—actively looking around. At the same time, they are becoming more comfortable in a reclining position because of the increasing strength of their back and neck muscles. In addition to visual interest, they also show what appears to be interest in mouthing objects. It is hard to be sure about this, however, since mouthing to relieve discomfort—which is very common as the teeth break through the gums during much of the first year—must be distinguished from mouthing to explore shapes. Thus, it is not clear how much of the mouthing of the fist and fingers during the first five or six months of life serves to satisfy curiosity about these interesting items and how much serves simply to relieve soreness in the mouth.

From nine weeks to four months, in addition to continued mouthing and looking, two new interests emerge: practicing hand movements under the guidance of the eyes—in the pursuit of mastery of the hand as a tool—and socializing. There is no question that the early smiles and apparent pleasure in face-to-face encounters are indicators of emerging social interest at this time (although the very first behavior of this sort are not so "social" as they may appear).

From four to five months—in addition to the aforementioned interests, which continue—children begin to experiment with their own sounds, most notably through playing with their saliva. They also begin vigorous exercises with their legs. From five to seven months, mouthing, looking, practicing hand movements, playing with sounds, and exercising their legs continue to be prominent in daily activities, and interest in mastery of the body spreads to the torso. Most babies spend a good deal of time turning onto their sides and from back to stomach (and vice versa) during this period.

From seven to thirty-six months of age, there are three overwhelming interests, which include several subinterests. The major interests are people, mastering the body, and satisfying curiosity.

The period from eight to twenty-four months is when home-reared babies concentrate on family members, and most of their attention is focused on the person who spends the bulk of the time with them during their waking hours. In addition, if there are closely spaced siblings, a special interest is forced upon the child by the jealousy problems that are normal when children are spaced less than three years apart. For example, an eight-month-old child with a sibling who is less than three years older is often forced to spend a great deal of time each day warding off hostile actions. This is a daily concern (rather than an intrinsic interest) that will persist throughout the balance of the first three years. Similarly, when the younger sibling gets to be seven or eight months of age and starts to crawl, the older child—who is still under three—ordinarily spends many hours each week coping with the resulting chronic intrusions on the daily routine. This older child will remain seriously concerned with the baby until at least age three and a half.

The second major interest in the seven- to thirty-six-month period is in mastery of the body. From seven to eighteen months of age, infants exhibit a very strong interest in gross motor challenges—starting with pulling to sit and crawling and moving on to pulling to stand, cruising (walking while holding onto something), climbing, getting down from a standing posture, and walking unaided. These emerging abilities—especially the more adventurous climbing activities—reach their peak during the period from seven to eighteen months of age. Subsequently, interest in gross motor activities continues, but less for the purpose of mastering a newly emerging skill and more for the simple pleasure of gross motor activities.

During this time, there is also an equally powerful interest in hand–eye activities for developing skills and learning about the world of small objects. This is a very strong interest throughout the entire two- to twenty-four-month age range. Hand–eye activities continue to be of interest to the child through to thirty-six months, with special concern for new challenges—for example, manipulating parts of puzzles and small gadgets, such as pencil sharpeners or paint brushes.

The third major interest, curiosity—is manifested in simple visual examination, especially during the period from seven to fifteen months of age. From fifteen months on—through the balance of the first three years—looking is supplemented by an increasing interest in listening to language.

Generally, all new objects, people, and scenes feed a child's curiosity from two to thirty-six months of age. However, the focus of a child's curiosity shifts with development. For example, books are of interest to the ten- to eighteen-month-old child as props to be used in practicing hand–eye skills or for labeling sessions (when a parent holds a child on his lap and engages in a social/language experience by simply naming the pictures). Once the child reaches eighteen months of age—and for the balance of the first three years—books become much more interesting for their story content than for their more primitive uses. Of course, a child's social interest also continues during storybook sessions, with the greatest potency coming during the first half of the eighteen- to thirty-six-month period. During the second half of that period, as children become more interested in agemates, there is a lessening of the intense interest in their parents that is common to the second year of life.

Anyone concerned about living with and/or teaching a baby should have a reasonably precise understanding of the evolution of interests during the first years of life. This information is needed by those who want to help shape the behaviors of young children, design materials to aid the developmental process, or simply provide fun for babies.

10
The "Amazing" Newborn

For many years now, people studying young children have reported a wide variety of hitherto undiscovered abilities in the very young child. Indeed, remarkable capacities have been ascribed to the neonate and even to the fetus. Some students of human development would have you believe that babies are busy "tuning in" on their mothers' thoughts and feelings for months before birth. Others claim that babies actively appreciate the experience of the birth process. Still others would have you believe that infants see, hear, compare, and make decisions—followed by intentional behaviors—within their first weeks of life. What *can* fetuses and very young infants do? What goes on in their minds between their conception and their first birthdays? Clearly, the younger the creature and the more amazing the ability, the more interesting, fascinating, and exciting the findings are.

The problem is that many of these findings turn out not to be valid. Sometimes it is several years before a claim is either confirmed or reputed. Until the late 1960s, claims about infants' abilities could stand a long time, because comparatively few people were doing research with children under three years of age. With the tremendous increase in such research activity in recent years, however, many claims are now examined more quickly and more closely.

Some claims may never be examined closely, but professionals should maintain an open mind regarding them. Sometimes, all we can do is judge whether a claim is consistent with related, well-founded information about children. For example, in *The Secret Life of the Unborn Child* (1981), Dr. Thomas Verny claims that a neonate can somehow absorb and retain language—indeed, even a foreign language. Most knowledgeable people resist this idea, and the work of Piaget in particular—which in my opinion stands as the most respectable information about mental capacities in the first years of life—directly contradicts any such claims for mental power of the neonate. I hasten to add, however, that many people still believe Verny's claim.

In the 1960s, the prevailing picture of early human abilities was first modified significantly by studies of vision, especially those of Fantz (1963), who demonstrated that babies could "discriminate" among targets during their first months of life. The issue of whether they were actually comparing targets or merely looking at the ones they could make out became one controversy. Another was whether they were perceiving "faceness" or complexity. In any event, Fantz convinced most people that babies could see better—especially after they were two months old—than others had thought they could.

As for hearing, although it is true that a newborn *can* orient to sound, given highly restricted conditions (see Muir and Field, 1979), we cannot expect much behavior of this kind before the fourth month. Unless they are held in the prone position and exposed to a particular kind of sound, infants routinely do no more than blink, startle, or pause in their activities in response to sound during the first weeks of life.

Again, for most students of human development, Piaget's analyses of intellectual development remain the most accurate. The picture he created from continuous observations of his own three children has been supported by many studies over several decades.

Piaget's work on the origins of intelligence in the first two years of life has never been replicated completely, but there have been many attempts to replicate small portions of his work. In particular, studies of the development of object permanence have proliferated during the past fifteen to twenty years. Aside from some minor details, Piaget's findings have been successfully replicated in virtually all cases. In my own work with institutionally reared babies under six months of age, my colleagues and I have replicated many elements of his early findings on hand–eye behavior and other basic phenomena, except for some minor differences regarding the influence of sucking behavior.

In 1977, Meltzoff and Moore reported that two- to three-week-old infants opened their mouths more frequently following a mouth opening model than following a tongue protrusion model. Similarly, the infants produced more tongue protrusions after the tongue protrusion model than after the mouth opening model. This claim, apparently documented by films of the episodes, left advocates of Piagetian theory confused. In Piaget's system, imitation of a very primitive kind—behavior he called *pseudo-imitation*—first surfaces during the fourth month of life, when a few behaviors a baby *has already engaged in* may be protracted when an adult simulates or imitates the baby. Imitation of the sort described by Meltzoff and Moore is not supposed to surface until the end of the first year, when Piaget refers to it as *imitation of seen models.*

How do we resolve this discrepancy? It would be relatively easy simply to state that Piaget was the master and that findings not consistent with his must therefore be false. This would attribute infallibility to Piaget, however, and though I consider him the only genius in the field of human development research, that would be folly given what we have learned from the history of science.

On the other hand, we could say that imitation in the first weeks of life is a reality and that, therefore, Piaget's views of the intellectual power and behavior of infants must undergo a substantial revision. However, most researchers would not want to move toward such revision without first having replications of the new findings, preferably by other investigators.

One factor that has to be considered when an unusual finding is claimed is the credibility of the investigator. It happens that Meltzoff and Moore both have reputations that are beyond question. They both are very capable and very knowledgeable with respect to research on neonates. This makes dismissal of their claim even more difficult.

A later study by Hayes and Watson (1981) first attempted— unsuccessfully—to replicate the Meltzoff and Moore findings on neonatal imitation of tongue protrusion and mouth opening. A second experiment—to assess whether the experimenter's determination of the onset of data recording might have been influenced by the infant's ongoing behavior with a pacifier held by the experimenter—again provided no evidence of imitation. The results indicated that the type of mouth movement on the pacifier just before its removal (i.e., tongue pressure or passive release) was a reliable predictor of subsequent infant behavior. This could have contributed to artifactual results interpreted by Meltzoff and Moore as evidence of neonatal imitation.

Thus, it seemed clear that the Meltzoff and Moore results did not warrant a revision of Piaget's picture of intellectual development in the first years of life. It was still possible, of course, that others would discover that imitation does take place in some form at two to three weeks of age. In fact, in 1982, Field et al. reported just such a result. They claimed that in their study of 74 neonates (average age thirty-six hours), three facial expressions were both discriminated and imitated. However, until the overall weight of the evidence favors acceptance of such claims, I recommend that judgment be reserved.

Finally, in 1984, Abravanel and Sigafoos did something a bit unusual. They tested for several types of imitative responses with children four to six weeks of age and others up to twenty-one weeks of age at four different points, and their procedures were most impressive in their thoroughness and care. These researchers found some evidence of incomplete imitation of one gesture—tongue protrusion—but only at four to six weeks of age. Their studies of slightly older children did not indicate a growth in the capacity to imitate; rather, they found virtually no imitative behavior beyond the first age period. Their explanation of the limited amount of imitative behavior that was found is consistent with much of the literature on innate organized behavior patterns that have been found to exist in the first two or three months of life, then disappear and be replaced by more sophisticated forms of the same sort of behavior. Included in these behavior patterns are coordinated arm and leg movements, the so-called swimming patterns of the newborn, stepping patterns, rooting behavior, and the centralizing reflex in vision.

We can conclude, then, that the earlier reports of Meltzoff and Moore are confirmed in part, but that the interpretation they proposed—that imitative ability is present from the first months of life and that Piaget's views of the growth of imitation are incorrect—has limited validity. It may be fair to say that Piaget missed these short-lived examples of imitation during the initial two months of life, but it is not appropriate to recast our understanding of when and how imitation develops during the first years of life.

The question of how to deal with new claims applies not only to the issue of neonatal imitation, but also to Verny's statements about the registration of language in the newborn (and, indeed, the sensing of maternal perceptions by the fetus), some of the claims of the Brazelton group concerning the conscious awareness of the child in the first months of life, the claims of others about the decision-making capacity of children in the first months of life, and so on. These claims represent but a few of the many that surface regularly from time to time. It is our recommendation that they all be treated with caution to the extent that they are markedly inconsistent with more numerous and long-standing reports on early human capacities.

In Piaget's view, babies start pretty much from scratch at birth. They do not think or process specific experiences in the aware, conscious style of older children or adults. They have no innate memories or appreciations of the world around them. They make no decisions and perform no intentional acts for several months at least. The first intentional problem solving appears at about six or seven months, when a baby moves an obstacle aside in order to procure a desired object. It is not until eight or nine months or so that babies develop the first short-lived memory capacity. By eighteen to twenty-four months, they begin to solve problems by thinking about them.

This picture of the developing mental capacities of the infant is far more consistent with the existing evidence than any other claims for the fetus and young infant. Claims of "amazing" capacities in the newborn may be powerful and seductive because of the eternal fascination for poorly understood, long-standing puzzles. But to accept such claims without due regard for legitimate and substantial evidence to the contrary makes little sense.

Furthermore, uncritical acceptance of such claims may have detrimental consequences for new or expectant parents. For instance, the film *The Amazing Newborn,* which depicts neonates engaging in imitative behaviors and other atypical activities, has a brief disclaimer at the end to inform viewers that they should not expect to elicit similar behaviors from their own babies at home. I cannot imagine new parents *not* attempting to replicate various demonstrations shown in the film and *not* being disappointed or upset when their babies do not respond in the appropriate manner.

Another hazard involves the claims by proponents of the Le-Boyer method of childbirth. The LeBoyer method—which involves a quiet setting, soft lighting, gentle handling, and the like—seems like a very nice way to be born. Furthermore, encouraging close contact between parent and child for the first few hours after birth is probably a good idea. However, claims that the newborn is aware of what is going on, that he will remember the circumstances and events, and that these memories will have significant, long-term effects on his mental and emotional development simply are not substantiated by hard evidence. Yet parents who, for one reason or another, do not have LeBoyer-type childbirth may believe that they have failed their children in a fundamental way.

Perhaps the most potentially hazardous claims are those currently being espoused by people who contend that the fetus is capable of perceiving the mother's thoughts and feelings in utero and that these perceptions will have significant, long-term effects on the child's mental and emotional health after birth. Besides citing well-established evidence that various maternal activities, such as taking certain drugs or smoking, may adversely affect the fetus physically, the claim is made that development can be dramatically influenced by mentally processed experiences as well.

After years of trying to convince people of the importance of experiences during the first years of life, I find it a bit strange to be in the position of resisting claims about the importance of experiences prior to birth. Nevertheless, resist I must, because there are potentially negative consequences of such claims and because the claims are inconsistent with the knowledge base.

I urge professionals to adopt a conservative stance with regard to claims about "amazing" mental and emotional capacities in newborns and fetuses, and I urge caution about premature incorporation of revolutionary new ideas into work with families.

11

What We *Don't* Know about Early Development

I f you scan the topics covered in this part, you will notice that several interesting, important, and popular subjects are not mentioned—such as the development of creativity, values, character, artistic talent, and musical talent. Also missing is information about the origins of sex-role identity and the self-concept. The reason these subjects have been omitted is simple: little useful and reliable information has actually been discovered, at least in a manner that would allow people in general to use the information.

For example, consider the concept of creativity. There is no doubt that something like creativity is being enhanced by the child-rearing practices of parents and professionals somewhere in the world. Also, certain programs promise that children receiving their guidance will develop into more creative people. In some situations, there is apparent success. However, there are no *proven* practices.

Over the past century, a wide variety of research projects have clearly demonstrated or proved that certain childrearing or teaching practices routinely produce certain kinds of outcomes in young children. The best information of this kind comes from rather rare, high-quality psychological or educational research—research in which professionals create a clear plan, control the activities of the adults and/or subject children, and employ first-rate measurements of the children's abilities both before and after, along with measurements of the childrearing or teaching experiences involved.

For example, learning theorists have manipulated the rewards that infants experience when they look in certain directions or when they suck more rapidly. Studies featuring this kind of experimental control have demonstrated certain effects repeatedly, and these demonstrations have been described in a manner that will allow other qualified professionals to repeat the experience with other children. This is what I mean by proven practices.

In my own work, my colleagues and I have had considerable success demonstrating how to accelerate the development of visually directed reaching during the first months of life. The power of our model parent education programs in Missouri is of the same sort; that is, we have followed standard practices and have demonstrated that when *A, B,* and *C* are done, the benefits are *D, E,* and *F* for a wide variety of children.

This simply has not been done with respect to creativity, nor has it been done for any of the other subjects listed earlier. Furthermore, we have an even more fundamental problem in dealing with these important topics: Many of them have yet to be properly defined. No one has come up with a generally accepted definition of a creative six-month-old or of a truly masculine fourteen-month-old. It happens that creativity and gender identity are, by any standards, very difficult concepts to define. In contrast, height and weight are trivially easy to define and measure, and even language and intelligence have been defined rather well. But emotional states, such as joy or fury, and such notions as self-concept, character, and the like, present an as yet unmastered set of challenges for child development research.

The result, sadly, is that no one is really able to promise good results in these areas. The best we can do is make educated guesses. Some of our guesses will be pretty good, and others will be very shaky. Ultimately—perhaps forty or fifty years from now—we will know more about these subjects. In the meantime, what we *do* know about helping a child develop into a healthy social creature— with genuine enthusiasm for learning, fine language and intellectual skills, and so on—is far more than anyone knew until as recently as twenty years ago and offers substantial and remarkable opportunities for parents and professionals to provide much better beginnings for children.

Part II
Developmental Variations, Influences, and Problems

12
Developmental Divergence

A lthough I have never been fond of technical terminology when it gets in the way of the communication process (and I think it often does), there are times when a special label seems helpful in conveying a complex idea. *Developmental divergence* is such a term. For many developmental processes—such as growth (in height), spoken words, or problem-solving abilities—the levels attained by a group of children at any given age vary quite a bit. So, for example, two-year-olds will vary in height by several inches and in the number of words they speak by several dozen. For any group of children, there is some number that describes the average or central tendency for the group for any measurable acquisition. For groups of children free from gross pathology, the scores for individuals will vary from below to above average and, when plotted on a graph, will usually form a "normal" curve. A small number of scores will diverge widely—either well above or below the average—whereas many scores will approach the average.

If the average scores for several ages between birth and age three are collected and plotted, the result is a picture of the development of a measured attribute, such as height or speech. We have a great deal of information on the growth in height of normal children, and pediatricians use such information to gauge the normality of an individual child's stature at any point during the early years. Minor divergence from the average is expected; indeed, it is the rule. Major divergence usually calls for a closer look.

We use developmental divergence to describe deviations in ongoing developmental processes that are likely to have lasting significance. For example, if a child of two or three years of age lags substantially behind the average in the acquisition of abstract thinking ability or receptive language skills, we call that an instance of developmental divergence or delay. Correspondingly, a child who is well ahead in such developments would also represent developmental divergence, albeit a more welcome kind.

Although our knowledge is not perfect by any means, many educators believe that developmental divergence with respect to language and higher mental abilities in three-year-old children is very significant. (There is reason to believe that low social skill achievement levels at age three are also of major significance, but our data on this are rather weak so far.) There are two major reasons for this belief. The first is based on evidence that has been abundant for many years. In groups of normal children (i.e., those free from serious pathology but not necessarily at the average level for any particular ability), scores of three-year-olds on tests of intelligence and language begin to predict later test performance reliably. Although the predictive power of any *single* test for any *single* child is only fairly good, it is useful, especially for children who score quite high or quite low.

The second reason some educators are very interested in developmental divergence at age three is that poor levels of achievement at that age seem remarkably difficult to deal with using current methods of remedial education. In other words, a child who is weak in intellectual and language skills at age three is not often or easily brought to average or above average levels of function on those abilities by special programs.

Therefore, for anyone interested in good development in children, the question of when children first begin to reveal how well they are progressing is of fundamental importance. The highest priority in the minds of most concerned people is the earliest possible detection of any significant problem. A more subtle concern is the early identification of underachievement. In addition, for many practical reasons, we need to know how well each child is acquiring basic abilities during the early years. For example, the timing of remedial or preventive services can be planned only on the basis of such information. Whereas some thought Head Start was a preventive program, test data later demonstrated that, for many three-year-olds, it turned out to be remedial work.

For language and intellectual development, at least, the knowledge base on developmental divergence is more than adequate to provide vitally important guidance for educational policy. The situation is as follows.

A small fraction of children (exact number unknown, but likely to be less than 5 percent) are born with serious physical handicaps—for example, blindness, deafness, or other severely debilitating congenital defects. For such children, performance on general tests of early achievement, such as the Gesell Schedules, the Bayley Scales, or the Denver Developmental Tests, produces consistent indications of very poor development from the earliest months of life. For such children, *the tests of development during infancy are predictive.* According to what we now know, such children never will acquire the levels of intellectual and linguistic abilities of physically normal children, regardless of educational efforts.

A second small group of children (again, exact number unknown) are born free from serious physical defects but are seriously damaged during infancy. Such serious damage can result from abuse by disturbed parents, from environmental conditions such as lead poisoning, and so forth. These children may also perform well below national averages, consistently, on the aforementioned tests during infancy. For them, too, the prognosis is generally poor, although we rarely can be sure that they will never come back fully.

For most children born in this country (75 percent to 85 percent), the general tests of achievement administered during the first eighteen months of life *do not predict* to later tests of language and intelligence. This finding has also been reported for large numbers of children around the world. In general, the first predictive power of early achievement tests for such children is seen at about two years of age, although recent research suggests that receptive language testing as early as fourteen months of age can identify children who are already moving ahead or falling behind. For example, in the Harvard Preschool Project's longitudinal research, the Bayley Mental Index (as distinguished from the Motor Index) correlated at the $+.41$ level with Binet scores at three years and at the $+.63$ level with language scores at three years. This is by no means an isolated finding. In addition, much older research has indicated genuine (though far from perfect) predictive power of scores on the Binet and the Wechsler tests of intelligence from three and four years on, respectively.

What this information seems to mean is that children begin to indicate their future levels of achievement increasingly from the second birthday. At first, only the most and least precocious produce reliable indicators of their developmental trends; a greater fraction of noteworthy children is revealed by the third birthday, and so on. It should be noted, however, that a score of 135 on an achievement test (with an average score of 100) attained by a child on the first birthday is no more predictive of a high score at three or four years of age than a score of 95. Hence, we say that developmental divergence begins to become clear from the second birthday on.

The reasons underlying this state of affairs are also becoming clear. Since recent research has shown that language and higher mental abilities have barely begun to develop by the first birthday but often move ahead very rapidly during the second year, these results should come as no surprise.

13
Developmental Risk

Developmental *risk* is the possibility that a human achievement will not come into a child's repertoire to the best degree possible, given the child's innate potential. Since our focus here is on education, we will discuss the common, postnatal, environmental bases for risk, rather than such other factors as genetic anomalies or extreme pathological circumstances (e.g., psychopathology or chronic, severe abuse).

It is interesting that across the full array of achievements children can acquire during the early years, there is wide variation in the degree of risk under the range of circumstances American children routinely encounter. For instance, the degree of risk with respect to the acquisition of visual skills is quite small during the early years, as is the degree of risk with respect to mastery of the body—that is, the capacity to hold the head erect, sit up, crawl, walk, climb, and so forth. In contrast, a high degree of risk exists with respect to language acquisition, the ability to manipulate ideas and to solve problems through mental operations, and the development of a healthy personality.

How professionals know about the degree of risk depends primarily on two sources of information: research and experience. Despite significant weaknesses in the knowledge base, there is ample evidence to enable us to gauge the degree of risk involved in most of the major areas of early development. Clearly, we should put our greatest efforts where the degree of risk is high. If resources are limited, it becomes quite important to know whether some areas do not require the efforts of professionals, parents, or children.

The following table indicates the degree of risk found among the general population with respect to major human achievements during the first three years of life:

Low	High	Unclear
Gross muscle skills	Personality	Creativity
Fine muscle skills	Social skills	Artistic talent
Vision	Language	Athletic talent
Sensorimotor intelligence	Higher mental abilities	Sex-role identity
(0–24 months)	Hearing	
Taste	Curiosity	
Smell		
Kinesthetic sense		
Vestibular sense		
Interpersonal security		
(0–6 months)		

There is a great deal of confusion about the subject of risk—not only in the popular articles in various parents' magazines but also among professionals, including some of the most substantial in the field. For example, one of the most impressive students of compensatory education for three- to five-year-old children from low-income families, David Weikart of the High/Scope Foundation in Ypsilanti, Michigan, has also worked in the area of infancy. In his studies and programs, he has concentrated on helping the very young child acquire normal sensorimotor intelligence, as defined by Piaget. However, many studies have indicated that sensorimotor intelligence is not at risk for the vast majority of children. Although it is true that children with severe innate deficiencies or environmental circumstances can fail to achieve the highest levels of sensorimotor intelligence by their second birthday, it is not at all likely that the 85 percent (or more) of the population not included in such categories will have any difficulties of consequence—regardless of the wide variability of childrearing conditions found among families.

In other areas, we have comparable kinds of confusion. The subject of bonding has recently thrown many parents and professionals into a tizzy, on the assumption that interpersonal security in the first months of life is very much at risk with ordinary variations in childrearing practices. In recent years, some professionals have insisted that the first days of life are extremely important with respect to bonding; and some have strongly urged parents to pay attention to the establishment of good communication patterns during the first weeks of life. Neither of these claims seems to be supported by substantial evidence.

However, there is ample evidence that other, equally important basic human achievements are very much at risk in the general population. For instance, language and higher mental abilities repeatedly have been shown to be vulnerable to ordinary variations in early experience. Mild to moderate intermittent hearing losses during infancy and toddlerhood is also an area in which risk has been well established.

There is also confusion represented by the category labeled "unclear" in the foregoing risk table. There are several subjects that are dear to the hearts of some people, but even indirect information on these subjects is hard to interpret with respect to risk.

The most conservative path for professionals to take is to pay a good deal of attention to guidance for parents in regard to helping a child achieve a solid personality, a collection of effective social skills, the highest possible degree of receptive and expressive language ability, the highest possible degree of intelligence and problem-solving ability, intact hearing, and the highest possible degree of pure curiosity by the third birthday. For those with special interests in creativity, artistic or athletic ability, or sex-role identity, I urge caution. The knowledge we have with respect to risk in those areas of development is far too skimpy for us to provide guidance with confidence.

In regard to the achievement areas for which risk seems low, rather than overburdening either professionals or parents, I suggest that parent educators provide basic information, but without an air of urgency. It is surely important for parents to know when their children will acquire gross muscle skills—if for no other reason than that safety is a general concern during infancy and toddlerhood. If the parents do not know such basic facts as when a child is likely to start crawling, climbing, and the like, accidents are more likely to happen.

The problem with explaining all of these risk factors to parents and others is that people have a limited capacity to absorb and act upon information. If you try to get parents or professional childrearers to absorb a huge amount of information, the result will be chaos. It is better to keep the focus on the highest priorities and do a good job with them than to muddy the waters and do a poor job across the board.

It should also be noted that many parents—particularly first-time parents—are in a state of chronic anxiety. It would be a disservice to them to convey the message that they have many things to worry about.

14
Bonding

B onding is the rapid development of an intense and healthful attachment between a newborn and an older person—usually the mother—in the first hours of the infant's life. The concept of bonding came into the limelight primarily through the work of two physicians at Case Western Reserve University in Cleveland, Marshall K. Klaus and John H. Kennell (Kennell et al., 1974; Klaus and Kennell, 1970). They reported that when mothers were given sixteen extra hours of contact with their children immediately after birth, the relationship between those mothers and their infants seemed to become generally more beneficial for both mother and child—as compared with the more common situation in which the mother of a newborn infant spends relatively little time with the infant during the first day of the baby's life.

Klaus and Kennell also reported that several years after birth, the mothering behavior of those mothers who had had a chance to spend time in close contact with their brand-new babies was generally of a more desirable quality than that of mothers without such special experience. The mothers who had had the closer contact tended to be more affectionate with their children, more interested in them, and less harsh with them.

These dramatic announcements, which seemed to offer exciting new information, immediately received a great deal of publicity. Over the next few years, a number of hospitals modified their practices to allow young mothers and their newborn babies to enjoy as much close contact as possible from the very beginning.

Whereas the original reporters of the bonding phenomenon had studied women from low-income families, an attempt to repeat the findings with middle-class mothers was performed at Stanford University. The Stanford study found differences in the first months in childrearing styles of the mothers who had the extra contact with their newborn babies. They were more inclined to cuddle their infants and be physically affectionate with them, and they seemed more confident as mothers. However, by the time the children were one year old, there were no differences between mothers who had been given the extra contact experience and those who had not. Furthermore, the Stanford study found that factors such as the socioeconomic status of the parents and the sex of the infant were considerably more powerful influences on childrearing styles than the amount of early contact.

Another study was conducted at the University of Colorado Medical Center, this time with lower-middle-class mothers. The resupts were similar to those of the Stanford study. Beyond these three studies, there is little evidence regarding direct testing of the concept of bonding. Therefore, we should be cautious about accepting the claims with regard to the phenomenon.

A major factor to consider in deciding whether to accept a new finding is how it fits in with other known evidence, and a good deal of available information bears upon the issue of bonding. Some of the evidence concerns the general attachment process, which is thought to operate (with varying degrees of intensity) during the first two years of a child's life; the balance concerns the nature of newborn children and their mothers.

With regard to the attachment process, evidence from studies of children (and of many animal species) strongly indicates that early experiences are very important influences on lifelong emotional and social health. A good early attachment is vital for physical, emotional, and educational growth. However, there is a substantial amount of evidence that during the first three to four months of life, children are quite primitive; that is, their brains are not very well equipped to understand what is going on or to identify any individual near them with any accuracy.

It appears that newborn babies become attached to *any* older human who spends a lot of time with them. For survival, it is so important for them to become attached to an older human that, at first, they will respond with affectionate signs to just about anybody. It is not until the fourth month of life that babies begin to be particularly responsive to the people they have been living with. From that point on, the attachment becomes more focused, and by the end of the second year of life, the baby's entire day revolves around the mother or other primary caretaker.

This general picture of the process of developing attachment does not fit well with the notion that the first few hours of life are especially significant from the baby's point of view. However, it could be a special time from the point of view of the baby's mother. Although newborns are quite simple, undeveloped creatures from an intellectual, emotional, and social standpoint, that is not true of their mothers, of course. It is possible that mothers undergo some sort of uniquely important experience during the first day after the birth of their children that will somehow have lasting effects on their childrearing styles and on their feelings for their babies.

However, we must move on to the question of whether the bonding concept is a reality or, at this time, simply a speculation. In its favor, we have only one study on a small group of mothers, and we have two other studies that fail to support the first one. We can only conclude that the idea remains a speculation rather than a proved notion.

Moreover, we should consider the practical situation that would result if bonding were accepted as a thoroughly established phenomenon. If it merely caused parents to spend more time with their babies in the first hours of the babies' lives, no harm would be done. Indeed, it would probably be quite an enjoyable experience for everyone concerned. But there might be some bad effects, too. Any mother who was prevented from having close contact with her new baby might come to fear that there would be no way she could ever have a first-rate relationship with her child. Since, for a variety of reasons, many young mothers are unable to be with their babies in the first few days, the consequences of such fears would be widespread and harmful. The same would be true for adopting parents, who are almost never present in the first hours of their child's life. In the interests of all such parents, it is important that we treat the whole concept of bonding with reserve. It is no more than a hypothesis—and not a very well supported one at that.

15
The Father's Role

W hat do we want to know about the role of the father in the
development of the very young child? The ultimate question
is whether the *absence* of a father makes a difference. Since women
traditionally have had the responsibility for most of the direct childrearing activities with infants and toddlers, and since many women
today are raising children by themselves, it is not unreasonable to
ask whether a father (or other man) must participate in early childrearing for the process to be fully successful.

If the father is expendable, all succeeding questions take on a
different degree of importance, and the legions of women raising
babies alone can breathe a collective sigh of relief. On the other
hand, if the father has a significant role to play (either directly with
the child or indirectly through the mother), a host of questions surfaces. For example, are the childrearing styles of fathers different
from those of mothers? How much direct input from fathers is best?
How does the impact of fathering style affect mothering style and,
in turn, the child's development? The two basic questions regarding
the role of the father, then, are whether he makes a difference and,
if so, how?

One of the best sources of information on this topic is an article
by Allison Clarke-Stewart (1978), which reports on some first-rate
research by Clarke-Stewart herself and also contains a thorough review and discussion of the literature as of 1977. Since very little has
appeared since then, the review can be considered reasonably up-
to-date.

In the article abstract, the author states the purpose of her
study: "to expand our meager knowledge of fathers' behavior in
interaction with their young children and to explore their direct and
indirect contributions to children's development." In the early para-
graphs of the report, she expands on that statement by remarking

that "fathers are forgotten contributors to child development" and that "the nature of their role and their contribution to children's developmemt remains uncharted and unknown."

Clarke-Stewart cites a few studies (whose validity she questions) that claim that fathers are "as good at parenting as mothers." She moves on to a small number of studies that indicate that fathers' childrearing activities are different from mothers' activities; for example, fathers' roles involve fun and games and physical activities, whereas mothers' roles involve more caretaking and are usually more verbal in style. A few studies of differences in children's behavior toward fathers and mothers are also mentioned. The literature on attachment is perhaps the most substantial on the subject of fathers, although Clarke-Stewart lists only four studies. She also cites two small studies on the effects of fathers on children's development (no conclusions were reached).

Having reviewed the scanty existing reports, Clarke-Stewart presents her own study of fourteen families from a wide socioeconomic range. Children were observed at fifteen, twenty, and thirty months of age—with their fathers alone, with their mothers alone, and with both parents present. Both structured (a limited choice of activities) and unstructured (natural observations) situations were included. The major findings were that the children were equally attached to both parents, responded more to play initiated by their fathers in structured situations, and played much more with their mothers under natural conditions.

A difference was found in type of play selected by the parents, with fathers favoring social and physical games. Various other interesting findings are reported, but none presented as either very dramatic or thoroughly established. The primary conclusion is that the father's major impact on the fifteen- to thirty-month-old child is indirect, through his influence on the child's mother. There is no discussion of how substantial that impact is or of what the long-term impact of the father is.

Thus, existing research is simply too scarce to form a reliable basis for judgment on this issue. Someday, possibly, we may find real and interesting differences in childrearing behaviors of fathers versus mothers; then again, we may not. As of now, there are some modest indications in the literature, but not much has been firmly established. Whether such differences have significance for the child's development is yet another matter—at this point, totally unexplored. Older research has sometimes been cited to claim that prolonged father absence leads to sex-role problems for both boys and girls, with boys becoming less masculine and girls less feminine. However, that claim has not yet evolved into a generally accepted principle.

In the research of the Harvard Preschool Project, a few of the children who were developing very well were being raised without fathers at home, but the number was too small to allow for generalizations. Common sense would suggest that a process as complicated, stressful, and rewarding as childrearing would go better when shared by two parents. Beyond such shaky speculations, however, we can only conclude that firm statements about the importance of fathers for the development of infants and toddlers are not supported by evidence. They are more than likely another example of claims that people would *like* to be true, rather than reliable, proved judgments. Therefore, we must be cautious when reviewing information regarding this topic.

16
Sibling Spacing

The effects of various age gaps between siblings have been a matter of debate among laypeople for many years. Having children close together (a year or two apart) will hasten the day when diapers are no longer needed and might facilitate close relationships among the siblings. Having them at considerably longer intervals will avoid the heavy workload of caring for two or more very young children at once and will give parents more time to devote to each child during the first years of life.

Research on the effects of sibling spacing in the early years was virtually nonexistent until the late 1960s. The research of the Harvard Preschool Project included hundreds of hours of repeated observations in many kinds of families that had one or more very young children. We were most impressed by the apparent effects of various spacings. Among families raising children who had no special needs—such as developmental delays or abject poverty—the most commonly reported concern by far was sibling rivalry.

This finding was remarkably consistent. Many parents were tormented by the behaviors of their one- to three-year-old children toward each other. The older children generally were perceived as the greater source of difficulty, but as the younger ones moved into the second half of the second year, they were sometimes reported (and observed) to be hostile toward their older siblings. What does this finding mean?

In my opinion, the answer lies in the normal pattern of social development and in the power of parental attention during the first years of life. There is no question about the significance of the parent–child emotional bond, nor is there much disagreement that children devote a good deal of their time, energy, and passion toward the development of that bond during the first years. However, what has become clearer recently are the fine details of the process, which, in essence, are as follows:

> *Birth to two months:* The child displays virtually no social interest in adults, but her helplessness and cry are powerful factors that induce adults to care for her.
>
> *Two to three and a half months:* The child begins to smile and become accustomed to repeated episodes of distress, followed by the arrival of an adult, followed by the reduction of distress. By three and a half months, the primary caregiver's attributes (face, voice, odor, etc.) are better elicitors of attention and smiles than those of other people, although the baby is responsive to almost everyone.
>
> *Three and a half to eight months:* The baby remains adorable and continues to grow closer to the primary caregivers.
>
> *Eight to fifteen months:* The period of indiscriminate acceptance of approaches by others usually ends. "Stranger reactions" to non-nuclear family members who try to "cozy up" are common indicators of a new, more focused stage of the attachment process.
>
> *Fifteen to twenty-one months:* This is a period of intense concentration on the primary caregivers, featuring "testing" behavior, negativism, and shyness when out of the home. True socializing with agemates is still rare.
>
> *Twenty-one to twenty-four months:* The contest of the preceding months *may* recede, leaving the two-year-old with a stable working relationship with the primary caregiver, from which explorations of the wider world, including agemates, can begin in earnest.

This process is of fundamental importance to all children. Interruptions are not treated lightly. A younger sibling entering the picture at any time during the first two to two and a half years, constitutes a potential threat to the process, though not so during the younger child's first half-year of life. Especially in the first months, babies sleep most of the day and stay in one place unless moved. It is not until they get to be about seven months of age that problems begin to develop.

Newly crawling babies can easily get hurt. They break things, and they scatter magazines, clothes, cups, and almost any movable objects they encounter. Such realities must be coped with. Newly crawling babies require a lot of *attention*. This means that the older child, who may be as young as sixteen to eighteen months, no longer has maximum access to the primary caregiver. Worse than that, the older child's needs usually have to take a back seat to those of the new baby. The attachment process is very important, however, and the older child is too immature to handle this situation well. The normal reaction, therefore, is gradually increasing anger, jealousy, and hostility.

I have used the following kind of story to express just how difficult a situation the two-year-old finds himself in when he is living with a ten-month-old younger brother or sister. He is in the same situation a woman would be in if her husband one day made the following announcement: "Honey, I've got wonderful news for you. Next week I'm planning to bring home someone else to live with us. It will be a woman; she will be a bit younger than you, perhaps a bit more attractive. In any event, she will seem that way because I plan to spend more time with her than with you. Nevertheless, we are all going to continue to be a very happy family. You will get used to her presence, and I very much want you to love her and to show how much you love her."

I believe most women would have a very difficult time getting accustomed to such a situation. Yet that is pretty much what we are asking a two-year-old to do when there is a newly crawling baby in the same home. If a full-grown woman would find such a situation totally intolerable, how can we expect a two-year-old, whose life revolves around the home and particularly around the central person in the home during the day, to be able to cope with the feelings that result? The answer is that there simply is no way to avoid those feelings. The only two-year-old who would not be extremely jealous and unhappy about the presence of a ten-month-old sibling would be one who had very little to lose—that is, one who had not formed a solid attachment to the primary caregiver. In a sense, then, the nasty behavior of the two-year-old toward the younger sibling is reasonably good proof that the older child has had normal beneficial early attachment experiences and has formed a very strong tie to the primary caregiver.

After a few months of living with a seven- to eleven-month-old younger sibling, the older child's patterns of behavior and feelings become stable. Ironically, aggression by the older child toward the baby often leads to punishment by the primary caregiver, thereby worsening the situation. It is this scenario that underlies the conversion of happy (though testy) eighteen-month-olds to sour thirty-month-olds. It is not pleasant to observe.

The situation is quite different when the spacing is greater. The further the older child is beyond the two-year attachment process, the smaller the threat is from the new child and the more likely it is that there will be good feelings between the children. In our research, three years appeared to be the significant dividing line.

With the dramatic increase in the interest in early development during the last two decades, a few other studies of this issue have been performed. In perhaps the most important of these studies, Zajonc (1976) reported on the correlation between number and spacing of children in the family and intelligence test performance when the children were in their teens. The major finding in this study—which collected data on almost 1 million children in four Western countries—was that the more children in the family and/or the closer the spacing of the children, the lower the scores on intelligence tests.

Recently, a few studies of spacing effects have reported mixed results. Most are consistent with the foregoing analysis, but a few have reported little or no effects of narrow versus wide spacing intervals. However, these studies do not yet constitute a substantial body of evidence because of small samples and/or very limited contact with the subjects.

17
Spoiling

Between 1965 and 1978, the research of the Harvard Preschool Project featured a virtually unique set of observations. A team of some seventeen researchers observed hundreds of children from many kinds of families as they went about their daily activities during the period between their first and third birthdays.

One of our more important findings was that we could not properly call any of the one-year-old children unpleasant or spoiled in any but the most minor ways; however, it was all too common for us to report excessive undesirable behavior in two-year-olds. To be accurate, undesirable behavior surfaced routinely during the negativism period (beginning at about fifteen months). The interesting finding, however, was that although this behavior declined rapidly in many of the children we observed, it seemed to become stabilized—even characteristic—in the day-to-day lives of a considerable number of others.

As we proceeded with our research, we became quite convinced that it is comparatively easy to inadvertently create a badly spoiled child sometime between the first and second birthdays. However, it was several years before the picture of how this happens became detailed and reliable in our minds. I am pleased to report that we now feel very confident that we understand not only how spoiling typically takes place but, even more important, how it can be avoided.

How Spoiling Takes Place

Step 1. The first step in the spoiling process, somewhat ironically, is the first step that is required in helping a child become a wonderful person. It takes place during the first four months of life, and it consists of lavishing attention on a child when she shows the signs of inevitable, numerous instances of distress. As everyone knows, you cannot keep a newborn from being uncomfortable now and then. We probably will never devise ways of perfecting the parenting process to that point.

In the most common kind of parenting situation, the newborn's distress—signified by crying—is noticed by some older person and is followed quite promptly and naturally by attempts to comfort the baby. These attempts usually succeed—often in spite of the fact that the principal cause of the distress may not be identified. In other words, babies (especially newborns) are meant to be comforted. During the first four months of life, it is clear that thousands of such episodes take place in the lives of young infants.

As an accompaniment to the cycle of discomfort, followed by the cry, followed by the arrival of an older person, followed by reduced discomfort, there is learning. The learning that takes place is automatic; it does not involve higher mental processes but, rather, is some form of conditioning. Infants come to associate this cycle, especially the later stages of it, with the look, smell, sound, and feel of the people who comfort them. One consequence of this learning is that sometime during the fourth month, children begin to indicate the singling out of such people in their smiling behavior. Research at the Tavistock Clinic in Great Britain has demonstrated convincingly that during the fourth month of life, the favored adults in a baby's life can elicit smiles and keep them going longer than just about anyone or anything else.

A less well known but apparently equally inevitable consequence of these first four months of learning and of the growing abilities of the infant is that shortly thereafter, babies begin to use the cry *deliberately* to get attention. This means that during the first few months of life, the cry is an unintentional, unlearned behavior as a response to distress; it serves no other purpose. But from four to four and a half months on, the cry serves a second purpose at times, in that it becomes an intentional tool used to bring about the presence (and, it is hoped, the nurturing behavior) of the favorite older person. In more natural terms, from four months on, babies begin to cry to get someone to come over and pick them up and hold them as well as to indicate discomfort.

Step 2. The period between four months and the onset of crawling (which typically surfaces at about seven months but can vary from five months to never) is special in several ways. The special manifestation that is most appropriate for this discussion is the combination of curiosity and boredom. By four months of age, most babies are reasonably comfortable when they are oriented vertically (propped up in an infant seat, for example). They can see and hear almost perfectly, and they are possessed of a tremendous amount of curiosity, as previously manifested in their sustained hand-regard activities. Unfortunately, however, they cannot move about on their own. The result is a child who sits around a lot and does not have much to do, yet apparently is very much interested in situations and objects she can perceive from a distance.

The child has one tool to alleviate this frustration—the cry. When she makes noises, be they cries or other forms of sound, she will (if she is fortunate) be responded to in a variety of ways, including the arrival of an older person who will pick her up, play with her, and in many ways occupy her for a time. Therefore, it should be no surprise that during this particular period, babies increase their crying behavior, and many parents find that they are picking up their five- and six-month-olds more and more as the weeks go by. In a sense, we can now say that the baby has taken a step toward genuine spoiling, if we define spoiling, in part, as demanding of attention.

The situation takes a less than ideal turn a few months later, when the nine- to ten-month-old child begins to create problems for his parents at night when he is supposed to be sleeping. It is extremely common for such a child to begin to wake up anywhere from 9:00 to 10:00 P.M. on through to 2:00 or 3:00 A.M. and begin to cry. Of course, there are times when such crying is the result of some sort of illness or other significant, physically based distress. Commonly, however, crying of this sort seems to be based on the fact that the child is alone, usually in a dimly lit room, is not very sleepy, and does not have much to do. Therefore, he brings into play the one tool that has alleviated boredom before—the cry. In other words, this kind of crying often seems to be motivated by a desire to have the company of an older person rather than to be alone, awake, and without anything to do.

It is easy to see how this tendency can become ingrained as a result of the beneficial experiences of the responses to distress during the preceding months. However, it is just as easy to see that it is the beginning of inconvenience to parents that can become quite a burden as time goes by. Many young couples have spent many hours awake in the wee hours trying to deal with this situation. A while back, I had a long-distance emergency call from a dentist in Georgia, who was mildly embarrassed to describe the lengths he and his wife were going to with their ten-month-old child. They were taking a minimum of two auto rides after midnight and before 6:00 A.M. nightly. Like others in the same boat, they were beside themselves. Parenthetically, I should mention that they had discussed this problem with their pediatrician, and they were told that the baby was in fine shape physically and that they should simply let the baby cry it out.

Step 3. The next observable step in the spoiling process appears when children get to be a little over one year of age. Now, for the first time, children begin to use the whine skillfully to overcome resistance. We have observed many thirteen- and fourteen-month-olds very effectively insisting on getting their own way by using this little tool. At fifteen or sixteen months of age, with negativism and self-assertiveness surfacing, another stress is placed on parents, and they now have to cope with a child who very often deliberately tests their authority.

Many parents routinely make allowances for the fact that the child is "only a baby," and they allow unpleasant behaviors such as throwing objects, kicking or hitting people (usually the parents), and the like. They seem to make these allowances partly because the baby is the most wonderful thing they have ever experienced, partly because they are afraid that the baby might not love them so much if they are firm, and partly because of the difficulty of coping with a child who repeatedly seeks out situations in which she can challenge the authority of her parents. Whatever the reasons, a pattern of letting the child behave in a manner that is clearly unacceptable (at least to outsiders) becomes entrenched.

Closely associated with the problem of coping with negativism is the tendency of parents at this stage to allow a minor need of the child to inconvenience them. In their zeal to make sure that the baby's needs are always being satisfied, parents may get into a habit of chronically inconveniencing themselves.

Finally, there is a tendency on the part of parents not to follow through when they set limits during the second half of the second year. A parent may notice the child doing something objectionable, such as smearing food on a lamp, say something firmly to end the behavior, and then turn away and become reinvolved in cooking, talking on the telephone, and so forth. What the child learns from such experience when they are repeated regularly is that if he pays attention to his parents for a few moments when they are yelling at him, they will soon turn away and he can then continue to do whatever he wants to do, including the admonished behavior.

The net result of this very common path of development is a two-year-old who may very well have a good mind, great language ability, and excellent physical abilities but who is most unpleasant to live with. We have known parents who have left home for a couple of weeks simply to get a breather from such a child. The problem is aggravated by the tendency of the fourteen- to twenty-four-month-old child to stick close to the parent throughout the day, as the child is in the final stages of early attachment.

Such a child is very likely to move into the third year of life without having fully resolved the question of what he can and cannot do in the presence of his parents. Such a child is likely to throw temper tantrums, especially during the first half of the third year. Such a child is also likely to cause maximal grief if there is a closely spaced younger sibling. (For fairly obvious reasons, this problem seems to be greatest in the case of first children, as opposed to later-born children).

How to Avoid Spoiling

Can such an outcome be avoided? The answer is an emphatic *yes.* It is possible to produce a delightful three-year-old child rather than one who is spoiled, although it is a bit more difficult than we would like it to be. The appropriate ways of achieving this wonderful end are to be found in an understanding of the foregoing evolution of the spoiling process.

Of course, you *could* guarantee an avoidance of spoiling by neglecting the baby in the first months of life, but that would be extraordinarily ill-advised. A baby has to receive routine comforting and many fun experiences with other people during the first months of life in order to establish a lifelong capacity to love other people.

Two procedures are advised for avoiding spoiling. The first, of course, is to be aware of the fact that from four months or so on, the child will begin to use crying intentionally at times to get company, rather than only when he is in pain or discomfort. From that point to the onset of crawling or some other means of moving about, parents should do whatever they can to be mindful of the situation and to avoid excessive picking up and carrying of the child throughout the course of a day.

That is easy to say, but how can you do that without sentencing the child to long periods of boredom? One tactic is to use an infant seat or a jumpseat to move the child to different parts of the home. You also can bring small toys to the child for her to examine and play with. But none of this works well enough.

It is because of the comparative ineffectiveness of such tactics that we recommend the use of a well-designed walker, in spite of the opposition of some specialists in the field. A walker is the ideal solution to this problem. Babies love them. They can occupy themselves profitably in a walker for several hours a day, and the use of a walker in this manner does not in any way interfere with affectionate interplay between parent and child. There is, however, the reality that a five- or six-month-old in a walker is much more likely to suffer an accident than one who simply remains in a crib or playpen or on a blanket on the floor. This is why we have to repeat the warning that *a baby should be supervised every moment she is in a walker.* Also, once the child is able to get about on her own, the walker should be discarded.

The second point requiring attention is night-waking problems. Even if parents have acted on our advice in the four- to seven-month period, they may still find that the child is insisting on their presence late at night once she reaches nine or ten months of age. Our recommendations for parents (which have been shown to work repeatedly) are as follows.

Be watchful for the emergence of this kind of behavior. If it does emerge, respond promptly, and check thoroughly to make sure that there is nothing wrong with the child. If there is nothing wrong with the child, give her a hug and a kiss, and say, "Sweetheart, it is now time for sleep. We all need our sleep. I will see you in the morning. Good night." Then leave. Do not be surprised if the child continues to cry. Ignore her.

If they must, and we know this is sometimes a necessity, the parents should go back a half-hour later and repeat the same brief scenario. They should *not* provide a bottle for fear the child is going to be undernourished; they should *not* take the child into their bed. With the appropriate response style by parents, the child will routinely sleep through the night in a matter of seven to ten days under most circumstances.

I should point out here that some people who work with young parents disapprove of such advice. They claim that anytime a child cries, it is vitally important that those cries be responded to with a totally loving response, including the concept of the "family bed." My response to such an approach to the situation is that if that is what parents feel they want to do, they should go ahead and do it. But I firmly believe that it is not the wisest procedure.

The next step of the antispoiling process involves setting limits. One of the parents we worked with said of her one-year-old: "I love her enthusiasm and her curiosity . . . but she doesn't *have* to play in my makeup!" The healthy selfishness involved in such a statement is part of our recommended orientation toward setting limits.

Starting from eight to nine months on, children should know that there are some things that they simply will not be allowed to do. Anything that intrudes substantially on the rights of anyone else, especially the parents, should be forbidden in just about every situation. Children who are dealt with lovingly but firmly from the time they start to crawl until they enter into negativism during the second year are generally easier to live with throughout the balance of the negativistic period. I do not mean to say that it will be a picnic, but they will be a bit easier to deal with.

Waiting until a child is seventeen or eighteen months of age before beginning to set limits is a mistake, primarily because it becomes much more difficult to do. Also, during this time, the child should be taught that he is special, indeed, but no more so than anyone else in the world—especially his parents.

If parents stick with this prescription, and if they avoid overly stressful conditions by spacing their children three or more years apart, I am willing to guarantee that they will have a delightful companion by the child's second birthday and on through to the third birthday and that they will not have to suffer through temper tantrums during the third year of life.

18
Breast-Feeding versus Bottle-Feeding

In my early experiences in the field of child development, the question of breast- versus bottle-feeding was one of many practical issues of concern to professionals and parents. Until about twenty years ago, the popular consensus among professionals, in essence, was that there was little to choose from between the two methods. Although few objected to the concept of breast-feeding, many took pains to point out that the climate of love associated with the process could just as easily be created by a bottle-feeding mother, so long as she was aware of the importance of that condition. As for nutrition, there seemed to be little concern because of an abundance of apparently suitable substitute formulas.

There was some concern with bottle-feeding of an impersonal kind, perhaps most conspicuously in connection with infants reared in institutions. In such cases, it was not uncommon for babies to be bottle-fed in a manner that hardly involved other people. Sometimes, bottles were propped up on pillows or blankets so that a staff member, who may have had eight or more infants to feed, could handle a large number of them at once. The work of Spitz, Bowlby, and numerous others on the dramatic harm that could come to children who were reared in institutions with a minimum of human contact served to alert professionals to the vital importance of human contact usually available to home-reared children during the feeding experience. These ideas were widely circulated and, as a result, bottle propping was actively discouraged.

However, at the same time—during the 1950s and 1960s—there was no concerted effort to laud the advantages of breast-feeding over bottle-feeding. Unquestionably, professional opinion was influenced by some cultural disapproval of breast-feeding in developed nations as well as by the desire to support women who, for any number of reasons, could not or chose not to breast-feed.

Sometime toward the end of the 1960s, a change occurred. Medical studies began to provide substantial evidence that breast-feeding was superior to bottle-feeding in a number of important ways. Although specifics of the argument are beyond our area of expertise, in essence, babies were found to be healthier if breast-fed rather than bottle-fed. As time went by, few countering arguments were generated, and additional supportive evidence surfaced. Since then, most professionals, at least in the Western world, have become more firm in their advocacy of breast-feeding. In my own work, I, too, have consistently recommended breast-feeding, if possible, on the basis of the medical evidence.

A while back, I participated in the annual conference of the La Leche League, an organization started in the 1950s by some mothers who felt that they wanted to breast-feed but were unable to find support for that desire among their friends and professional advisors. By any standards, the League has become enormously successful. It now has well over 100,000 members and branches in two dozen countries. Members of the League currently are consulting in developing nations in an effort to help reinforce the concept of breast-feeding.

My own contact with the La Leche League had been very limited over the years. I had been aware of their organization, their newsletter, and their passionate devotion to breast-feeding. This passion had led me to be quite reserved about their work, however, because it seemed that overstatements and unsubstantiated claims were likely under such conditions. However, in general—from a distance—I valued the organization's humanistic goals, which have always emphasized close, caring relations between parents and children. Beyond such ideas, however, I knew little about the group.

During the conference, I had an opportunity to meet and talk with a number of leaders in the organization. We had a spirited discussion wherein I maintained the role of academically oriented skeptic. The people in the group were extremely warm and caring, and I heard relatively few outrageous claims for the benefits of breast-feeding. Nevertheless, as we talked, it became clear that they were surprised at how little I was willing to grant about the advantages of the activity. I maintained my long-standing position that breast-feeding was to be preferred over bottle-feeding because of the proven medical advantages—not only from the point of view of nutrition but also with respect to the prevention of allergic reactions during infancy. However, several members of the group insisted that there was much more to it than that.

Subsequently, La Leche League members sent me several articles reporting on differences between breast-fed and bottle-fed babies that I feel are worthy of very serious attention. It appears that something new and potentially very important seems to be surfacing in the research on this topic.

For a long time, we have been particularly sensitive to the importance of adequate hearing during the first years of life, along with the apparently widespread threat to such ability due to a condition known as otitis media, or middle ear disease, with associated build-up of fluid. There seems to be little question that chronic episodes of mild to moderate hearing losses occur in a goodly percentage of young children and that the consequences can be serious and long-lasting. Although these consequences usually are not life-threatening, they do include many problems concerning the acquisition of language, higher mental abilities, and effective social skills.

One of the most important research reports I received came from the University of Helsinki (Saarinen, 1982). In a study of 237 healthy children, with a follow-up from birth to three years of age, a strong association was found between recurrent otitis media and early bottle-feeding. In contrast, prolonged breast-feeding was found to have a long-term protecting effect up to three years of age. The study did not determine whether the prophylactic effect of prolonged breast-feeding is due to protection by human milk from infections or allergy or to avoidance of harmful effects caused by cow's milk. This link, which apparently has been found in several countries, is potentially of enormous importance for the development of young children everywhere.

As an important aside, I should mention that the researchers also noted that full-time group day care of very young infants—which in most cases precludes breast-feeding—also, quite understandably, is linked to recurrent otitis media. Clearly, in addition to the absence of breast milk, there is also a greater likelihood of infection due to the out-of-home circumstances.

Other factors also deserve attention. Two research reports from New Zealand describing studies with large populations indicated that breast-feeding was associated rather strongly with improved speech clarity and better reading ability in five- and six-year-old children (Broad, 1973, 1976). Such a claim, of course, is more difficult to substantiate, dealing as it does with older children for whom many other factors have had a chance to operate. Nevertheless, the claim is worthy of attention, especially since it is consistent with the evidence of the linkage between otitis media and bottle-feeding during infancy.

An interesting point in these reports from New Zealand is that, for the most part, the effects were limited to *male* children. This opens up another complicated subject. For years, it has been known that young girls generally are more advanced with respect to early language acquisition. A study of some 48,000 children tested for hearing between 1967 and 1971 in the Auckland health district of New Zealand indicated that boys are considerably more prone to hearing defects than girls (Broad, 1976). This finding is consistent with the others, but a large part of the story remains unclear.

Another important point running through these research reports is that for breast-feeding to be effective, it has to be prolonged (six months or more). Generally, breast-feeding for a month or two produces no particular advantages over bottle-feeding.

Another report, from Canada, describes a series of studies on the impact of changing infant feeding patterns in the Northwest Territories (Schaefer and Spady, 1980). The subjects were Eskimo, Indian, and nonnative infants. These studies were done in connection with a campaign by health services to increase breast-feeding during infancy. The article cites a number of dramatic benefits resulting from the increase in prolonged breast-feeding. However, from the claims regarding earlier walking, reduced morbidity, and the like, it seems obvious that the populations involved were in high-risk situations and that the benefits of breast-feeding probably were attributable to improved basic nutrition. Therefore, these findings cannot be fairly generalized to, for example, caring middle-class families in the United States. Nevertheless, they do represent another forceful statement of the advisability of breast-feeding.

Taken all together, this information has led me to modify my stance. I now believe that breast-feeding is clearly the preferred way to go if it is possible. Benefits are likely not only in the area of general nutrition but very probably in respect to learning as well. I believe it is now obligatory for professionals to advise mothers to do whatever they can to breast-feed, even if they have reservations about the practice. Mothers who do not breast-feed should be told to be especially alert for middle ear problems due to either infections or allergies.

Associated with these recommendations should be a warning about putting a child to bed with a bottle containing formula or any other fluids other than water, especially those that contain sugar. It has been well-established that such a practice commonly results in significant dental problems.

19
Hearing Impairment

I t is considerably more difficult for children to grow up to be fully developed human beings if their hearing is impaired during their first years of life. The ability to acquire language is directly dependent upon the ability to hear well. Children undergo rapid basic language learning during the first three years of life, and deficits in language development in three-year-olds are perhaps the most common important educational difficulties found in underachieving preschool children.

Severe or profound hearing impairment is defined as 70 or more decibels of loss. This is an extraordinarily difficult handicap for an otherwise healthy young child to overcome. Mercifully, such a degree of loss is comparatively rare. Far more common is the mild to moderate loss of from 20 to 55 decibels. There is good reason to believe that the presence of such losses not only is common in young children of all socioeconomic backgrounds but is a chronic deterrent to good language development.

For an older child or a young adult, a moderate hearing loss constitutes a relatively minor problem. Previous learning allows such people to fill in some of what is not heard clearly. In contrast, when language is being learned for the first time, even minor losses constitute significant obstacles to good development.

The development of higher mental abilities depends directly on the acquisition of language capacities, and most specialists would agree that optimal early language learning is a prerequisite of optimal early intellectual growth. The social developments of the first few years of life also are rapid and fundamental. Three-year-olds can be fascinating, delightful individuals in their interactions with others. Some, however, may be considerably less well-endowed socially and well on their way to lifelong difficulties in interpersonal relations. The development of social skills—such as the ability to gain someone's attention, to use an adult as a resource, or to exercise leadership—depends directly on the skill and concern of the child's early teachers (ordinarily the parents) and on the capacity of the child to understand the words through which the teaching takes place. We do not socialize our children through gestures or through grunts and groans.

It seems clear, then, that even moderate hearing losses during the first few years of life can be devastating or, at least, serious impediments to first-rate development of children.

The Problem

An extremely serious situation exists in this country with respect to the early detection and treatment of mild to moderate hearing losses in children from all levels of society.

It is first necessary to distinguish between severe and mild to moderate hearing loss. The profoundly impaired child is considerably less common than the child with a mild or moderate loss, and children with profound or severe losses are much more likely to be identified as hearing impaired than those with lesser degrees of difficulty.

The behavior of a child with a 60-, 70-, or 80-decibel loss, even as a newborn, will be quite different from what people expect. Such handicaps usually are noticed early in the child's life. Also, almost any medical examination will lead to the discovery of severe deficits. Mild or moderate loss also is fairly easily noticed in an older child or adult. Sometimes the person's speech is slurred; at other times it may be a bit louder than is called for. More commonly, a person with a mild loss simply is not as quick to respond or as accurate in understanding conversations. Unfortunately, none of these signals are apparent in a child under two years of age. Since we do not expect such a child to speak clearly or at a suitable level, and we do not expect such a child to understand speech well, early detection by parents and professionals is less likely.

Furthermore, our health systems function poorly in this area. Pediatric practice has always had to cope with the phenomenon of many symptoms of aberrant development during infancy that lead nowhere. At times, perfectly normal children behave in ways that suggest there is something significantly wrong with them. Time after time, however, such early symptoms simply vanish and the child develops normally.

Because of this peculiarity of the first years of life, and because of a desire to avoid needless anxiety in parents, medical practitioners often find themselves reassuring parents, telling them that one or another worrisome behavior is nothing to worry about and will be outgrown. Such a practice on the part of medical personnel infuriates people involved in pediatric audiology, because the consequences of inattention to hearing loss in the first years of life are quite large, and the consequences for the educational development of young children are real and substantial.

Early Detection

My recommendation for professional practice in this area is as follows. First, a distinction must be made between temporary and permanent difficulties in the area of mild to moderate hearing loss. Unfortunately, infants are more vulnerable to respiratory distress than older children are. Therefore, the presence of middle ear infection (otitis media) is quite common during infancy and toddlerhood. This condition often is accompanied by a build-up of fluid in the middle ear system and by a functional hearing loss. When the infection is cleared up, the fluid usually disappears and the child's hearing returns to normal.

Such episodes may occur once, twice, or considerably more often during the first years of life. For as long as the child is unable to hear normally because of such distress, the child is experiencing a loss no less important than if it were caused by congenital nerve damage. The second type of loss, the more chronic type, could be due to a congenital nerve loss, a conduction difficulty, or some other problem in the central nervous system.

I strongly suggest that temporary losses be treated in a manner similar to the treatment of instances of high fever. A pediatrician who finds that a baby's temperature is elevated significantly above normal is not likely to advise that the baby be seen again in six months. On the contrary, the physician generally does whatever is possible to see to it that the temperature returns to normal and that the condition does not persist.

From an educational standpoint, I believe that the same policy can and should be instituted with respect to functional hearing loss. If a child under three years of age has any difficulty that temporarily causes a functional loss, the medical or educational professional should inform the child's parents and then help them get the assistance they need to cope with the problem. Most important, the follow-up should be of the same sort that is provided in the case of a high temperature. There should be an attempt to see to it that the hearing loss does not persist longer than a few days. If it does persist for weeks or months, the consequences for the child's educational development can be serious.

For the kind of hearing loss that is more constant, I recommend that procedures be administered routinely with *all young children* for the earliest possible identification and management of mild to moderate hearing loss.

The field of early detection of hearing loss has been moving forward very rapidly in recent years. Although much study remains to be done, there now exist sufficient established procedures to see to it that any child with significant problems in this area can be identified reliably and early enough to make a substantial difference in the consequences for the child's development. Although there are some disagreements among leading authorities, most would agree that the following elements would be useful in any comprehensive early detection program.

A High-Risk Registry. New parents are asked to respond to from six to twelve questions of the following kind: Has there been a history of hearing loss in the family? Was the mother exposed to Rubella during the pregnancy? Was the child premature or of very low birth weight? Was there a blood incompatibility problem? Has the baby been given mycin drugs? Although the collection of questions varies somewhat across institutions, there is substantial agreement on the majority of them.

Orientation to Sound. Procedures can be used by parents, paraprofessionals, or professionals to determine whether a child orients to both loud and soft sounds accurately from the time he is four months of age.

Questioning of Parents. One of the most valuable and least expensive elements of an early detection program is periodic questioning of parents about the behavior of their children as it relates to hearing especially as the child moves beyond the neonatal period (0 to 30 days). Professionals repeatedly report that parents are surprisingly accurate as early detectors of mild to moderate hearing loss. Indeed, several claim that if a parent suspects that something is wrong, it is mandatory that there be a follow-up diagnosis.

Monitoring the Growth of Language Ability. By eight or nine months of age, children should begin to show that they understand the meanings of a few simple words, such as their own name, mama, bye-bye, bottle, and the like. Increasingly, as the weeks go by, the child's receptive vocabulary should improve to the point that a child of thirteen or fourteen months of age, though saying comparatively little, if anything, should understand at least twenty to thirty simple words and a half-dozen or so simple instructions. If a child is not speaking at that point, this should be noted by the parents and brought to the attention of medical personnel, but it is not necessarily a cause for alarm as yet. The delay of speech beyond the second birthday, however, is often an indicator of a hearing problem.

All of these elements, or at least a core collection of them, should be included in a comprehensive early detection program. Furthermore, surveillance of the development of hearing ability should be continuous. A child should be seen two or three times during the first year of life and twice during the second and third years, even if no signs of high risk or difficulty are noted. Whenever a sign of hearing loss is detected, careful diagnosis and close monitoring are warranted. Diagnosis should be done by specialists in testing, preferably pediatric audiologists trained in the appropriate medical techniques, such as acoustic or pneumatic otoscopy and tympanometry.

New Screening Equipment

Recently, two medical equipment companies, both located in Massachusetts, have come out with impressive equipment to help screen for mild to moderate hearing losses during infancy.

The D.A. Levow Network produces the MD System, which consists of three pieces of equipment. The first piece is called an *impedance analyzer.* Its principal purpose is to determine the presence of fluid in the middle ear, using air pressure to do tympanometry. Technically, it is very modern, apparently accurate, and much simpler to use than earlier equipment. It is currently being used mainly by medical practitioners, but it could be used by early educators as well. It does have a limitation in that the pressure produced in the administration of the procedure, though not harmful in any way, is impractical for use with babies less than seven months of age because of the flexibility of immature ear canals.

In addition to the impedance analyzer, a similar unit can be used for pure tone audiometry. Finally, an optional printer is available as part of the system.

The product developed by Endeco Medical is even more exciting. It is an *acoustic audioscope,* which is basically a hand-held gadget that uses a sound rather than air pressure as a stimulus. It appears to be much easier to use than the air pressure device, and it is less expensive. Furthermore, this device can be used with infants of any age.

I was very impressed by the sophistication of the people who demonstrated these products to me and by their awareness of the widespread existence of the problem of undetected mild to moderate hearing loss in babies. Thanks to their efforts, I would expect these devices to come into broad use very soon.

What to Do When Hearing Loss Is Detected

Again, the consensus among specialists in the field is that once a hearing loss has been detected, prompt action is very important. Treatment consists of two major elements: medical attention and special assistance to parents. Typical medical treatment includes the use of hearing aids on children as young as a few months of age or, possibly, minor surgery to relieve conductive difficulties (e.g., the insertion of small tubes to cope with the build-up of fluid in the middle ear system).

Even if nothing can be done medically, specialists agree that it is essential that parents be informed about a hearing loss immediately. If they accept the reality of the impairment and are willing to take guidance from specialists, parents can do many things that will help minimize the consequences of a hearing handicap for the rapidly developing child. A special difficulty is becoming increasingly clear as specialists pay more attention to this vital problem area. Parental resistance to acknowledging such a defect in their child is frequent. Such a response is understandable, but if it is not modified, it becomes a serious impediment to coping effectively with the handicap.

I have been delighted to find that truly outstanding facilities and personnel are working on this important problem in many parts of the country. Further information about where and how to get help for children with hearing impairments can be obtained from the Alexander Graham Bell Association for the Deaf, in Washington, D.C.

Concluding Remarks

For many difficulties that impede early human development, we have a limited capacity to act. Much of the knowledge we need about how to help each child develop well simply does not yet exist. In addition, the costs of dealing with certain unfortunate situations that occur often rise to prohibitive levels.

In the case of moderate or mild hearing loss, we have an altogether different situation. The consequences of the difficulty can be very serious. Although the loss in potential and in happiness for both parents and children is not fully understood, it is probably very great. Fortunately, knowledge and techniques actually exist that enable us to deal successfully with the vast majority of the children in need. Another fortunate aspect of the situation is that the cost of seeing to it that no child passes through the early years of life with an undetected and untreated hearing loss is rather small.

Therefore, it is clear that one thing professionals could do that would be both useful and effective is to make every effort toward the adoption of a national policy with respect to this issue as soon as possible.

20
Toy Selection

E very year, millions of dollars are spent on toys for young children. Unfortunately, infants and toddlers have very little control over how those dollars are spent. During the first three years of life, children are largely at the mercy of adults when it comes to the selection and purchase of their playthings. What can be done to ensure that the toys chosen will be appropriate for the children?

Basic Considerations

The first and foremost consideration is *safety*. During the past few years, the federal government has gone a long way to protect very young children from their playthings. There are now regulations that prohibit toys manufactured for infants and toddlers from having lead-based paint, removable parts that are less than 1⅜-inch in any dimension (which can be swallowed and gagged upon), sharp edges, corners, or protrusions, and various other hazards. Nevertheless, it is wise to double-check all toys to be sure. A good set of safety guidelines may be obtained from the U.S. Consumer Product Safety Commission.

It is also important to remember that many of these regulations do not apply to toys manufactured for older children, and accidents can happen when such toys find their way into the hands of an infant or toddler. For instance, Matchbox cars are fine for an eight-year-old child; however, an eight-month-old child is likely to pick up one of these items, pull off the little tires, and pop them into his mouth or be injured by the exposed metal axles.

The second consideration is *durability*. Whereas an older child can be instructed to take care of her playthings, this is an unrealistic admonition for a child under three years of age. Regardless of how the toy was designed to be used, infants and toddlers will chew on

it, pull at it, bang it, drop it, and otherwise heap abuse upon it—
and they will do so with a strength that seems disproportionate to
their small size.

During the past few years, several toy manufacturers have begun to offer lifetime guarantees on some of their products. This is
quite a credit to the toy industry, but well-made toys are still the
exception rather than the rule. Therefore, it is a good idea to open
up the box and check out just how tough the toy really is prior to
purchasing it.

Along the lines, it should be noted that very young children not
only will subject their playthings to physical stress but also will ex-
pose them to dirt, grime, and bodily fluids of all kinds. Since most
objects that reach the hands of such children eventually reach their
mouths, too, a toy that cannot be washed easily will soon become
a worthless health hazard.

The third consideration when choosing toys for infants and toddlers is *play value*. That is, does the toy match the child's interests
and abilities? Although this may seem to be a very obvious question, getting a straight answer can be extremely difficult. In designing and packaging their products, manufacturers often seem to be
more concerned about the adults who will select and purchase the
toys than about the children who will receive and play with the toys.

For instance, many articles, pamphlets, books, and "experts" on
choosing toys have suggested that one follow the recommended age
on the boxes. This sounds like reasonable advice. Unfortunately,
most toys for infants and toddlers that I have encountered have had
inappropriate recommended age ranges on the boxes.

During the first three years of life, children's interests and abilities change more rapidly than during any other period in their
lives—and the kinds of playthings that appeal to them change
quickly. Something that is too advanced and frustrating for a child
at a particular stage of development may be too simple and boring
for that same child within a matter of months.

Therefore, if toy manufacturers were being totally straightforward, in most cases, they would have to put very narrow recommended age ranges on the boxes. But this could be bad for business.
After all, how many people coming into a toy store would be shopping for a child in that narrow age range? And even if the child is

in that narrow range, how many people would be willing to spend a lot of money for a toy that is going to be appropriate for the child for only a short period of time?

As a result, the recommended age ranges that appear on toy boxes usually are significantly exaggerated; consequently, they are largely inaccurate. It is not uncommon to see something like "for children three months to three years." Can you think of anything (except mother and father) that will be appealing to both a three-month-old and a three-year-old?

Another thing to watch out for is adult perspective. Children and adults have different interests and abilities, and most adults cannot remember what they were like during the first three years of their own lives. Therefore, when purchasing toys for infants and toddlers, adults have a natural tendency to select products that are appealing to them for one reason or another; in many cases, however, that opinion is not going to be shared by the children. To complicate matters, many toy manufacturers, to sell more toys, design and package their products in ways that will primarily capture the attention and acclaim of adults, not very young children.

For example, one of the more popular ploys manufacturers use is to decorate their toys—even toys for babies—with Disney, Sesame Street, or Smurf characters. They have to pay substantial amounts of money for the rights to use these characters, and the cost is routinely added to the price of the product. Manufacturers find that it is usually worth the investment, because adults have strong, positive associations with these characters and thus tend to perceive the products as appropriate for the children. But when you think about it, how many babies really know (or care) who Donald Duck and Big Bird are?

One last warning concerns educational claims. If an object or activity arouses the interests and challenges the abilities of a child, the child will enjoy it and perhaps learn something from it. However, the notion that any toy has a special and unique power to "teach" a child anything is nonsense. Nevertheless, since the educational development of the children is of fundamental concern to the adults who are purchasing toys for them, many toy manufacturers are almost shameless when it comes to promoting the "educational" value of their products.

In advertisements, on toy boxes, and even inside toy boxes (in little pamphlets called "learning guides"), I have seen claims that a given toy will "teach" a child such things as "to distinguish shapes and colors" or "that things which disappear can reappear." Although it is true that children will learn these things during the first years of life, they do not need to learn them from expensive, store-bought items. My colleagues and I have spent hundreds of hours in the homes of many families, and we have kept careful track of the kinds of toys infants and toddlers spend a lot of time playing with—which, unfortunately, are not always the toys their parents spend a lot of money for. The following is some specific advice about choosing appropriate toys for infants and toddlers.

Age-Appropriate Toys

Birth to Six Months

Traditionally, a baby's first toy is a rattle—although I have no idea why. I have never seen a newborn baby pick up and shake a rattle. I *have* seen many new parents pick up a rattle, shake it in front of the baby, and then, after getting no response, pry the baby's fingers open (babies tend to keep their hands fisted) and put the rattle in the baby's hand. The baby usually does not even look at the rattle, much less shake it, and after a few seconds, drops it. The parent then repeats this process until it is obvious that neither adult nor child is having much fun.

So what kinds of toys do make sense for a newborn? For the first few months of life, children are primarily interested in their own comfort. They spend a great deal of the day sleeping, and a fair portion of their waking moments is spent eating or crying. There are times, however, when they are awake, quiet, and alert; during those times, they are interested in their surroundings and are able to interact with their surroundings through their eyes, ears, mouths, hands, and feet. Since they cannot get around on their own, a few simple items that they can see and/or reach easily will be appreciated.

A mobile is a good toy for children from about three to nine weeks of age—but only if they can see it. Most commercial mobiles are nothing more than nursery decorations. An adult may enjoy walking into the room and seeing the figures fluttering in the breeze over the crib, but the baby in the crib, even if she is lying on her back, will have her head turned (usually to the right) most of the time. Even if she looks directly up for a moment, she won't be able to focus well unless the mobile is between eight and twelve inches away. And even if the mobile is placed at the right distance, all the baby will see is the bottom edge of the cut-out figures (which will appear like black lines floating in space).

Recently, some manufacturers have come out with mobiles that can be positioned so that the child, not the adult, gets the best view. In addition to such mobiles, an unbreakable stainless steel mirror, placed on the side of the crib, is a good idea, as babies get hours of enjoyment from staring at their own reflections.

Starting at about three months of age, infants get a little more physical, so mobiles should be replaced with sturdy, well-designed crib gyms. A good crib gym gives a child in this age range something to pull, swipe at, or kick—in return for which the child gets visual and/or auditory feedback of some kind. The problem with many commercial crib gyms is that the target objects are suspended on string—rather than on something more stable, such as plastic—so that the process of making contact becomes very frustrating for the infant who is just learning to use his hands under the guidance of his eyes.

A few other items are appreciated by children in this age range. Teething rings, key rings, and other simple objects provide them with the opportunity to explore the properties of various materials with their eyes, ears, mouths, and hands. The objects should be too large to be swallowed. Also, it should be remembered that since infants cannot get around by themselves, when they drop or throw these objects, they will not be able to retrieve them. Therefore, it is a good idea to leave several such objects around and to be ready to return them to the baby often.

In addition, well-designed infant seats can be used to move children to different parts of the house and give them new and different things to look at and listen to. For children in the later period of this age range, well-designed walkers also enable to them to widen their exploratory horizons. However, children in walkers can get into more trouble then they otherwise would, so they must be carefully supervised at all times.

That's about it. Surprised? You should be. With all the talk about "infant stimulation" and with all the busy boxes and other such gadgets that are designed to go onto or into the crib, some babies look like they are sitting in the middle of a high-tech hardware store. The fact of the matter is that during this period of life, normal, healthy children neither need nor enjoy a great deal of artificial stimulation, and I have rarely seen any of those fancy gadgets hold their attention for more than a few minutes.

Six to Twelve Months

During this period, children achieve locomotion—first crawling and pulling to stand and, shortly thereafter, walking and climbing. They become more adept at manipulating their hands and fingers, and they acquire a deep affection for small, portable objects as well as an intense fascination with the characteristics and operations of all sorts of devices.

There are many appropriate toys for this age range, but you should realize that toys simply cannot compete with the "real" world (so long as the child is allowed to explore it). To an adult, there is nothing spectacular about a typical house and its furnishings, but we forget just how wonderfully exciting it is when one is getting around it and into it for the first time.

I once saw a one-year-old girl spend several hours over the course of a few days just pushing and popping two small buttons on the door of an electric dishwasher. Of course, I am not suggesting that anyone go out and buy a dishwasher for a one-year-old, but be aware that whatever toys are bought will play second fiddle to light switches, stairs, pots and pans, toilets, and a host of other household items.

Bath toys—from the traditional rubber duckie to sponge puppets, boats, floating soap bars, and even more complex water toys—provide a child of this age with a lot of squeezing, pouring, and splashing fun in the tub. Water wheels, containers, and squirters are features that provide added attractions.

Simple mechanical toys are appealing to children in this age range. One of the best we have encountered features a "light switch," a telephone dial, a push button, and a pull lever. When the child operates one of these, it triggers a jack-in-the-box-type mechanism so that a corresponding door opens and a figure pops out. Unlike the standard jack-in-the-box, which requires two hands and an adult to reset, the doors on this toy can be closed very easily.

Sorting and nesting toys—such as a set of measuring cups that fit one inside the other and the old "square peg in the square hole" game—are fine choices. However, do not get upset if the child seems to be having more fun just carrying the pieces around or using the toy in a manner other than the way the child on the box is using it. A child can learn just as much, if not more, by trying to get the square peg into the round hole or by dropping the peg off the highchair. Toys that feature interlocking parts that can be pulled apart and pushed back together without much effort are a big hit as well.

Sometime near the first birthday, children begin to show an interest in books. However, the first interest in books is not the stories or even pointing at and naming the pictures. Hinged objects, such as doors and book bindings, are absolutely fascinating to children at this stage of development (why, nobody knows). What turns them on at this point is simply turning the pages. Books with stiff cardboard pages are preferable, because it is hard for little fingers to separate cloth or paper pages.

Twelve to Twenty-four Months

During the second year of life, children continue their interest in exploring the environment, and they are now able to get around and into it with greater confidence and ease. They enjoy anything that feeds their innate curiosity, and they welcome opportunities to practice their large and small muscle skills.

This stage of development also is the time when children become fascinated with language. They love to listen to it, even though they may not begin to speak very much until later in this period. Social interest blossoms as well, featuring an intense focus on the key people in their lives, especially their primary caretakers. As they approach their second birthdays, their imaginations start to grow, and they begin to mimic adult behaviors and activities.

The most popular toys for children in this age range are balls—the bigger the better. An inexpensive plastic beach ball is an excellent investment. Toddlers very much enjoy just carrying a ball around, and they get a big thrill from kicking or throwing it, watching it roll, and then retrieving it. The fact that they usually can get their favorite adults involved in this game is a special added attraction.

Riding toys are fun for children at this stage. They still do not have the coordination to manage pedals, so low, four-wheel trucks, wagons, or riding horses that are powered by pushing feet against floor are preferable. Boxes are appreciated, too, both large ones for crawling over and into and small ones for carrying around and collecting things. Sandboxes and/or shallow wading pools with all the fixings—pails, shovels, and so forth—are appealing and appropriate.

As memory and attention span increase, picture books featuring the alphabet, animals, or any favorite theme become quite popular—particularly when favorite adults can be involved in pointing and naming games. A toy telephone is a wonderful item for this age range, first for just playing with the dial and later for "make believe" conversations (consisting of a few words and a lot of babbling).

By the middle of the second year, simple puzzles begin to appeal to toddlers. Now, instead of just gumming the pieces, they begin to try to fit them into the appropriate spaces. As they mature, they can be given increasingly more challenging versions.

Some children also develop a fondness for one or more stuffed animals that they enjoy carrying around and talking to. Then again, some do not. Regardless of what many psychiatrically oriented professionals say about "transitional objects" and what the "Peanuts" cartoons would lead you to believe, not all children form such attachments. In our studies, less than half of them did. In any event, there certainly is no need to go out and buy a special item to ensure the child's emotional well-being.

Twenty-four to Thirty-six Months

During this period of life, imagination blossoms. Children become heavily involved in—and rather adept at—role-play, fantasy, and artistic activities. They continue to appreciate opportunities to practice both large and small muscle skills, and as they move toward their third birthdays, they begin to show increasing coordination and grace.

The memory and attention span of children in this age range are now rather well-developed, and their language and intellectual skills are growing in leaps and bounds. They still prefer to interact primarily with close family members, but their sociability does expand to include other adults and agemates on a regular basis. They also are content to play by themselves for extended periods of time.

Simple art supplies—including crayons, finger and brush paints, clay, and play dough—are good choices. Although children in this age range should be beyond the "eat everything" stage for the most part, it is a good idea to buy only nontoxic materials to be on the safe side.

Musical toys can be fun, too. One of the better buys in this category is a children's record player that is easy to operate and virtually indestructible. I have seen many children spend a lot of time with this toy. Blocks also provide much enjoyment, whether they be the standard wooden ones or the more modern versions.

Indoor and/or outdoor gyms, swing sets, and even a tricycle can be introduced during this period. Tricycles should be low, sturdy, and designed specifically for very young children. Also, play on such devices should be restricted to safe areas and should be carefully supervised. An interesting toy of this kind is the "Sit and Spin," which holds up to four children. Its major appeal is that it is not powered by batteries or adults; the children make it go around by turning the wheel themselves.

Storybooks come into their own during the third year. Children now are able to understand and follow the plots, and they will recognize and remember characters and scenes.

Theme toys are very popular with children in the third year of life. Now that they can combine all they have learned about people and small objects with their new imaginative capacities, they have a lot of fun with "pretend" houses, fire stations, farms, parking garages, and the like.

Along the same lines, children at this stage appreciate dolls, cars and trucks, tools and appliances, costumes, and anything else that allows them to act out adult roles. Since their hands and fingers still are not as agile as those of older children, it is a good idea to stay away from complicated items and stick to the basic models. Also, there is no need to have a lot of detail included in the materials. A three-year-old can take a simple hat and turn it into a major, long-running theatrical production.

Concluding Remarks

Buying toys for infants and toddlers, though tricky and trying at times, can be a wonderful experience. With a little time and talent, *making* toys for them can be even better. Most products on the toy store shelves can be equaled or surpassed by putting together simple household items and materials. It is amazing how much fun children can have with the container from a pair of pantyhose. Either way, following these guidelines, adults who have bought toys for a child should be able to avoid that terrible experience of watching the child play with the box for hours while ignoring the toy.

Part III
Child Care
Education

———

21
Education for Parenthood Programs

Education versus Social Services

As more and more education for parenthood programs have come into existence, a difficult problem has been emerging—the problem of professional identity. Our orientation to these programs is educational. We want to see education for parenthood become the cornerstone of society's educational effort.

This goal is a direct result of what we have been learning during the last three decades. Put simply, we have concluded that the educational experiences of the first years of life are too consequential to be ignored by the national educational system. A secondary reason for educational support programs for new parents is to benefit family life. Such programs can reduce stress and deepen pleasure in important ways for all concerned.

What, then, is the problem? The problem is that the distinction between education and social work easily becomes blurred in professional work with parents of infants and toddlers. The problem is most acute in the case of families with special needs. It is rooted in the fact that a family's capacity as an educational delivery system rests upon its general capacity to function in society.

This fact was brought home to me dramatically when I was participating in international meetings at UNESCO in 1976. After I had presented my position on the significance of educational experiences during the first years of life, the delegate from India took the floor. She did not disagree with the position I had taken but, rather, pointed out that her first concern for India's children was not optimal or even adequate education during the preschool years. She noted that 9 million children are born each year in India (about three times the number born in the United States) and that half of them die before their fifth birthday. Her first priority, therefore, was their survival—not their early education.

In his first-rate analysis of early intervention programs, Dr. Urie Bronfenbrenner (1974) called for programs to assist the family as the child's primary developmental delivery system. In his view, *all* the conditions necessary for the family to function as a childrearing system had to be met by society—including adequate health care, nutrition, housing, employment, and so forth.

In their book *All Our Children* (Kenniston, 1977), the Carnegie Council on Children went further, urging less talk about parent education and the substitution of a vigorous, government-led program of societal reform. The council pointed out that low-income families simply do not have any real chance of successful childrearing given the intrusive, exploitive, and selfish nature of current society. According to the council, parent education efforts are beside the point, at best, and in fact help people avoid facing the more central issues.

I want to emphasize two points. First, Dr. Bronfenbrenner and the Carnegie Council were referring to low-income families exclusively. Second, there is no refuting the argument that the extra-educational factors they refer to play a basic role in a child's development. The practical consequences of these facts are what can lead to trouble. Any professional who sets out to educate parents would be well-advised to keep the following points in mind:

1. *Educational programs have limited utility.* They are no substitute for multifaceted social service programs. A family's minimum basic needs have to be met as a precondition of programs intended to assist the family as an educational system. The satisfaction of these other needs is a matter for other professionals and programs. It also is a costly affair, usually beyond the modest funds available for educational services. Moreover, it usually requires training in fields other than education.

2. *Educational programs cannot address their greatest efforts to the greatest needs.* Families with the greatest educational needs often are those with the greatest extra-educational needs as well. The Brookline (Massachusetts) Early Education Program (BEEP), a

large-scale education for parenthood program, easily could have exhausted its budget on 30 of its 300 families.

3. *When working with families whose needs may be too great for an educational program alone, a strong social work referral mechanism is highly advisable.* A beautiful example of how this works can be found in the Child and Family Resource Program (CFRP), based in Jackson, Michigan. BEEP and Missouri's NPAT project had good results as well.

4. *A family that will welcome someone into their home to help them raise their baby is likely to ask for help in areas other than education.* Educators must resist the temptation to offer it themselves. They must steer the family to the appropriate specialists. This policy will help them maintain your professional identity, credibility, and focus.

It will take time for educators, psychologists, social workers, physicians, and others to sort out their responsibilities. The process will be painful at times. But for the time being, in addition to the important task of figuring out how to assist families, educators will have to be conscious of the hazards involved in working in a field that touches on several other disciplines.

The Role of the Pediatrician in Parent Education

Are pediatricians appropriate parent educators? Over the past fifty years, the two most influential books dedicated to helping parents raise their young children were written by physicians—Drs. Arnold Gesell and Benjamin Spock. When we were helping to plan the Brookline Early Education Project (BEEP), it was very clear that several kinds of physicians saw themselves as parent educators. In addition to pediatricians, general practitioners and child psychiatrists often considered parent education to be a routine element in their work. It also was clear that, in some instances, visiting nurses and public health nurses saw themselves as parent educators as well.

What does all this mean? Should parents expect someone in medicine to provide information they need about living with and raising a child on a day-to-day basis? I believe that every family with young children needs information about the nature of children to some degree. Two major needs for information that goes beyond the children's physical well-being have to do with management of the children and with helping them develop their abilities to the fullest extent. Providing information to parents can also heighten enjoyment and reduce stress for all concerned. Parents and children seem to get more pleasure and less pain from living together when the parents are reasonably well informed about early development. It is unfortunate, but true, that chronically anxious people, when given information about childrearing (even if it is good information), can become even more anxious. In such cases, additional information actually may hurt rather than help; however, such situations are not very common.

Ideally, I would like to see professionals in education—properly trained in the details of early human development and in working with parents—made available to every person who is trying to raise a young child. Unfortunately, such an ideal situation is not likely to exist for many years to come. What can we do under the present circumstances? I recommend that parents take the best advice they can get wherever they can get it. It is because the ideal system does not exist and the need is so strong that parents reach out for help to people in pediatrics and general medicine—indeed, to anyone they respect who is within reach. It is as if every home with inexperienced parents constitutes a vacuum of sorts, such that anyone who happens to be in the vicinity when anxiety starts to rise is drawn in to help. At times, help is sought from friends, relatives, or virtually any person who might know something useful. Professional help is most often sought from medical people, as they have been the only professionals in regular contact with parents of young children for many years. The concept of a professional educator who is seriously interested in babies is quite new; but new or not, that is the concept that makes the most sense to me.

Over the past decade or so, I have had a good deal of first-hand experience with professionals at varying levels of the medical field. The majority are quite willing to admit that they do not have extensive training in the areas that would be useful to parents who are interested in their children's educational development. Several have told us that they would be delighted if there was some other professional who would provide that kind of clearly needed help and allow them to return to what they were trained for—maintaining the physical health of the child. There are exceptions. Some physicians look upon child development as a subspecialty of pediatrics. Also, some people in pediatrics, with a very strong orientation toward psychiatric issues, feel strongly that training in pediatric psychiatry qualifies a physician to do all sorts of counseling concerning childrearing.

I am not trying to rule parent education out of bounds for medical personnel. That would be ridiculous. What I am trying to do is reduce the confusion. At the very least, if programs for training medical practitioners were more aware of the distinctions between educational and medical issues, they could begin to take advantage of important recent advancements in knowledge about the behavioral and experiential development of young children.

In my view, most people in medicine—whether they are in nursing, psychiatry, or pediatrics—have a comparatively modest background for helping parents with respect to educational issues during the first years of children's lives. Since the reality of our society is that education for parenthood programs will not be universally available for some time to come, it makes sense for people to continue to seek information on the topic wherever they can get it—which includes medical as well as educational personnel. However, medical people who are actually working with the families of very young children, especially those who are working with first-time parents, would be well-advised to pay attention to the newer information about babies that has been generated during the past twenty years, rather than to assume that the educational material in the textbooks previously used in medical training is adequate. Often, it is not.

The First-Time Parent

In our research and training programs over the last three decades, one vital fact has become quite clear: first-time parents are unique. Not only are they different from people who are not parents, but they are also different from those who have had children before, even if they have had only one.

This fact was brought home to us shortly after we began our home-based research in the mid-1960s. In those studies, my colleagues and I used stopwatches to time the behaviors of parents as well as babies. One of the most striking outcomes of that collection of information was that, on the average, parents of second, third, and fourth children were spending a total of about an hour and fifteen minutes in the course of the day in direct interactions with their babies. We were rather surprised by that number, which applied to the period when the babies were between twelve and thirty-three months of age. A striking finding that followed was that first-time parents were spending approximately *twice as much time* in direct interactions with their babies. First-time parents put much more time into the job than other parents—interestingly, much more time than is absolutely necessary in order for the child to do very well. From this and other experiences, we have concluded that the motivation of first-time parents with respect to the parenting process is the highest of anyone we have ever worked with.

A second very important characteristic of first-time parents is their responsiveness to training and their flexibility with respect to parenting behaviors. In our research, we are able to sample the behaviors of parents with their children while these parents were enrolled in our educational programs. We were quite surprised to find that parents of second, third, and fourth children rarely seemed to modify their parenting styles substantially as a result of being in our programs. In contrast, first-time parents tended to follow our guidance very closely.

The consequences for program planning are clear. For the best prospects for a program's training to have effect—that is, for the parents actually to absorb and act upon the guidance—the chances are substantially greater if the program involves first-time parents. Work with these people appears to be more likely to produce good results for babies than work with parents who have had children before.

I believe that both this heightened investment of time and this responsiveness can be attributed to the normal emotional state of first-time parents, which is a combination of extraordinary excitement and chronic anxiety. Indeed, the normal anxiety of first-time parents is what seems to underlie so much of the work of

Dr. T. Berry Brazelton. His neonatal scale, for example, was created in large part to help the professional demonstrate the individuality of babies from the first days of life, in order to alleviate the typical concerns of parents (see Brazelton, 1973). Many parents have tended to view virtually all behavior in their three- and four-month-old children as being due to parenting practices.

This emotional state of excitement and anxiety is of fundamental importance to educators. Of course, we are not the only people who have concluded that first-time parents are prime candidates for attention. So, too, have the major toy companies, the producers of baby products (such as baby food, diapers, powders, etc.), the publishers of magazines for parents, and the people who are offering various organized programs for young children. All of the aforementioned concentrate their marketing efforts on the first-time parent. The people who subscribe to the most magazines and buy the greatest number of baby products and enroll in infant exercise and achievement-oriented programs are more often the first-timers than the more experienced parents.

It is interesting that there are both good and bad consequences of this special condition of first-time parents. Clearly, a program of parent education—or anything else having to do with the well-being of a baby—is well-advised to orient its efforts toward first-time parents. This is not to say it should exclude others, but for the best results in recruiting, for faithful commitment to a program that features more than a single contact, and for clients who are more forgiving than others (that is, who will accept flaws in the offerings and stay with the program), then by all means, a program should aim for the first-time parent. If professionals want to feel that they are really doing valuable work, they should work with the first-time parent. The level of appreciation and loyalty received will be maximal.

Unfortunately, there is at least one disadvantage to the first-time parent's state—and I think it is of extraordinary importance. The normal anxiety state of inexperienced parents is the fundamental source of their vulnerability. This vulnerability of first-time parents, especially during the first months and years of their children's lives, probably accounts for a good deal of their open-mindedness, but it also makes them more exploitable than most people. In addition, it constitutes a potential threat to the success of parent education programming, because it often converts the relationship between parents and educational professionals from a learning/teaching situation to a situation that, in my opinion, features too much dependence. It is very important for professionals in education for parenthood to be aware of this. When professionals work with first-time parents of infants and toddlers, they are in a situation that is loaded with much more emotion than that of, for example, a preschool teacher working in a nursery school or a teacher in elementary, secondary, or other levels of education.

This unique state of first-time parents gives us the opportunity to provide information and support that means a great deal to them. There are no happier clients than those in the New Parents as Teachers project in Missouri, for example. They are in the middle of a once-in-a-lifetime, magical experience. They are not victims of anxiety to the degree that unsupported new parents are. In addition, they are being helped to enjoy the parenting process even more than they otherwise might because the information coming in to them makes the development of their child even more exciting and interesting than it would otherwise be. Also, they have support at hand if they should run into problems. However, it is equally obvious that people who are either unknowing or exploitive can take the same emotional situation and use it in a manner that is not helpful and may even be damaging to the family.

22
Educational Goals for Infants and Toddlers

I always have believed that the only appropriate starting point for any educational program is the establishment of goals. There are several reasons for this position. At times professionals and parents hold differing views on goals. At other times, people adopt goals that cannot be achieved with the current "state of the art." More often, the key problem is that educational program operators and parents do not really know the degree to which the goals are being achieved—if, indeed, they are.

In a program I was involved with during the late 1960s—the Brookline Early Education Project (BEEP)—the staff agreed that the parents were the appropriate people to choose the program goals for their children. My colleagues and I then had to find out what the parents wanted from the program. We also wondered how much they knew about what could be delivered by an early education program.

We held a series of meetings with two purposes in mind. First, we tried to describe what we could and could not do as educators. For example, we could fulfill the promise that no child would pass through the preschool years with an undetected learning handicap. However, we could not fulfill any promises for increases in creativity or self-confidence, mainly because we could find no proven ways of measuring or encouraging the development of either characteristic.

The second purpose of the meetings was to find out which goals were valued most by the parents. We were particularly interested in differences among the parents and between the parents and the staff. Unlike most early education programs, BEEP served families from almost all areas of the socioeconomic spectrum (SES), from welfare recipients to high-income professionals.

We found that the lower-SES families were much more oriented toward academic readiness and "good manners" goals than were the families from the upper end of the SES. The former wanted their children to learn "their numbers, colors, and the alphabet" and to learn "to be good." The latter were not at all concerned with such goals; instead, they wanted their children to be "socially adept, confident, and individualistic." The goals favored by the staff were closer to those of the high-SES parents than those of the low-SES parents.

What can be done when the goals of the parents do not coincide with the goals of the staff? First, an attempt should be made to explain the staff's goals to the parents in an effort to decide on mutually agreeable goals. Failing that, the staff either has to accept the parents' goals or look for other work.

In general, in determining educational goals for infants and toddlers, I recommend the following steps:

1. Professionals should explore the knowledge base to learn the full range of possible goals for early education programs.

2. Professionals should judge which goals actually are capable of being achieved, given what we know and what we don't know about how to help a child develop well.

3. Professionals should then select program goals they value and choose to work with, keeping an eye out for new developments in the field.

4. Parents in a prospective program should be provided with reliable information about program goals and should be asked to make their choices, with due consideration of those selected by the program's staff.

5. Whenever possible, some form of testing should be incorporated into the program so that staff and parents can gain some idea of whether or not the program goals are being realized.

I favor "general competence" goals for children who are free from significant delays. I believe that special needs children should be in programs specially designed to deal with their particular handicaps. I also prefer not to work on programs designed to develop either genius or precocity in some specific activity, such as early reading, mathematics, piano playing, tennis, and the like.

The range of possible goals is quite broad once we go beyond the general "well-developed, happy child" level. The selection of goals for programs I have worked with—which include social skills goals as well as intellectual and linguistic development goals—has always been based on our extensive studies of preschool children who were judged to be outstanding in all aspects of development. I urge all professionals to examine closely the explicit and implicit goals they are working toward and the bases upon which these goals rest.

23
Programs That Promise Precocity

G lenn Doman's Better Baby Institute, based in Philadelphia, promises parents smarter, more capable babies if the parents attend the institute's brief training program. Several years back, Doman and a colleague were urging parents to help their children learn to read by using their kit. A fair number of parents are very interested in such ideas. Indeed, the Doman's work has been featured in several popular magazines and television shows lately.

Professionals in early education are either puzzled or enraged. Does Glenn Doman know a dramatically better way to raise a baby? Are parents making a mistake if they are not closely monitoring and stimulating their babies' development from birth? Or are we going too far? Are parents' typical anxieties and exaggerated ambitions for their children being exploited?

The national YMCA is concerned about the hazards—such as water intoxication—involved in programs designed to teach swimming to infants. On the other hand, many people have been bowled over by the violin and piano virtuosity of preschool students of the Suzuki method. What does it all mean?

Parents' interest in their children's extraordinary early achievements is not very different from the general interest most parents have in their children's welfare. For some parents, however—for reasons that vary and are not clearly understood—such interest becomes unusually strong. Some people object to such high ambition in parents of infants and toddlers. Setting aside such objections for the time being, we can turn to practicalities. What results are these people seeking? Can anyone really produce such results? If they are produced, what would be the costs?

The results these parents are seeking range from the conventional to the extreme. Most parents want their very young children to develop free from handicaps, capable, well-balanced, confident, and comfortable with people. "Capable" usually means as far above average as their congenital potential will allow. Most parents' aspirations for their children do not include development of pre-professional skills in such areas as tennis, ice skating, or music, or genius levels in mathematics. That is not to say that parents would not value such skills, but they usually do not set such goals and pursue them avidly.

However, some people very much want very high levels of achievement for their children as soon as possible. Such desired achievements range from the ability to read before three years of age, the acquisition of prodigious amounts of factual material (including remarkable vocabularies), learning to swim during infancy, and the ability to play a musical instrument.

Can anyone really produce such results? We can look for the answer in research and in established practice. In research, as noted earlier, the most widely accepted knowledge about the growth of intelligence is the work of Piaget. Nothing in that work directly addresses the question of how to help a child become very bright very early. Piaget simply was uninterested in the subject. Although there are large numbers of studies of gifted children taking place at this time, no substantial body of knowledge has yet been acquired on *how to bring about* giftedness.

One closely related study was our own Harvard Preschool Project. With a large staff and generous funds, we spent thirteen years examining the details of early development in children who developed unusually well during the preschool years. However, we were interested in *balanced* development. In fact, we deliberately excluded intellectually or artistically precocious children who were not equally capable of interacting with others or who were weak in any other major area of development. Thus, there is no direct basis in research for any program that promises intellectual giftedness.

Is there a basis in well-established practice? In Montessori preschools, the teaching of reading and writing to preschoolers has been demonstrated—*for all to see*—repeatedly over several decades, in many places, by many practitioners. At the University of Kansas Preschool, teaching preschoolers to tie their own shoelaces (no mean task) has been demonstrated repeatedly—*for all to see*—and the method is transferable.

However, there is no basis in well-established practice for any program that promises intellectual giftedness. That does not mean that Doman or any number of other people might not have discovered some effective procedures; rather, it means that no such methods have received widespread examination or approval. Indeed, Doman's group has refused to allow any professional group to evaluate his procedures. Furthermore, his earlier, equally dramatic claims of success in working with brain-damaged patients have never been supported or replicated by others in the field. Therefore, I am unable to recommend his services to parents.

What about the Suzuki procedures? The Suzuki method, unlike Doman's Better Baby Institute, does not claim to produce extraordinary achievements in all major facets of development. Furthermore, it has been in existence in many locations with conspicuous success for many years, and there is nothing secretive about it. The procedures are available for examination by anyone. Although some teachers of music no doubt have objections to the Suzuki method, I see no obvious reason to be concerned. In contrast, a program that requires regular, lengthy drills to induce learning at a fast pace and in great quantity during the early years is a matter for concern.

What are the likely costs of special teaching programs for the very young, and why should we be concerned? If the costs involve several hours of drilling each day for parents and children over long periods of time, I believe that the children's spontaneous interest and pleasure in learning are likely to be jeopardized. If large portions of time are spent in a narrowly focused direction—such as tennis, ice skating, violin, or reading—I believe the children probably will pay a significant price in other developmental areas as well as in motivation to learn.

During the early years, some of a child's most important learning is in the social realm. Children learn to relate to people in fundamental ways during the first six years of life—and that learning takes a lot of time. They also learn to use their bodies during that time—and that learning takes time. Children spend a great deal of their time in experiences that are not dictated by any lesson plan but nevertheless seem to be an important part of their healthy early development. They also spend a lot of time in a relaxed mood. Any program that promises precocity ultimately must be evaluated in the light of all its effects on the broad pattern of development in the young child. I therefore urge a conservative approach to any such program.

24
Nursery School

During their third year of life, most children begin to show that they are ready for regular out-of-home experiences. Traditionally, nursery schools have set two and a half years as the age at which they will first accept children. Equally traditional has been the orientation of such schools toward middle-class families. What is the role of the nursery school today? What are the responsibilities of the parent educator in this area?

It is my opinion that the ultimate responsibility for a child's education rests with a child's parents, except in cases where the parents are either unwilling or unable to do the job. I believe most parents want the job, and with some information and support, can do it well. I define nursery school as an out-of-home, educationally oriented, part-time group experience for two-and-a-half- to five-year-old children who are free from serious educational handicaps. As a starting point in discussing the role of the nursery school, I suggest (as always) a consideration of goals. The primary avowed purposes of nursery schools seem to be as follows:

1. To provide a transition experience between the early years at home and the formal school experience that usually begins during a child's sixth year.

2. To enrich the social life of a child who has limited access to agemates.

3. To give a child a lasting educational advantage or a head start.

4. To help deal with minor educational handicaps.

5. To provide parents with some relief from the responsibility of caring for a child for a few hours a week or considerably more.

Not all of these goals are attainable. Some research has been done on the subject, though not much in recent years. Virtually all of the research on preschool education since the early 1960s has focused on compensatory education for children from low-income families (see Weikart, 1980). However, the results of such research are only indirectly relevant to the subject under examination here.

The standard reference regarding nursery schools for nondisadvantaged, nonhandicapped children is an article by Joan Swift (1964). Information in that report should be understood by parent educators because it serves as a legitimate (and rare) basis for family guidance on this often confusing topic.

Although some nursery school advocates will swear otherwise, there is no evidence to support the claim that a child who attends nursery school will be more comfortable entering kindergarten or first grade than one who does not. Indeed, there is no substantial evidence of lasting benefits—social or intellectual—from any type of nursery school experience. Apparently, a child who comes from a caring, normal family will learn as much within the social and intellectual climate of her own home as she will from experiences in good professional schools during the preschool years.

Children can and do learn—often in impressive ways—from preschool experiences. For example, as noted earlier, the Montessori curriculum uses proven methods for teaching reading and writing to preschoolers. Researchers at the University of Kansas have created effective techniques for teaching preschoolers to tie their shoelaces. Suzuki principles, properly applied, will produce violin and piano playing skills in very young children. Fitness curricula can lead to swimming and other special motor skills in the early years. It is even possible that Glenn Doman's Better Baby Institute is producing equally impressive results (although, as mentioned earlier, he has not allowed impartial evaluations of his work).

The fact that preschoolers *can* learn much that they would not ordinarily learn until later does not mean, however, either that the effects are lasting or important or that the experience is advisable. Some parents want precocious musical ability and are willing to pay a substantial price for it. Other parents would rather not enter their three-year-olds into a regular pattern of lengthy, daily practice sessions.

In my view, preschool education for children who are developing normally should be decided on with due consideration of *all* the goals of early childhood and *all* the costs to both the children and their parents. If early reading or musical ability, for example, is attained at the expense of the child's pleasure in learning or in a manner that interferes with good social development, I would not recommend it. Some parents will choose the path toward the development of special talent even when the price is high; others will not. In either case, the responsibility of the professional is to point out the options, the possibilities, and the costs, as well as to make recommendations.

Regarding the role of nursery schools in remediation of educational handicaps, the concept of special education becomes relevant. By two and a half years of age, developmental delays in language and higher mental abilities are often clear. What is needed in such situations is a program designed to cope with special needs. Nursery schools ordinarily are not equipped to offer special education programs. Such programs are usually affiliated with colleges, universities, mental health centers, or similar institutions, and their services cost considerably more than nursery schools in general.

I believe that relieving parents of some child care responsibilities is an undervalued and important function for nursery schools. Nursery school personnel are often sensitive about serving this function because it can be seen as a demeaning comment on their work. If nursery school were merely babysitting, their extensive teacher training would be largely wasted. There is no denying, however, that trained nursery school teachers have valid professional skills and that nursery schools provide relief from child care for parents who need time off from their children. However, the issues of whether families need child care and whether nursery schools offer more than child care are quite separate.

Lately, there has been a dramatic increase in the demand for full-time child care—both from those who run nursery schools and from other early childhood professionals. Nursery school professionals have long insisted that they are not child caretakers; they prefer to focus on the child's education. Many other child care professionals, on the other hand, insist that their work is educationally sound as well as useful for child care purposes. Families often need professional help in sorting out these confusing cross-currents.

Where, then, does that leave the parent educator on the subject of nursery schools? First, parents should be informed about the world of education for the two-and-a-half- to five-year-old. They should learn about different types of preschools—including the "traditional" forms, such as Bank Street and Pacific Oaks, as well as Montessori, Doman, and other available models. They should be given details about the various goals, costs, and likely effects of each of the different approaches.

Second, if the child has a special need, the parent educator should provide the parents with comparable information about the world of preschool special education. Third, the parent educator should make recommendations and give reasons for them.

In my opinion, a child who does not have a special educational need does not have to attend a nursery school to be prepared for school, either intellectually or socially. A good nursery school can offer a child enjoyment from good social experiences, attractive equipment, and other facilities. It also can challenge and motivate a child. In some communities, certain nursery schools may even be a necessary first step in a long-term private school program. In most situations, however, a nursery school should be selected on the basis of answers to the following questions:

1. Is the child comfortable in an away-from-home program?

2. Do the parents want such an experience for their child?

3. Is the child free from any special educational needs?

4. Are the key personnel loving and knowledgeable, and are they aware of what they *don't* know?

5. Is the cost reasonable?

6. Are the conditions—such as location, transportation, and hours—convenient for the parents?

Of course, if a child has a special educational need, that should take precedence; in any event, such needs cannot usually be dealt with by a typical nursery school. The need for full-time day care should not be confused with the educational needs of the child. Claims that a full-time group experience is educationally desirable for preschoolers are not supported by evidence at this time, but the needs of the parents for full-time day care for their preschoolers should be given full consideration in their own right and should be weighed in with their children's educational needs.

25
Full-Time Day Care

The subject of full-time day care for infants and toddlers first began to attract widespread attention about fifteen years ago. I remained comfortably uninvolved for several years as the issue grew warmer. Today, however, it is a very warm issue, and I find myself very much involved.

My public involvement began during the summer of 1979 as a result of an interview published in the *Los Angeles Times*. Among the many questions put to me was what my views were on full-time day care for very young children. My response was essentially negative. I suggested that babies are very probably better off when they are cared for by family members. Consequently, I was approached by a small California foundation and asked to conduct a public information campaign on the topic.

I spent some time considering whether or not to take an active role in the day care issue. I knew I would be causing pain to young parents who had already placed their infants in full-time day care. I knew I would anger people who were working hard to fund day care operations. Yet I also felt deeply about what infants and toddlers need to get off to their best possible start in life. In addition, I felt a special responsibility to speak to the issue of the impact of full-time day care *on the child*. Aside from Selma Fraiberg (1977), most of the voices I heard were focusing solely on the needs of the parents, especially mothers.

There are many indications that the use of full-time child care for infants and toddlers has increased substantially during the past few years, and it also seems clear that earlier implicit taboos against the practice are being actively contested. Like many issues involving babies, families, and the role of parents, full-time child care is a highly charged topic. Also, like many issues involving the development of babies, hard evidence is scarce, opinions are plentiful, and the need for reliable answers is deeply felt.

No single answer to the question of whether or not to use full-time child care is possible. Some important considerations are as follows:

Do the parents want to be fully responsible for the care of their children?

Do the parents have the resources to do the job?

Do the parents have any real choices?

What kinds of child care are available?

If, for example, the parents do not want the job, or if they are unable to do it minimally well because of severe emotional problems, physical disabilities, alcoholism, and the like, I would favor full-time care. If, on the other hand, parents seek full-time child care because they are not aware of potential significant losses to their children or themselves that might result, that is another matter.

I have been studying the role of experience in the development of children for twenty-eight years. Important information on this subject has come from several sources, including research in developmental psychology, psychiatry, and education. Much of that research has been done with children, and a considerably greater amount has been done with the young of numerous other animal species. In addition, I have learned something about the effects of full-time child care in such long-standing institutions as the Israeli kibbutzim and the British practice of the use of nannies.

The results of all these endeavors constitute my knowledge base on the subject of full-time child care. Few people would be bold (or foolish) enough to claim to understand the subject in full. Nevertheless, some judgments have to be made. What follows are my best judgments, based on what I think is known about the subject and with the conviction that a conservative position is the only sensible one when it comes to the welfare of infants and toddlers.

1. The experiences of the first few years of a child's life have special significance for the entire life span.

2. Given the wide variations in the quality of available child care, most children are better off when most of their waking time

during these first years is spent with their parents, grandparents, or someone else who has a special feeling for them.

3. Full-time day care for children under three is *not* generally advisable, except when the family is either unable or unwilling to handle the task themselves.

4. Inevitably, some families will be unable or unwilling to shoulder the primary responsibility for rearing their own children. In such cases, the child will probably be better off in a day care system.

5. For *most* families *part-time* child care, *after* the first six months of life, is probably a good idea. The normal stresses of child-rearing, especially when there are several closely spaced children in a family, are better dealt with when they are not continuously imposed on a single person in the household.

6. There is no evidence that a parent has to be female to participate in or take major responsibility for raising a baby.

7. Full-time child care reduces the opportunity for parents to receive some of life's greatest rewards. The pleasure and excitement of sharing their own child's daily life as he or she experiences the wonders of the first years can be as valuable as any life has to offer.

8. If full-time child care is to be used, I recommend the following order of preferences: a caretaker in the child's own home; a caretaker in the home of the caretaker; nonprofit family care, with no more than two other children under three years of age in the care of an adult; nonprofit center-based care; for-profit family care, with no more than two other children under three years of age in the care of an adult; for-profit center-based care. In any event, the person or persons who will be caring for the infant or toddler should be very carefully selected for warmth, intelligence, and experience—not merely for degrees or other academic credentials.

In summary, the topic of full-time child care is currently of great concern to many people, and it is difficult to predict where it will end up. There is no question that for many families, the economic pressure for both parents or a single parent to work is enormous. It also is a reality that the cost of high-quality center-based care for infants and toddlers is very high, and we cannot expect either government or industry to pay for very much service at such high rates.

I really do not know an easy solution. As a professional edu-

cator, my role in the issue is necessarily a limited one. Having studied what infants and toddlers need to build the best foundation for
later life, I have no choice but to continue to urge parents—those
who have a choice—to see to it that their children spend the majority of their waking hours with either their parents or grandparents
during the first three years. I also continue to urge government authorities to help young families achieve this goal.

Part IV
The Shape
of the
Future

26
The Missouri
New Parents as Teachers
Project

Origins

The remote origins of the Missouri New Parents as Teachers (NPAT) project lay in my long-standing interest in the development of competent people. That interest first surfaced in the early 1950s and led to my doctoral work in psychology. From 1957 to 1965, my work concentrated on infants between birth and six months of age. It was that work that led to the opportunity to create the Harvard Preschool Project in 1965.

The Preschool Project was a rather unusual research enterprise. The School of Education at Harvard had been awarded a $1 million per year research contract from the U.S. Office of Education. Part of that money was to be spent exploring the newly created target area of preschool education. My suggestions on how to approach that problem led to the creation of the Harvard Preschool Project.

In 1965, the conventional approach to preschool education was to develop curricula for center-based compensatory education programs for low-income minority children between three and five years of age. In contrast, the Harvard Preschool Project's orientation was to explore the question of how children could receive experiences between birth and the sixth birthday that would allow them to develop to their fullest potential. This orientation came directly from Abraham Maslow's (1970) studies of self-actualized people.

By the late 1960s, the Preschool Project had narrowed its focus to the period between birth and the third birthday because of the simple conclusion that the major distinguishing characteristics of the outstanding six-year-old could be found in the outstanding three-year-old. At about that time, Dr. Robert Sperber, the superintendent of schools in Brookline, Massachusetts, requested my assistance in developing a program to help Brookline's children prepare for public school. The result was the Brookline Early Education Project (BEEP). BEEP was designed as a cost-effectiveness study. Its goal was to help all children born within a specified period of time in Brookline to receive the best possible beginnings in life during the preschool years, starting at birth, through a program of training and assistance for their parents—the children's first teachers. BEEP, which was sponsored by Harvard, the Carnegie Corporation, and the Robert Wood Johnson Foundation, received a good deal of national publicity, which attracted the attention of two women from Missouri: Mildred Winter, head of the State Department of Elementary Education, and Jane Paine, a program officer at the Danforth Foundation in St. Louis. Mrs. Winter visited BEEP and held extensive conversations with me, which led to her commitment to the BEEP concept and a strong desire to create such a program in Missouri.

Although this book is not the place to go into the details of the BEEP experiment, a few descriptive remarks and comments are warranted. Initially, I directed the planning of BEEP while simultaneously maintaining continued supervision of the Harvard Preschool Project. There was a concerted attempt to translate the emerging findings of the Preschool Project research, along with those of other relevant studies, into programs of training and support for parents. Since the size of the BEEP task was considerably larger in many ways than the Preschool Project research enterprise, it soon became clear that it would be most difficult for me to maintain the direction of both enterprises, and a director for BEEP was hired. I then became the senior consultant to BEEP while maintaining directorship of the Preschool Project. As the BEEP project evolved, several of its characteristics began to develop in ways that I thought were ill-advised. For example, too many parents were selecting themselves for entrance into BEEP, a classical flaw in studies of this sort that is called a "self-selected sample." Such samples invalidate these studies because the target population does not include a fair representation of all kinds of families in the community;

rather, it becomes overweighted with those who are most sensitive to and most interested in new educational programs. Despite strong recommendations to the contrary, the BEEP personnel continued to allow self-selection to take place. A second critical problem was that the BEEP management team insisted on evaluating themselves, a task for which I thought they had neither the special abilities nor the resources. Because of these and additional difficulties, I resigned from BEEP early in the 1970s.

In the meantime, Mrs. Winter and Mrs. Paine invited me on several occasions to help them convince the authorities in Missouri that a BEEP-type program made sense for them. Every year-and-a-half or so, I addressed groups of legislators and advocates of better education in an attempt to help convince them that three years of age was quite late in a child's learning process. These results led to the establishment of planning efforts for NPAT in the summer of 1981. An administrative structure was created, and preservice training began during the fall of 1981. The administrative groups consisted of an executive management team that included the state's commissioner of education, Dr. Arthur Mallory, Mrs. Winter, Mrs. Paine, and myself. A second group, known as the Advisory Committee, was established. This larger group included a medical advisor, a speech and hearing specialist, and representatives of the superintendents of the four school districts that were selected to operate the pilot programs.

Preservice training was accomplished between October 1981 and January 1982. Personnel from the Center for Parent Education traveled to Missouri for three-day sessions on six different occasions. These sessions were designed mainly to train the key operating personnel for the pilot programs. A library of more than 150 items was provided by the Center, and readings were assigned during the nineteen-day training period. In addition to the readings, the work included supervised home visit sessions and training in conducting group sessions.

Training of staff did not end with the beginning of service delivery but continued with in-service activities six times each year for the next two and a half years. The total training time in contact with the Center staff was approximately fifty days.

Goals

The goals of NPAT were identical to those of BEEP. Both programs were designed as cost-effectiveness studies to seek information regarding the desirability of training and support for new parents as their children's first teachers. Although we were interested, of course, in whether the parents became more knowledgeable about children, whether they enjoyed the program, whether the community valued the program, and so on, the key evaluation question was whether, at three years of age, the children whose parents had gone through the program were better developed in all major characteristics than they otherwise would have been.

For good reason, many early childhood programs that were created in connection with the Head Start project concentrated on helping children develop high levels of intellectual and linguistic skills. The focus of the Missouri program, which was considerably broader, was on what I have called *general competence*. General competence includes intellectual and linguistic skills, but it also includes—and ranks more highly in a basic sense—social skills. The full definition of a competent three-year-old, derived directly from the research results of the Harvard Preschool Project, included some seventeen distinguishing qualities of the outstanding three- to six-year-old child (see appendix 26A, following the text of this chapter).

Participants

The Missouri NPAT project focused on first-time parents. Also, although the program attempted to include all first-time parents in the pilot areas, it excluded *for evaluation purposes* families whose situations were beyond the capacity of a modestly priced program. For example, the family of a thirteen- or fourteen-year-old single parent would not be excluded from receiving services but would not be included as part of the evaluation sample, because it was expected that the needs of that family would go beyond the regular capacity of the project. The same was true if English was not the first language spoken in the home. What this meant was that a small minority of all first-time parents, certainly no more than 10 percent, were not included in the evaluation sample.

Concentrating on first-time parents is of very great importance in projects of this kind. In many years of work with young couples, we had learned that first-time parents are by far the most highly motivated, receptive, and flexible of all parents. The Harvard Preschool Project routinely noted that people who were in training with us but who already had one or two children tended not to adjust their parenting styles to reflect our recommendations nearly as much as first-time parents did. A key indicator of the enthusiasm and devotion to the task of first-time parents was that the actual time spent by them in direct interactions with their children in our studies was consistently about double that spent by second- and third-time parents.

Recruiting: Avoiding the Self-Selected Sample

Many programs designed to help young children develop have fallen victim to the problem of self-selected samples because they were not careful enough in their attempts to recruit a representative sample of the population in question. Consider the practical situation. They go into a community and try to recruit families to a new and potentially valuable assistance program. They announce that they are seeking families to participate. They publicize the opportunity. People who volunteer are much more likely to be those with an unusually strong interest in the subject and an unusually high degree of awareness of events taking place in their community as compared to other young couples. In fact, couples who most need help are often less likely to become aware of and volunteer for such new programs. (Remember, however, that neither BEEP nor NPAT was designed for the most needy young families in a community. For example, if a young couple consists of two people who are alcoholics or drug abusers, these programs are not likely to make much difference.) Therefore, many young couples who could profit a good deal from these programs have to be actively sought out.

In the NPAT project, we were very sensitive to this issue. In each of the four pilot areas, we made a serious effort to recruit every young couple expecting their first child. Throughout the ten-month recruiting period, from the beginning of January to the end of September 1982, we routinely examined the birth records in these communities to see if we had missed anyone; when we found that we had, even though the child was then several weeks old, we tried to recruit that family into the project. An examination of our four samples in comparison to the comprehensive records of all births during the recruiting period indicates that we rarely missed a family.

Four communities were involved in the project. An attempt was made to represent the bulk of Missouri's families in these four communities. Therefore, there was one urban center, which included among its families young single parents as well as intact two-parent families in which both parents had advanced degrees. There were two bedroom community sites, one in the eastern part of the state and one in the western part. Finally, there was one rural site, where the level of education often was less than high school and where per capita income was much lower than in the other sites. We ended up with some 320 families that, in most major characteristics, truly represented the young couples starting to raise families across the state of Missouri.

Methods

Our purpose was to create a sensible and comprehensive educational system to help parents guide the learning processes of their children from birth to the third birthday. Our model for building this system was adopted from conventional educational practice in the public schools. It included teacher training—both preservice and in-service—and support, assessment in the form of regular screening of developmental status, and referral for special services if needed. There was to be special emphasis on hearing ability and the development of receptive language and social skills.

By initiating the program in the third trimester of pregnancy wherever possible, we were able to provide a modest amount of preservice training to the expectant parents. Through monthly contacts with parents from the time of the birth of the child through to the third birthday, we could provide regular in-service training and support. Additional support came from other parents, who would interact with the client families in small group sessions. An added important outcome of these group contacts was the opportunity for cooperative baby-sitting, which allowed each of the parents to avoid 100 percent "on duty" circumstances. In other words, there would be an opportunity, for a minimum of at least a few hours a week, for any parent not to have to be responsible for his or her child.

The screening program was designed to fulfill a promise we made to each of the parents—that if they participated in this free, school-based program, nothing could go wrong with the early learning process without their learning about it promptly and without their being provided assistance in procuring whatever help they needed to cope with the difficulty. It turned out that fulfilling this promise was not very difficult or costly.

Note that we did not use the term *testing*. First-time parents, though in many ways ideally suited to the task of raising babies, are at the same time, and for very good reason, easily alarmed. It appears that the supreme importance of the well-being of their first baby, combined with the responsibilities involved and the total helplessness of the child, among other things, leads to a normal state of chronic anxiety for such parents. Furthermore, they seem to be on guard against what they dread—that is, any sign that something might be wrong with their child. We tried to avoid using the word *test* unless it was essential. *Screening* is a more appropriate term anyway, and it is tolerated much better. Screening is also much less expensive than testing, since it requires less training for the staff.

The NPAT design parallels that of public school systems for older children in that extensive diagnostic work is undertaken only when a student shows signs of a significant educational problem. So, too, NPAT provided for referral to proper diagnostic testing of any child for whom the staff or parents had a serious educational concern.

The targets of the screening effort were determined by the particular goals of the project. Because the project was oriented toward general competence rather than simple intellectual achievement, screening had to be a multifaceted proposition. At the top of the list of priorities was screening for interpersonal skill acquisition. Of course, we also screened for intellectual and linguistic progress. Since all of the aforementioned depend directly on the capacity of infants and toddlers to hear well, and since approximately 25 to 33 percent of all infants and toddlers suffer from temporary mild to moderate hearing losses several times in each of the first two years of life, we initiated a careful program of screening for mild to moderate hearing losses from the time the child was four months of age through the first years of life. Table 26–1 illustrates the screening schedule that was followed.

Table 26–1
NPAT Monitoring Schedule

Age	Procedures	Administered by
3 weeks	Questionnaire: family history of hearing and vision problems and information on the birth process	Staff
4 to 5 months	Denver Developmental Screening Test (modified)	Staff
	Ewing Hearing Test (modified)	Parents
8–30 months	Harvard Preschool Project Social Competence Rating Scale (modified)	Staff
12 months	Denver Developmental Screening Test (modified)	Staff
	Ewing Hearing Test (modified)	Parents
14 months	Harvard Preschool Project Language Abilities Test (modified)	Staff
24 months	Denver Developmental Screening Test (modified)	Staff
	Ewing Hearing Test (modified)	Parents
	Harvard Preschool Project Language Abilities Test (modified)	Staff
30 months	Denver Developmental Screening Test (modified)	Staff
	Ewing Hearing Test (modified)	Parents
	Harvard Preschool Project Language Abilities Test (modified)	Staff

Parent Education and Support

It should be noted, first, that in administering training and support to our client families, we did not simply create written curriculum materials and hand them out to the parents. We have learned over the years that the most effective way to get information across to parents is through talk and pictures. Therefore, we made heavy use of audiovisuals and face-to-face contacts. We did create superb written materials (see appendix 26B for samples), but we did not expect everybody to read and understand them.

We have found that some 10 to 15 percent of most populations that we deal with not only read what we hand them but seem to have an insatiable appetite for reading material. Such people are part of every population, but they represent a small minority. Professionals should not be misled by their behavior into thinking that the majority of new parents are avid readers. In our experience, at least, that has not been the case.

We communicated with our clients through two means: the home visit and the group visit. Home visits were private sessions approximately one hour long. Group visits took place at our centers, and generally lasted about an hour-and-a-half. Each type of visit has advantages and disadvantages.

Group Visits

Group visits are, of course, less expensive than private visits. We recommend that the groups consist of seven or eight couples whose children are within a month of each other in age if possible. Having more couples in a group reduces the effectiveness of small group discussions, and having a wider age spread among the children makes it more difficult to hold the attention of all the parents simultaneously. It is very difficult to maintain the attention of a parent of a six-month-old when you are talking to the parent of a one-month-old about her child. To facilitate two-parent participation, it is advisable to hold some group visits in the evenings and on weekends.

It is important not to try to cover too much material in a session. We aim for about one-third of what could be covered in a high school or college class. Group visits allow the parents to form friendships and compare experiences, so the group visit situation serves an important social function. Our group visits featured refreshments as well as education. Occasionally, there would be a guest speaker, sometimes there would be a toy-making session, and very often there would be a video or film presentation. Sample group visit agendas appear in appendix 26D.

Private Visits

Private visits are usually done in the home and are structured around four segments. The staff member who has an appointment examines the family's folder, which contains all materials collected from the beginning of the family's involvement in the project. Particular attention is paid to concerns, either recent or long-lasting. Once the folder has been reviewed, the staff member selects the standard agenda for the particular visit and then heads for the home. Samples of agenda for private visits are shown in appendix 26E.

After entering the home and greeting the parent, the staff member begins the observation period. The usual beginning is to say to the parent, "Would you please make believe that I haven't arrived as yet for the next 10 or 11 minutes?" This observation period, which can be mildly disconcerting to both staff and parent, is a very valuable element in the program. After proper training, staff members can accumulate a remarkable amount of information about a baby in just these few minutes of observation—information that will give them greater ability and confidence to talk about developmental issues with the parent later in the visit. Teaching takes place much more effectively when it can be related directly to the child's developmental status, rather than being done in the abstract. The observation is done from eight to ten feet away, with the observer playing "fly on the wall" rather than interacting with the baby. The baby's attempts at interactions, which are inevitable as the infant matures, are gently discouraged. When interactions are discouraged skillfully, within a few minutes the child under two and a half years of age will begin to act as if the observer were not present.

After ten minutes or so of observation, during which time the parents sometimes have to be discouraged from "putting on a show" with the child, the second segment starts. This segment is designed with several purposes in mind. It consists of a series of questions to the parent: Are you concerned with anything having to do with the child's learning processes? What is new about the child's behavior since our last contact with you? Are there any favorite places in the home where the child spends a lot of time? Are there any activities the child favors? Are there any particular objects that the child plays with frequently?

When asked about their concerns, if parents try to get the staff members to comment on some physical ailment, like a rash or a feeding problem, the staff members are advised to identify such issues promptly as noneducational, rather than to attempt to offer advice outside their principal professional role. First-time parents are very much inclined to try to use staff members as all-purpose experts, and staff members often are tempted to provide information that goes beyond their principal role. We believe it is very important for them *not* to do so. The professional identity as an educator is vital to the success of the program. Four or five months down the line, when a medical person tells the parent not to be concerned about a suspected hearing loss, our staff then can insist that the hearing loss be dealt with on educational as well as medical grounds, while gently pointing out that they are the educational specialists and the medical doctor is the principal resource for the family with respect to issues of physical health.

In asking questions about the child's new behaviors and current favored activities, we are painlessly teaching the parents what they should know if they are to be good observers of their children. Finally, asking parents to talk about their own first child seems to make them feel more comfortable with the visit. After all, to talk about the most precious person in their lives is generally both easy and very enjoyable.

The third segment of the one-hour private visit consists of about twelve minutes of delivery of information by the staff member to the parent. We have learned to keep the information as simple as possible. Staff members are often inclined to stuff the twelve minutes with dozens of notions about the child. The problem with this approach is that it can confuse and intimidate the parents. One has to be on guard continually to keep this segment simple and to the point, with the highest priority items receiving special emphasis. The content of these sessions is described in each of the standard lesson plans, or agendas.

The last segment is about four or five minutes long. There is a repeat of the opportunity for the parent to raise any educational concerns, and then the staff member leaves the parent with predictions regarding what to look for in the baby's development over the next several weeks. Once staff members have been properly trained and have had some experience, they soon become able to predict accurately what is coming with respect to mastery of the body, vocalizations, social skills, and so on. Providing this information is part of the professional's role, and parents find living with their child even more fun than it might otherwise be when they have a sense of what is coming next. (Figure 26–1 recapitulates the procedures of the private visit.)

The staff member then says good-bye, leaves the home, drives around the block, turns the car motor off, and fills out a simple one-page report. (A sample report form appears in figure 26–2.)

Early in the NPAT project, staff members often sat in their cars in front of the home and started to fill out lengthy reports. At times, they would find parents drawing the curtain and looking out at the car with concern. Once again, we were seeing a manifestation of the normal anxieties of first-time parents. Their assumption was, "If that staff member is writing something down, it very probably means that something is not going right with my child, and she was too kind to mention it to me." The remedy for this problem is to drive the car around the block before stopping to make out the report.

Early on, staff members were turning in reports four or five pages long, but we have learned that a standard report form, on which the staff member notes only what was unusual, is all that is required. It takes no more than ten minutes to complete.

Schedule of Group and Home Visits

The typical schedule of group and home visits appears in figure 26–3. Our central goals for the period from our first contact with

---

NEW PARENTS AS TEACHERS

Procedures for Home Visits

I. Establish rapport

II. Observation period

    A. Observe the child for Phase _____ development ⎫

    B. Observe for parent–child interaction   ⎬ 10 minutes

    C. Make observation notes on development ⎭

III. Parent discussion

    A. Comments regarding observation period

    B. Questions to parents: "What's new?" or child's current interests

    C. Parents' questions/concerns

IV. Lesson

    A. Special topic of discussion or screening

    B. Suggested activities

V. Summary

    A. Brief summary of visit

    B. Suggest what's ahead

    C. Necessary announcements and reminders

Figure 26–1. *NPAT Home Visit Procedures*

the family until the child turned seven months of age were to help guide the child

1. to a solid state of feeling loved and cared for,

2. to the achievement of each of the modest skills possible for a seven-month-old,

3. to a healthy interest in exploring the environment.

We put a great deal of emphasis on the first goal, since it is the unanimous opinion of mental health specialists that the lifelong capacity of a child to trust and love another human being depends largely on this achievement. For this reason, we actively discouraged the use of full-time child care during this period.

NEW PARENTS AS TEACHERS PROJECT
Personal Visit Record

Family name _____ Visit # _____ Age of Child _____

Visitor _____ Place: Home _____ Center _____

Date _____ Approximate Length of Visit _____

* *

Objectives:

Topics Discussed:

Parent Questions/Concerns:

Comments/Observations on Child and Parent (How's it going?):

Plan Completed: Yes _____ No _____ If not, why not?

Follow-up—Plans for Next Time, Consultation Needed:

Figure 26–2. *NPAT Home Visit Report Form*

Prenatal	Birth	5 mos.	36 mos.
1 PV and 1 GV during late pregnancy	PVs start when baby is three weeks old	1 PG per month	
	GVs start when baby is five weeks old	1 GV every six weeks for the period from five to thirty-six months	
	Next PV at seven weeks		
	Next GV at nine weeks		
	PVs and GVs continue at four-week intervals until child is five months of age		

PV = private visit (at home); GV = group visit (at Center).

Figure 26–3. *NPAT Schedule of Group and Home Visits*

Our central goals for the period between seven and thirty-six months of age took three forms:

1. Helping the child become a delightful, competent three-year-old whose typical behavior manifested the seventeen distinguishing qualities mentioned earlier (see appendix 26A).

2. Maintaining a balance of three major interests—mastery and enjoyment of the body, interest in people, and interest in exploration.

3. Optimal development of learning foundations—language, intelligence, curiosity, and social skills.

We emphasized three parenting functions.

1. Providing developmentally appropriate learning opportunities.

2. Providing assistance as needed.

3. Providing encouragement and shared enthusiasm.

We strongly recommended that parents or grandparents be with the children for the majority of their waking hours from seven months until at least thirty months of age.

In the Missouri pilot programs, we continued the program until the child's third birthday. In retrospect, however, we think that two and a half years is adequate. If a program has not significantly helped shape the parenting style by the time the baby is thirty months old, another six months is not going to make any difference. Furthermore, by the time the children are thirty months of age, most parents have managed to get through the difficult, negativistic stages of the children's behavior reasonably well.

As the schedule in figure 26–3 shows, there is a shift in frequency of contacts after five months of age. This shift is important. In our understanding of the early learning process, we make a major distinction between the child's development before the onset of crawling and the development that follows. The onset of crawling most commonly occurs at about seven months of age. Crawling is generally accompanied by the beginning of receptive language learning, accelerated social learning, and a variety of other developmental processes that are far more likely to fail to go as well as they might than the learning that takes place during the first seven months of life. Therefore, we emphasize that change by shifting gears when the child is about five months of age. We then begin a two-month preparatory period in which we try to prepare the parent for the dramatic developments and increased stresses that crawling ushers in.

The Curriculum

What information did we want to convey to the parents in our project? Simply put, we wanted them to know what any teacher of important material has to know to do the job as well as possible. Therefore, all major processes involved in the development of a delightful, capable three-year-old were the core of the curriculum. These include development of interpersonal skills, language, problem-solving ability or intelligence, along with basic information about the development of sensory skills, such as vision and hearing, and control of the body through both large and small muscle abilities. We wanted to teach them *what* happens *when*, starting at birth and moving right through to the third birthday.

We also wanted to teach them about the principal influences on each of the developments. We wanted to teach them the difference between developments that were likely to go quite well almost regardless of what they did versus others that depended considerably more on the particulars of their childrearing practices. An example of the former would be learning how to master the body in basic ways, such as achieving the abilities to walk and climb. An example of the latter would be language acquisition, which depends directly on adult activities, such as how and when language is addressed to the baby. It is interesting that language acquisition also depends directly on how carefully parents and other adults see to it that the child is able to hear well throughout the first years of life.

We also believed that our young parents ought to know something about assessment. Therefore, one feature of our work was the exposure of parents to screening procedures. Watching the ways in which a professional determines how much language a one-year-old understands, for instance, turned out to be an enjoyable and educational experience for the parents.

Of course, overriding the importance of all this information was the message we wanted parents to receive from the program—that they have a wonderful opportunity to make a substantial, lasting difference in their child's future. The trick is to convince parents of this without making them overly anxious or, for that matter, overly pushy.

The content of the curriculum was derived largely from the many years of research of the Harvard Preschool Project and my prior work focusing on the first six months of life. That extensive material was combined with outstanding products of other research workers, such as Piaget, Mary Ainsworth, Alan Sroufe, and Konrad Lorenz. Of all that material, the most germane and useful was probably the material that came from the Harvard Preschool Project, which was derived from analyses of the childrearing practices of families who were having wonderful results with their children. We owe a substantial debt to those many different kinds of families whose natural styles of parenting provided the direction for our attempts at understanding how to help a child get the most out of the first six years of life.

The emphasis of our curriculum was consistent with the scheduling of contacts with the families; that is, it was oriented in one way between the period of late pregnancy and the child's fifth month, and then the orientation shifted substantially from then on. In the first period of the project, we were oriented toward the "introduction to parenthood" issues, including support for somewhat nervous parents and a general introduction to the parents' opportunity to make important contributions to their children's futures. As the age of crawling approached, we moved toward a very specific delineation of the developmental processes that were about to surface. For example, we talked of four major developmental themes in the period from seven to eight months on to the third birthday: language acquisition, the development of intelligence, the development of curiosity, and the acquisition of interpersonal skills.

The Missouri project benefited from our many years of previous experience during which we evolved effective teaching strategies. For example, we learned many years ago not to try to cover too much territory in any single session. We also learned the value of limited redundancy. A certain amount of repetition is necessary, but too much can be counterproductive. We learned the importance of being entertaining as well as informative. We learned how easy it is to confuse parents by trying to convey too many details, resulting in a loss of focus on what is most important to understand.

All of these learnings were combined with the help of an extraordinarily good staff in Missouri into a collection of curriculum materials and lesson plans that cover the entire time period from the third trimester of pregnancy through to the child's third birthday.

We made extensive use of audiovisual products in our attempts at delivering the curriculum. The most basic audiovisuals we used were five hours of video and film material entitled "The First Three Years of Life." This material essentially converts my book, *The First Three Years of Life,* into pictorial form. Although it is not a complete parent education program, this high-quality pictorial material provides a constancy to the curriculum that is most helpful. Indeed, several hundred programs in Missouri are now using the same video material. To that extent, what they are communicating to their parents is constant across programs.

In addition to "The First Three Years," we have used films showing how other animal species raise their children as well as films illustrating some of Piaget's ideas on the development of problem-solving abilities in babies, and the like.

While we certainly did not assume that our written materials would be read by even the majority of the parents, the staff did produce superb products. These were created by senior staff, under the direction of the State Department of Education personnel, principally Mrs. Winter and Mrs. Marion Wilson of the Ferguson-Florissant school district. The best of the material from each of the four pilot programs was integrated into a collection of beautifully illustrated materials, which was provided to the families to help them incorporate the core information of the curriculum. Besides descriptions of developmental processes and parenting techniques, supplementary material about enjoyable activities linked to the developmental level of the child also proved useful.

We found that some of our parents were most anxious to learn about activities that would be particularly helpful to their children. For example, some believed that certain kinds of puzzles or texture toys are important for learning (we do not believe they are). At times, some parents seemed to want specific "recipes" to follow with their children. They might say, for example, "My child is fourteen months of age and right on target, perhaps somewhat advanced. Over the next month, what shall I do on a daily or weekly basis in order to improve sensory perception or fine motor coordination, etc." We strongly discouraged such requests. We explained to parents that there really are no specific learning games that anyone has proved effective in moving the developmental process forward. Instead, we explained to them that we were teaching parenting *styles,* the specific content of which was much less important than the general form. For example, we explained that if the home had been made safe for a baby to crawl around in and climb, they could count on the one-year-old to begin to explore. We also told them to expect the baby to seek out a parent frequently in the course of the day as the result of three types of situations: (1) if the child bangs her head and needs comforting; (2) if the child finds something very exciting, such as an empty cigarette package, and wants someone to share the thrill of discovery; or (3) when help is needed, perhaps with a stuck toy. Our parents were taught to expect such overtures from the child, provided that they gave the child the opportunity to explore the home.

We described a particular type of reaction to the baby's overtures that we believed would be most effective in helping the child learn well. It consists of a prompt response, featuring identification of a child's interest at the moment and provision of the service or the behavior, whenever reasonable, accompanied by a good deal of natural, normal language and a related idea or two. Occasionally, when common sense dictates, the prompt response should be of the following form: "I hear you, but you are going to have to wait a minute because I'm busy now, and what you need does not seem to constitute an emergency." We have found that this kind of response, starting when the infant is about eight or nine months of age, is quite important in beginning to teach the child that he is not the only one with needs.

This reactive response pattern is a central feature of the parenting style we have tried to teach. Another major feature of the parenting style consists of specific guidance on how to avoid over-indulging a child (see chapter 17). Not to be forgotten is that element of the parenting style which emphasizes the desirability of having at least one parent or grandparent present for the majority of the child's waking time in the period from six months or so to three years of age.

Staff Requirements

The staff unit we used in NPAT (and the smallest desirable one, in our judgment) consists of two full-time-equivalent parent educators and a half-time secretary. These two full-time equivalents should be a half-time director/half-time parent educator and two half-time parent educators. The resultant group of three makes for very effective functioning. The staff members support each other and, in general, seem to make a better working unit than either one person working alone or even two. We firmly believe that such a staff should not be asked to deal with more than fifty to sixty families—fewer at the beginning of their work and then perhaps a few more as they become more experienced. We believe that, in the long run, overloading them will prove to be a false economy.

The first qualification we look for in a staff member is an appropriate personality. Young couples need to be able to feel comfortable with the staff worker. After all, the staff worker will be dealing with the most precious part of the lives of these parents. Yet, although we want a comfortable relationship, we do not want parents to become overly dependent on our staff. It is very easy for staff members to develop into all-purpose amateur therapists for young couples. We think that is a mistake.

Second, we want someone who has experience with babies. We prefer to use parents whenever possible, simply because most of the families we have worked with seemed to appreciate receiving guidance from people who not only have had training but also have had first-hand experience raising children.

Staff training and academic credentials are more complicated issues. Because the field of early human development is incomplete and only recently developing into maturity, our experience has been that people who have degrees in early childhood development can create a good deal of difficulty for our programs. The reason is that their training generally has not included the very recent detailed information needed for the work. Also, the people who trained them were trained themselves many years earlier, in most cases, and their own backgrounds have suffered from the neglect of the subject of early human development until the late 1960s. Therefore, we are in favor of reserving the bulk of the staff training for up-to-date preservice and in-service training, rather than assuming that someone with a bachelor's or a master's degree in early childhood or family studies is already appropriately trained for this work. We hope that this situation will change in the near future.

We believe it is important, for several reasons, that each of the parent educators deal with every one of the families in the project. If we were to assign twenty families to a single parent educator, a variety of problems would surface. First, there would be a rather strong tendency for some of the parents to form a deep dependence on the parent educator. This is inevitable under the circumstances.

Since we are not doing social work or psychological counseling, we think that the development of dependence should be strictly limited. Second, we have learned that staff members tend to form strong likes and dislikes for various parents. If only one staff member visits a particular home, it is likely that a distorted picture of the family situation will be presented. When three staff members rotate their contacts with the families, the result is a much more balanced and accurate picture. Third, some staff members are inevitably stronger than others. We believe it is best to distribute such strengths and weaknesses evenly over families. Fourth, having three part-time parent educators gives the project some protection against inevitable staff turnover. For all of these reasons, we recommend rotating a staff of three part-time parent educators in this kind of work.

The Physical Facility

Since the majority of the work of projects like NPAT is done in the home, the requirements for a physical facility are modest. We have used classrooms in elementary schools, renovated apartments, small educational buildings, and so forth. The center is the location for administrative work—making appointments, keeping records, and the like. The center is also used for educational displays featuring toys, magazines, and books. Finally, the center is used for group meetings and, since audiovisuals are relied upon heavily, is the site for viewing films and videotapes.

Costs

As in most programs of this sort, approximately 85 percent of the costs are for personnel. Although salaries have traditionally been very low in the field of early childhood education, because of our total conviction that this work is the most important educational work anyone can do at any level, we believe that the staff should be well compensated. That translates to the notion that parent educators should be paid on the same scale as elementary school teachers—including fringe benefits as well as salary. The director/parent educator should receive compensation equivalent to that of an assistant principal of an elementary school. If the project grows and the director's responsibilities become greater, the work should be considered equivalent to that of an elementary school principal. Naturally, the unit cost of the program will vary with prevailing wages in the communities involved. Given current salaries across the United States, the least expensive programs might cost as little as $700 or $800 per family per year, and the most expensive might go as high as $1,100 or $1,200 per family per year. On the surface, this may seem like a lot of money for this kind of program, but when one considers both the importance of the program and the level of funding of elementary and secondary education programs across the country it is obvious that such a program is remarkably inexpensive. The principal reason for the low cost is that the bulk of the work of educating the children in this program is done by parents and grandparents.

Results

The NPAT pilot programs have been remarkably successful. To our knowledge, they constitute the strongest evidence supporting the value of guiding the early learning process that has ever been developed anywhere—stronger than the Head Start evidence, stronger than the BEEP evidence. Furthermore, the evaluation of its impact was of very high quality. A principal reason for the high quality of the evaluation was that NPAT's evaluators could profit from the experiences of earlier workers in the field of early childhood education, especially in the period from 1965 to 1984. The second significant element in the strength of the evaluation was that NPAT did not evaluate itself. The reputations of other outstanding programs, such as David Weikart's Perry Preschool Project, would have been even stronger if their evaluation had been done by a first-rate independent organization. In general, this is an important principle in considering the significance of research results.

The NPAT evaluation was contracted out to Research and Training Associates of Overland Park, Kansas. The principal evaluators were Dr. Judith Pfannenstiel and Dianne Seltzer. They created an evaluation that featured a post-hoc control group. In the

more common matched pre- and posttest designs, the ideal evaluation design for some purposes would be as follows: A large representative sample of the target population would be identified. These
people would be told that some of them were going to be receiving
a program of services designed to help their children develop well,
while others would receive other kinds of services. Yet another
group would receive no services other than some form of interim
evaluation of their children's progress parallel to that of the other
groups. All these people, including hard-to-reach families, would
then have to agree to accept whatever assignment a random selection process would give them. Therefore, some parents would have
to accept being assigned to what appeared to be a very attractive,
helping program, while others would have to accept the notion that
they would receive no substantial help in raising their child. It is
obvious that this would lead to several kinds of practical problems
in a community.

This sort of ideal design works quite well when we are dealing
with laboratory animals, such as mice. But in educational field research, it often cannot be done. In Missouri (and probably anywhere else) it would not have been feasible. Instead, the post-hoc
control design was used, wherein control (nonproject) families
matched to project families were selected as the project family children approached their third birthdays. The developmental status of
the three-year-olds in the control group was then compared to a
matched subsample of project families. There are numerous complications to this design, and for information as to how the evaluators dealt with them, I refer you to the full evaluation report.[1] At
this point, I can only indicate that the evaluation design was very
sophisticated and did indeed meet most of the requirements to be
considered an absolutely first-rate piece of work.

The principal target of evaluation was quite simple: Did the
three-year-old children whose families were involved in NPAT actually develop into better educated three-year-olds than they would
have if their families had not been enrolled in NPAT? We also gathered data on whether the parents valued the program, whether the
communities accepted the program, whether the parents knew more
about child development, and other relevant issues. The bottom

line, however, remained simple and singular: Were the children better educated as a result of the project?

Table 26–2 presents the principal data comparing the scores of a representative sample of 75 of the project's original 320 children with those of 75 matched comparison children. The superiority of the project children was substantial and dramatic in nearly all linguistic, intellectual, and school-related areas. Also, these benefits were present regardless of socioeconomic level of the family. In assessing intellectual performance, after an extensive search, the evaluators selected the Kaufman ABC Scales. For the assessment of language abilities, the Zimmerman Test was selected. Both tests are of recent origin and are widely perceived to be among the most up-to-date and outstanding procedures for these purposes. Unfortunately, no comparable test was available for measuring interpersonal skills, and, frankly, the evaluation is weak in that regard. Ratings were gathered by independent psychological testers of the social development of all children. As shown in table 26–3, the ratings clearly favor the project children; realistically, however, we cannot make nearly so firm a claim for benefits in the interpersonal area as we can in the intellectual and linguistic areas.

The intellectual and linguistic areas are very important, of course, especially with respect to later academic work. The link between outstanding intellectual and linguistic abilities at three and comparably outstanding levels of ability at school entrance age of five and a half or six years has been thoroughly established. The NPAT results indicate that on their third birthdays, the project children were remarkably better off as a result of the project experience than they otherwise would have been.

As for secondary results, the parents loved the program; 99 percent of the responding parents reported a high degree of satisfaction with all project services (group meetings, private home visits, screenings). Home visits were identified as the most valuable service. Furthermore, 97 percent of the parents felt that project services made a difference in the way they perceived their parenting role.

During the first years of their lives, project children had received much more attention to the possibility of early, educationally relevant difficulties, especially in the area of mild to moderate hearing

Table 26–2

Average Scale and Subtest Results for NPAT Sample and Comparison Group

Scale	Overall Mean	Standard Deviation	NPAT Sample	Comparison Group	Difference	Significance[a]
Kaufman Assessment Battery Scales						
Sequential Processing (standard score)[b]	104.6	10.6	105.3	103.7	1.6	ns
Simultaneous Processing (standard score)	106.0	14.8	109.8	101.6	8.2	.001
Mental Processing Composite (standard score)	106.1	12.5	109.1	102.4	6.7	.003
Achievement (standard score)	109.6	13.6	114.7	103.8	10.9	<.001
Sequential Processing (age-equivalent)	3.5	0.6	3.5	3.4	0.1	ns
Simultaneous Processing (age-equivalent)	3.4	0.6	3.5	3.2	0.3	.003
Mental Processing (age-equivalent)	3.4	0.5	3.5	3.2	0.3	.001
Achievement (age-equivalent)	3.5	0.6	3.7	3.3	0.4	<.001
Zimmerman Preschool Language Scales						
Auditory Comprehension	24.2	4.8	25.7	22.6	3.1	<.001
Verbal Ability	22.0	5.1	23.4	20.3	3.1	<.001
Language Ability	46.2	9.1	49.1	42.9	6.2	<.001
Auditory Comprehension Age	4.0	7.2	4.2	3.8	0.4	<.001
Verbal Ability Age	3.7	7.6	3.9	3.5	0.4	<.001
Language Age	3.9	6.9	4.1	3.7	0.4	<.001

ns = nonsignificant differences

[a]Probability levels for statistical significance are commonly accepted at the .05 level. Most findings for this study were found to be significant at the <.001 level. This means that there is a less than one in one-thousand probability that the differences between NPAT and comparison groups were due to chance.

[b]The KABC has been scaled to yield a mean of 100 and a standard deviation of 15.

Table 26–3

Psychometrists' Observations of Social Development by NPAT
Sample and Comparison Group
(percentage distributions)

	Never or Almost Never	Infrequently	Occasionally	Frequently (at Almost Every Opportunity)	Probability
ADULT INTERACTION					

. Uses Adult as an Emotional or Instrumental Resource (after first determining s/he can't do it himself/herself)

A1. Seeks explanation or information by asking for further clarification on test tasks

	Never or Almost Never	Infrequently	Occasionally	Frequently (at Almost Every Opportunity)	Probability
NPAT	37	29	29	5	ns
Comparison	46	30	19	3	

A2. Asks examiner to actually do the task for him/her

NPAT	51	25	22	1	ns
Comparison	66	14	11	6	

A3. Asks for positive feedback on performance

NPAT	22	30	36	12	ns
Comparison	19	33	37	9	

A4. Shows reluctance to ask examiner for help when needed

NPAT	30	36	14	20	ns
Comparison	26	34	13	24	

A5. Seeks comfort or reassurance after unsuccessful performance on test task (either verbal or nonverbal)

NPAT	24	42	25	9	ns
Comparison	24	37	21	13	

A6. Responds to examiner's praise or encouragement (either verbal or nonverbal)

NPAT	0	5	38	57	.01
Comparison	9	6	43	41	

. Capability for Expressing Emotion to Adults
B1. Establishes eye contact

NPAT	0	0	18	82	.03
Comparison	3	1	26	69	

B2. Smiles or laughs

NPAT	1	4	17	78	.01
Comparison	9	7	23	60	

Table 26–3 continued

	Never or Almost Never	Infrequently	Occasionally	Frequently (at Almost Every Opportunity)	Probabili*
B3. Makes friendly statements					
NPAT	4	11	32	54	.04
Comparison	13	13	31	41	
B4. Physical expression of affection towards examiner—touching, patting, hugging, etc.					
NPAT	28	34	18	20	.05
Comparison	37	34	20	7	
B5. Shares or makes friendly gestures (such as taking examiner's hand)					
NPAT	25	33	26	14	ns
Comparison	33	33	26	7	
B6. Makes statement of personal dislike (e.g., "I don't want to do that")					
NPAT	51	16	22	9	ns
Comparison	57	13	10	19	
B7. Demonstrates unprovoked out-of-control physical behavior (hits, grabs, throws objects, tantrums, etc.)					
NPAT	84	8	7	0	ns
Comparison	87	3	4	4	
B8. Rejects physical affection from examiner					
NPAT	75	16	7	1	.05
Comparison	66	16	7	10	

2. COPING SKILLS

A1. Separates easily from parent(s)					
NPAT	7	17	24	51	ns
Comparison	19	9	30	41	
A2. Appears easily frustrated by errors or inability to perform tasks					
NPAT	37	32	25	5	ns
Comparison	30	40	19	9	
A3. Participates readily in new testing situations					
NPAT	5	13	32	49	ns
Comparison	13	16	27	43	
A4. Follows directions easily					
NPAT	1	12	36	50	.04
Comparison	7	16	39	37	

ble 26–3 continued

	Never or Almost Never	Infrequently	Occasionally	Frequently (at Almost Every Opportunity)	Probability
EXPRESSES PRIDE IN CREATIONS, POSSESSIONS, OR ACTIONS					
A1. Smiles at his/her accomplishments					
NPAT	1	5	22	70	.01
Comparison	11	3	30	53	
A2. Asks examiner to "see" what s/he did					
NPAT	29	32	16	22	ns
Comparison	39	30	16	13	
A3. Points to or shows examiner the results of his/her work					
NPAT	22	34	18	24	ns
Comparison	29	34	17	17	

= nonsignificant differences

loss, than comparison children. They were therefore more often referred to specialists for diagnostic and corrective procedures than were members of the comparison groups.

All in all, the results were wonderful and, quite frankly, exceeded our expectations.

The Significance of NPAT

Even before the NPAT evaluation results were published, the Missouri legislature passed an extraordinary law. In June 1984, they made it mandatory for all 546 school districts in the state to offer programs like NPAT to all people living in the community with children under three years of age. This law, which I am confident will exist in every public educational system sometime in the future, is at the moment the first of its kind in the world, to my knowledge. Unfortunately, however, this exciting news turned out to be less than meets the eye. Having passed the law, the state of Missouri then proceeded to fail to implement it in an effective way. The state insisted on implementation of the law quickly everywhere, even though opportunities for good quality training of personnel did not exist in adequate supply and the monies allocated at both the state and local levels were nowhere near the $800 to $1,000 per family per year needed in Missouri to properly fund the programs.

The fact remains, however, that the NPAT pilot projects were extraordinarily successful. The materials and procedures created by the personnel of the State Department of Education exist and are available for anyone who cares to pursue the topic. This situation has enormous potential for the future of education of children everywhere. Over many decades, school policy has always waited until a child was five and a half or six years of age before funds were directed toward the educational process. The first educational task has conventionally been the teaching of reading, and teaching reading to groups of young children probably would not be feasible if they were much younger than six or seven years of age. Traditionally, considerably more money has been spent as children reached high school age as compared to the early grades. Yet the results of attempts at helping children from poor families prepare for school, personified in the Head Start programs begun in 1965, make it very clear that a child who is nine months or more behind national averages in the areas of language and intelligence at age three is very likely not to do terribly well in school subsequently. The good news is that a child who is well ahead of the typical three-year age levels in these two critical areas is very likely to do quite well in just about any later educational situation. These realities point to not only the likelihood but the inevitability of programs like NPAT everywhere sooner or later.

Note

1. The full evaluation report is available from the Missouri State Department of Education, attention: NPAT, P.O. Box 480, Jefferson City, MO 65102.

Appendix 26A:
Distinguishing Qualities of the
Outstanding Three- to
Six-Year-Old Child

Note: The examples used here were taken directly from the protocols recorded by the observers in the schools. Consequently, they are often brief descriptive phrases rather than complete sentences. The following abbreviations are used throughout the appendix: A = adult; S = subject; M = mother; T = teacher; AT = assistant teacher; PF (or FP) = female peer; PM (or MP) = male peer; O = observer.

Social Abilities: Labels, Definitions, and Examples

To Get and Maintain the Attention of Adults in Socially Acceptable Ways

Definition: The ability to get the attention of an adult through the use of various strategies (e.g., moves toward and stands/sits near A; touches A; calls to A; shows something to A; tells something to A).

Examples:

(Five-year-old boy) S stands up and walks out of the closet, walking only on his heels. S yells, "Hey, Miss T!" (T doesn't answer.) S talks to PM. He shouts "Hey!", but no one pays attention. S walks over to T and says, "Hey, Miss T, look," and holds out his hand, which is holding the piece of ice. (T says something.) S says, " 'cause it's hot in here," and laughs.

(Five-year-old boy) S looks at PM, listens to T, and utters something under his breath. He looks at his long line of letters—rocks his chair. Standing, smiling, calls out, "What's this, T? What's this?"

while looking toward front of room and T. S repeats, "T, what's that?" indicating his picture and rocking on his chair. T guesses, "A lamp post?"

(Five-year-old girl) (T is sitting on a chair and most of the children are sitting around her discussing the things they did on their vacation.) S stands up on her knees. She calls out, trying to get T's attention. S talks to PM next to her (he shows her pencils in a pencil case that he has). S sits and looks at the pencils. S holds the pencil case and gives it back to PM. They talk. S pushes her hair back with both hands. She bites her nails, stands on her knees, and raises her hand trying to get T's attention. (T calls on S.) S says, "Guess what! Natalie is such a pig, she ate everybody's Easter eggs, she's a pig." (T comments that Natalie is a pig.) S repeats again, "She's a pig."

To Use Adults as Resources

Definition: The ability to make use of an adult in order to obtain something by means of a verbal request or demand or a physical demonstration of his need. His object may be to gain information, assistance, or food, and he may demonstrate this by declaring what he wants, making a request, making a demand, or by gesturing, acting out, or pointing.

Examples:

(Four-year-old boy) S sees a new crayon box. He gasps as if excited, takes the new crayon box, and then takes a piece of paper (written or scribbled on back). He looks up at AT and tries very hard to open the box. He places his tongue out and tries harder to open it but can't. (AT passes and taps him affectionately on the head.) After she passes, he touches his head a few times. He then watches T put up pictures along the wall, looks at O, smiles at O (O smiles back), looks again at O, and smiles at O. He then tries to open the crayon box again. It still will not open. For the next minute he tries again and again. Finally, he says loudly, "I can't open it." He looks at T, but she does not hear and just walks into the porch room to dry some pictures. (It is raining outside.) He says to T, "This screen is wet." T walks back into room and passes S. He

looks up at T and puts his face on her apron. (She just walks away.) He then watches the boy opposite him crayon. (AT comes near.) He says to her, "I can't open this." (AT opens it for him.) He smiles.

(Five-year-old boy) S glances at T and asks, "Teacher, how do you make a letter that goes like girl and helicopter? I forgot the letter that goes with helicopter and little girl." He looks at T while he grasps his pencil and moves it about. He continues to move the pencil about and slides around his chair. Then he calls again, "Miss T, how do you make a little girl and a helicopter?" (T walks over to his table and points to the girl. She asks, "What's this?") S responds, "A little girl." (T asks, "What sound does it have?") S responds with the correct sound of *g*. (T then asks the same questions about *helicopter*.) S answers all these questions correctly. (T then asks, "What's the problem?") S responds, "I don't know how to write it." S stands, his pencil drops, he bends down to pick it up. (T turns his paper over and prints *H*. She then turns it back to its original position and indicates that he should try to print one.) He looks at a girl, looks at the other side of the paper, then at the teacher, and succeeds in printing an *H*. (T then points to the picture of the girl and asks, "How do you make this letter?")

To Express Both Affection and Hostility to Adults

Definition: The ability to express affection and/or hostility through verbal and/or physical means (e.g., friendly statements, such as "I like you," "You're nice," or hugging A; statements of dislike, such as "I hate you," "You're bad," hitting A, or physically resisting A).

Examples:

(Three-year-old boy) T pulls S and says, "Do some work." S hangs down limp while T pulls him. He does not stand or move his legs. S says, "No, I don't want to." T continues to pull him up and yells, "Stand on your feet!" S just hangs and slides back and forth. (T drags him to work room and to a table where another T is. The other T says that she should give him the cylinders, since they are new—he may be interested in them.) T drags him to the shelf to get the set of cylinders. T takes set and S follows T to the table.

(Four-year-old boy) In library time, children at different times kept on saying, "I would like this book. I would like *Swimny*. I would like *Red Riding Hood*," etc., etc. AT kept on saying, "Yes, here it is, what would you like?" S then said in a loud, angry voice, "Would you like to be quiet, then I'll read the *Fire Engine Book*."

(Four-year-old girl) T sits down at table where S is working. S looks up at T and smiles warmly.

To Lead and Follow Peers

Definition: The ability to assume control in peer-related activities (e.g., to give suggestions, to orient and direct, to set oneself up as a model for imitation); the ability to follow the lead of others (e.g., to follow suggestions).

Examples:

(Three-and-a-half-year-old boy) S comes into view with several other children. They all appear to be excited about something. He is hopping and jumping as he enters the playroom, goes over to the AT talking excitedly, and says something about the window being stuck. He talks some more and then says something about "we saw fire trucks." PM1, who is sitting next to the AT, says, "What did they come for?" S says, "To put out the fire." S turns to walk out of the room, then turns back and comes back and says to PM2, "Come on, let's go." S starts to walk away. He turns back and says again, with more irritation in his voice this time, "Come on. Let's go." PM2 and the other children follow him out into the hallway, out of sight.

(Four-year-old boy) PM walks over to S. S makes a funny face at him. PM copies S. Imitation game with S as leader. S, always first, hits his face, then head, etc., while the other boy follows.

(Four-year-old boy) S is drawing a picture. He says, "I'm making a clown." PF looks up and says, "Make his hat red." S picks up the red crayon and draws a red hat.

To Express Both Affection and Hostility to Peers

Definition: The ability to express affection and/or hostility to peers through verbal or physical means.

Examples:

(Five-year-old girl) S walks around the playground with her arm around PF, who in turn has an arm around S. In this manner they walk together to far side of yard where the swings are.

(Four-and-a-half-year-old boy) S notices peer taking S's letter from the floor area. S yells, "Hey, put that back, put it back—supposed to be over there." (The child is still picking up the letters.) S walks over to him and says sternly, "Put that back."

To Compete with Peers

Definition: The ability to exhibit interpersonal competition.

Examples:

(Four-and-a-half-year-old girl) Attaching sequins to styrofoam balls for Christmas decorations. Says to PF, "I'm the first one done."

(Three-year-old boy) Children are punching holes in paper. S asks PM if he can have some red pieces of punched-out paper. PM says, "OK." S picks up some red and blue pieces of paper out of PM's bowl. S then drops the pieces on the table, picks up a larger piece of red paper, and asks PM if he can punch holes in that piece. (PM says, "Yeah.") S says, "I'll punch more holes than you ever dreamed up."

To Praise Oneself and/or Show Pride in One's Accomplishments

Definition: The ability to express pride in something he has created, owns or possesses at the moment, or something he is in the process of doing or has done.

Examples:

(Four-and-a-half-year-old girl) Children are making Christmas decorations by pinning sequin beads onto styrofoam balls. S says (to PF), "I need them too. How do you stick these on?" (PF replies, "I'll show you how I put the other color in.") S says, "I know how." (At this point S refuses to follow the advice of PF and concentrates on accomplishing her task.) After having successfully attached some sequins to the ball, she looks up and says to PF, "Look what I did!"

(Four-year-old boy) Upon T's instructions, S traces over the G, turns the page over, and writes. He looks up and loudly states, "I did my best." (T says, "That's a better improvement.")

To Involve Oneself in Adult Role-Playing Behaviors or to Otherwise Express the Desire to Grow Up

Definition: To act out a typical adult activity or verbally express a desire to grow up.

Example:

(Four-year-old girl) S sits down on the floor with the phone beside her. She pushes her hair in back of her right ear, takes the receiver with her right hand and puts the receiver on top of her hair—which has now fallen over the right ear. She kicks her foot on the chair to the left of her and then whispers into the receiver. She says "Yes" and laughs and twists cord around her fingers. S sits on her knees and continues to do this. (Observer comments that S is play-acting as if a teenage girl.)

Nonsocial Abilities: Labels, Definitions, and Examples

Linguistic Competence (i.e., grammatical capacity, vocabulary, articulation, and extensive use of expressed language)

Definition: Self-explanatory.

[No examples]

Intellectual Competence

1. The ability to sense dissonance or note discrepancies

Definition: This is a critical faculty on the part of the child, an ability to indicate one's awareness of discrepancies, inconsistencies and other forms of irregularity in the environment. It is almost always expressed verbally, but occasionally takes nonverbal forms as well. It is observable whenever a child comments upon some noticed irregularity. The effect that generally accompanies it usually involves mild confusion, a look of discovery, or a display of righteousness in pointing out and correcting the irregularity.

Examples:

(Three-year-old girl) S is sitting at a table working with play dough and glancing up periodically from one peer at the table to another. S turns to an FP beside her and asks, "Is your name Margot? Do you have a haircut?" (The FP has had her hair cut from shoulder-to ear-length.)

(Three-year-old boy) S is coloring at a table with several peers. An MP holds up his picture, announcing that it is the moon. S looks at the picture and remarks, "A moon doesn't have hair," noting that the moon in the drawing seems to have hair.

2. The ability to anticipate consequences

Definition: This is the ability to anticipate a probable effect on, or sequence to, whatever is currently occupying the attention of the child. It is usually expressed verbally, but also takes nonverbal forms. It can take place in a social context or in relative isolation. It is not simply an awareness of a future event—e.g., "Tomorrow is Thursday"—but must somehow relate that event to a present condition. The relationship may be either casual—e.g., "If X, then Y"—or sequential—e.g., "Now 1, next 2." The second half of each relationship *must* be an anticipated future outcome. It cannot actually occur until after the child anticipates the occurrence.

Examples:

(Three-year-old girl) S has been waiting for her turn at the juice table and checks on it periodically. MP is sitting there now. S comes and observes MP for a few seconds, then says, "He's finishing his cracker and after him I'm going to eat, okay?"

(Three-year-old girl) S has just finished washing her hands of paint and is drying them in a room with T and several peers. FP asks what time it is, and S then asks, "Is it time to go home now?" T answers that it is only 10:20 and not time to go home. S then says, "Just one more hour then it's time to go home, right?" About five minutes later, S refuses a task with the rationale that that particular task will take too long to do by the time she finishes the task with which she is presently occupied. S says, "I'll match them next time, okay?"

3. The ability to deal with abstractions (i.e., numbers, letters, and rules)

Definition: To use abstract concepts and symbols in ways that require building upon what is concretely present and showing mental organization of what is perceived. The term *concept* means "a mental state or process that refers to more than one object or experience"; the term *symbol* means "an object, expression or responsive activity that replaces and becomes a representative substitute for another."

Examples:

(Five-year-old boy) In a spelling game with Scrabble tiles, S asks, "Does she get two turns?" "I have 5 tiles—supposed to have 7." Asks T what his letters spell and repeats this (a nonsense word). S asks, "Does anybody have an A?" Attentive to others' moves as well as his own.

(Four-year-old boy) Class is doing a number exercise with collections of fingerprints on the board. Tasks are selecting the set that corresponds to a number, subtracting and adding ("How many more?" "How many too many?"), and making correct number of prints. S answers the counting questions, says, "I know where six

is"; sometimes answers with others but seems to answer more questions than the rest of the class.

4. The ability to take the perspective of another

Definition: To show an understanding of how things look to another person whose position in space is different from the subject's, or to show an understanding of a person's emotional state or mental attitude when they are different from the subject's (the opposite of egocentricity).

Examples:

(Five-year-old boy) In a word game, another child is having difficulty deciding where to place a letter. S watches her and smiles reassuringly, in a way that convinces the observer that he understands the girl's problem.

(Five-year-old boy) S is given the job of passing out cookies. He checks carefully to see that all are served, watches their selections, and assures a child, who is worried, that he will get a cookie.

5. The ability to make interesting associations

Definition: When presented with visible scenes, objects, or verbal descriptions, a person with this ability shows a capacity to produce related kinds of objects or themes from either his own realm of past experience or some imagined experience. These productions are characterized by the ingenuity of the relationships or the elaborateness of the representation. Another form is the ability to build upon these events by assigning new and interesting labels or building coherent stories around the presented elements.

Examples:

(Four-year-old boy) "Miss T, this is the simplest work, simple as a bee can fly."

(Four-year-old boy) T suggests building pictures with letter squares and makes a circle. S immediately builds a "Prudential Building" and asks T, "What's that?" She asks for a clue. "It stays in the same

place." She gives up and he tells her, "A Prudential Building." Peer: "What are you building now?" S: "Same thing, not a Prudential Building, a giant building." P: "Empire State?" S: "It's pretty big anyway. There's something wrong with this building. Supposed to stand up, not supposed to fall down . . . I gonna make the biggest American building in the whole wide world . . . outta these blocks."

Executive Abilities

The Ability to Plan and Carry Out Multistep Activities

Definition: This designation applies to largely self-directed activities, rather than activities in which the child is guided. At earlier ages, it would develop through gradual refinement of the use of means–ends relationships and the ability to plan and execute longer sequences.

Examples:

(Five-year-old girl) S fills a jug with water in another room, carries it back to main room, and carefully waters all the plants.

(Four-year-old girl) S sets up various materials in order to play store, getting others to participate and playing role of storekeeper.

The Ability to Use Resources Effectively

Definition: The ability to select and organize materials and/or people to solve problems. An additional feature is the recognition of unusual uses of such resources.

Examples:

(Four-year-old girl) Some drinking glasses and a box of crackers have been brought into the classroom in a paper shopping bag. S and PM use them to set up a store game—moving a table, arranging the glasses on a shelf, deciding on prices, and imitating storekeepers.

(Four-and-a-half-year-old girl) S is having trouble blowing up a balloon. She tries and fails, then takes her problem to another girl. S takes over her friend's job, setting out napkins for snack time, while her friend blows up the balloon.

Attentional Ability—Dual Focus

Definition: The ability to attend to two things simultaneously or in rapid alternation (i.e., the ability to concentrate on a proximal task and remain aware of peripheral happenings; the ability to talk while doing).

Examples:

(Three-year-old girl) S is sitting at a table pasting. S glances frequently at MP across table and 2 MPs standing by the door. S is obviously listening to their conversation while she works, and occasionally makes a brief comment to one of them.

(Three-year-old boy) S is cutting paper into a bowl with scissors. S talks incessantly to both MP and FP while continuing to cut.

Appendix 26B:
Sample NPAT Curriculum
Materials

The following pages are representative of the high-quality curriculum materials prepared for and used in the Missouri New Parents as Teachers project. Complete curriculum materials may be obtained upon request from NPAT, Missouri State Department of Education, P.O. Box 480, Jefferson City, MO 65102.

Phase I

birth–6 weeks

During these early weeks the infant is adjusting to life in the outside world. Baby will spend most of his time sleeping.

What is special about my baby during Phase I?

- Baby's periods of wakefulness will increase from 2–3 minutes an hour to an average of 6–7 minutes an hour.

- This phase is an adjustment to life rather than growth.

- The newborn infant totally depends upon others.

What is my baby like during this phase?

Your baby shows sleepiness and irritability. When not asleep, the newborn is easily irritated but an infant can change from great distress to comfort very quickly. Quick changes in mood continue for several months.

Your baby likes to be comfortable. Anything that disturbs baby's sleep causes him to be irritable.

Your baby likes being handled and moved gently through space. One way to comfort a distressed baby is to pick him up, hold him close and walk with him. This experience is so soothing to a Phase I baby that it will usually relieve all kinds of discomfort, at least temporarily.

Your baby enjoys sucking on his fists. During the first six weeks, the baby's ability to get his fist to his mouth and suck increases. Sucking on a pacifier or his hand is very common and is a satisfying activity.

Your baby's behavior is fragmented. The newborn's behavior consists of a small number of clumsy, unfinished and isolated reflexes. These behaviors—rooting, sucking, grasping and occasional glances at nearby objects—are the foundations of later intelligence. The first signs of coordination begin as the baby brings a fist to his mouth and sucks on it.

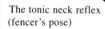

The tonic neck reflex (fencer's pose)

Your baby lacks mobility. When on his back the Phase I infant cannot ordinarily move his body. Occasionally, if angry, the baby may manage to propel his body the length of the crib by digging his heels into the mattress and kicking out with his legs. A bumper pad around the inside of the crib is a good idea.

Beginning at about one month and continuing for six to eight weeks, the common position of the baby, when on his back, is the tonic neck reflex or "fencer's pose." Both hands are fisted and the head is usually turned to the right. When on his stomach, the baby is only able to lift his head enough to clear the surface of the mattress for a moment or two. It is important to support the head when lifting or holding the baby.

Your baby is hypersensitive. The baby is unusually sensitive to any abrupt changes in light, sound or handling. A Phase I baby is especially sensitive to bright lights and is much more likely to open his eyes in a dimly-lit room.

Your baby begins social smiling. Toward the end of Phase I the infant will begin to look at a parent's face with increasing interest. The area between the eyes and hairline attracts the baby most. This interest is the first step towards true social smiling.

Your baby begins the visual discovery of the hands. At the end of Phase I the baby continues to lie in the tonic neck reflex position when on his back. The hand on the side to which baby's head is turned begins to attract a brief glance. With each passing day baby will notice his hand more often and for a longer time.

What will my baby learn during this phase?

During the first weeks of life the baby becomes more skillful in the behaviors that were present at birth such as finding and sucking the nipple, bringing his fist to his mouth, and tracking objects.

Learning to learn: There is little reason to think that a Phase I baby is able to think in the ordinary sense of the term. However, his simple actions like grasping and glancing at objects are the beginnings of intelligence.

Language development: Although hearing is not fully developed, the Phase I baby can discriminate a range of sounds. The baby will make simple sounds when awake and not crying.

Physical development: Head control will continually improve throughout Phase I. At birth baby can track (follow an object with his eyes) in a limited way. By the end of Phase I the baby will be able to track with great skill. He will be able to get his fist to his mouth with increasing ease.

Social development: Phase I babies are not sociable in the ordinary sense of the term. The first sign of sociability is the interest in looking at the eyes of the person holding him. The second indication is the first modest "smile" while looking at a person's eyes. All human babies smile at human faces or drawings of them.

Emotional development: When baby is awake his mood shifts quickly. He may be quiet, groggy, sober and his body still; or he may be bright eyed with little expression on his face and quiet; or he may be alert but active (kicking legs, moving arms, etc.) and happy; or he may be alert, active and upset. The pleasure gained from rocking and sucking seems to comfort babies.

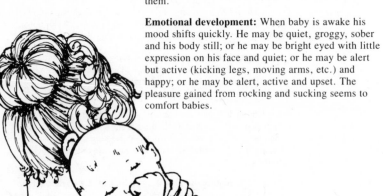

What can I do to encourage my baby's development?

Give the infant a feeling of being loved and cared for. It is important to handle the baby often and respond quickly to his cries as much as you can. A rocking chair and a pacifier are two especially useful items to use during Phase I.

Encourage interest in baby's surroundings. Toward the end of the first month babies begin to show more interest in their world. The infant will enjoy looking at a suitably-designed mobile and changes of location during the day.

Help baby with head control. Placing baby on his stomach occasionally will provide your baby with the opportunity to lift his head clear of the surface on which he is lying.

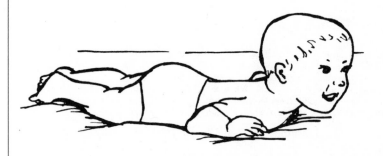

How will I know that my baby is nearing Phase II?

Signs that your baby is nearing Phase II are:

- most babies begin to smile regularly during the third month. However, you may see smiling as early as 6 or 7 weeks.

- the infant will begin to notice his hands briefly as they pass his line of vision. Gradually, he will look for longer periods and study his hands more intensely.

- most babies will increase the amount of time spent awake and alert from five minutes an hour at 1 month to 15–20 minutes an hour at 2 months.

Mobile or Stabile

A mobile or stabile can attract the attention of your baby when he is 3 to 9 weeks of age; it is important to have a mobile that baby is interested in and can see.

Baby's interest: According to Dr. Burton L. White, one universally inherited human behavior of infants is the tendency to be interested in and smile at another human face (or something that looks like a face) when it is within 6 to 12 inches of the baby's eyes. This face can be either the person who feeds the baby or a suitably designed mobile or stabile.

What babies can see: Commercial mobiles are colorful and attractive but not always of interest to, or useful for, babies. Commercial mobiles are primarily designed for adults to see when they are in the baby's room. When baby lies underneath most commercial mobiles and looks up, he merely sees several "knife-blade" edges of objects and not the objects themselves.

HOW TO MAKE A MOBILE OR STABILE

Pattern: Babies are interested in the forehead and upper portion of the human face; babies will smile at a pattern of that part of a face. (See attached pattern.) Cut out the circle and hang it by string taped to the back of the pattern.

Placement: *Hang the mobile where the baby tends to look when lying on his back.* Since a baby this age tends to look at the far right or left, hang the mobile off to one side of the crib, not over the middle. *Hang it at a distance the baby prefers.* Since a baby tends to avoid looking at objects closer than 8 inches and farther than 18 inches, a distance of 10 inches from the baby's eyes is recommended. The face pattern may be strung from a commercial mobile hanger or the side rail of the crib. If necessary, tape the mobile to a side rail to keep it steady.

Remove the mobile around 9 weeks of age or definitely before the baby is able to reach and grab it with his hands or feet.

6″

Phase V

**8 months–
14 months**

Your Phase V baby is curious to learn about and explore his surroundings. From now on you can encourage or discourage his learning.

What is special about my baby during Phase V?

- During Phase V your baby starts an important time of learning. From this point his experiences with people and his environment will have much greater influence on his development. Your attention to learning opportunities at this time is important.

- Your baby continues his fascination with small objects and the effects his actions have on them.

- Phase V is often the beginning of a stressful and challenging period in the life of the family. Babies this age are curious, mobile, active and capable but definitely not concerned with safety or neat houses.

What is my baby like during this phase?

Your baby is curious and learns about the people, places and things around him. He likes to spend time exploring everywhere he can go and everything he can find. If he has a chance, he will enjoy investigating every room in the house. Around the middle of this phase he may begin to have favorite activities and favorite places for doing them.

He continues his fascination with small objects and the effects his actions have on them. He spends time looking, touching, holding and gumming everything—toys, household items and things he should not have. Dirt, lint, dust, crumbs, or other small particles he finds on the floor still captivate him as his ability to pick them up improves. He loves to watch the effects of his actions. He frequently bangs, strikes, drops, or throws objects just to study what happens. One of his favorite activities might be watching what happens to objects he pushes off his high-chair tray.

His curiosity sometimes causes accidents or problems. Even though he is able to get hold of many things, he is completely unaware that some things are dangerous. If he gets hurt by something he finds, he often will not remember or be able to control himself so that he does not get hurt with the same thing again. He is completely unconcerned about any mess he makes during his investigations. Often while you are busy cleaning up one mess, he will be somewhere else making another.

Your baby enjoys practicing and mastering his large muscle skills. During this phase he may start to pull himself up and stand. He may begin to move about while holding onto stable objects such as chairs or low tables. This is known as cruising. It changes to walking without help, and later, running. Some Phase V children begin to straddle four-wheeled toys and drag them about.

Climbing stairs, furniture, or other objects one to two feet high is usually possible for the Phase V baby and is not related to whether he can walk. At this age he is not aware of danger and is not afraid when climbing to any height. He is capable of climbing to high places if he can climb to one or two feet. For example, he may climb onto a chair and then onto a table without hesitation. If he can climb from a chair to a countertop, he may climb from that countertop to the refrigerator. With this new ability he can explore many more areas of your house. If you do not supervise him closely, he definitely runs a greater risk of getting hurt.

During this phase your baby also begins to feel proud of his achievements. He enjoys other people noticing his accomplishments.

Your baby develops a strong liking for you. Generally he is friendly and excited about being with you. He might be spontaneously affectionate with you. Sometime after the middle of this phase, he begins to make simple requests for help. Instead of crying or whining, he uses gestures, vocalizations or simple words. At first these requests are quite often for things such as food or milk. As he gets older he will request help from you when he is having trouble.

Throughout this phase your baby continues to study you and your actions. He is curious to find out what you are like and exactly how you handle various situations. He learns if you are a person of action or words. He learns whether to expect consequences from the warnings or limits that you set for his behavior.

From his experiences with you and from watching your dealings with other people, he begins to learn how people act with each other. These experiences influence the way he behaves with you and other people later.

Even though he is interested in watching other people, he still may become upset if a person he considers a "stranger" gets too close to him. If left with a babysitter, he may be uneasy at first but will usually quiet down a few minutes after you have gone. During a later phase his "stranger anxiety" will probably disappear.

Your baby is a quiet looker. He loves to spend time silently studying people and his surroundings. Many times you will notice your baby quietly staring or looking at people or things with fascination.

Your baby begins to understand and respond to a few simple words. If not concentrating on something else, he usually will turn toward you when you say his name. When you say familiar names of other family members or a pet, he will usually look at or for them. During this phase he will follow simple instructions such as "play pat-a-cake" or "wave bye-bye." He can follow simple requests for doing things with familiar objects such as picking up a ball. During the later part of this phase he may make certain vocalizations for particular things or say a few simple words such as "Mama" or "Dada." He will not talk but will definitely begin jabbering.

What will my baby learn during this phase?

Learning to learn: Your baby's learning can definitely be encouraged or discouraged by you during this phase. He needs opportunities to explore his surroundings and experiences with you and other people. His "playing" with objects helps him find out about them and what he can do to them—how they can be used, put together or taken apart.

Language development: During this phase your baby begins to learn the meaning of a few simple words and instructions. Baby needs people to talk to him. He also needs a chance to respond to them. These experiences will prepare him for understanding words and actually talking during the next phase.

Physical development: During this phase your baby may progress from pulling up and standing, to moving about while holding onto large stable objects (cruising), to talking and running without assistance. Sometime during this phase baby may start to climb. Many babies climb before they cruise.

Social development: During this phase your baby learns more about you and any other person he is frequently around. He continues to study how to get and hold your attention. He learns when you are in a good mood or are unhappy with him, and how he needs to ask for help. Several social skills begin to develop now: how to use an adult as a helper, how to show pride in his achievements, and how to make believe or pretend.

Development of curiosity: During this phase your baby has a lot of natural curiosity about people and his environment. However, his curiosity and new physical abilities make life harder for you and dangerous for him. Your reaction to his energetic explorations and your protection of him for his safety can encourage or discourage his desire to learn in the future. If you allow and encourage his natural curiosity about people and his surroundings while protecting him from getting hurt, he will learn that it is alright and fun to be interested in his world.

What can I do to encourage my baby's development?

At the beginning of this phase a parent assumes three different roles, designer, consultant, and authority, in the development of his child. These jobs continue to be important to your child's growth during the next several years.

The parent as the DESIGNER of his child's experiences and world. During this phase it is important that your child's surroundings are interesting, accessible and safe. He needs to explore and become acquainted with many things and to readily and freely move about. However, you need to be constantly mindful of his safety. You may have "baby-proofed" your house, but it is still important to continually watch for harmful situations.

As the person in control of your baby's world and experiences, part of your job is encouraging his language development. Remember to talk to him about what is happening, explain what you are doing, and what he is doing or wanting at the moment. Read simple, colorful books containing stories and nursery rhymes. Imitate sounds he makes and encourage him to imitate your sounds. His experiences with words and sounds will influence his later language development.

The parent as a CONSULTANT providing advice and help to his child when needed. While it is important to help your child whenever he asks for and needs assistance, he should be encouraged and allowed to do things for himself whenever possible. When he accomplishes a task or learns a new skill, it is helpful for you to share heartily in his joy and excitement. When you have an opportunity to help him learn about people and his environment, it is good for you to talk to him about it at the moment. Simple sentences and words that are on his level will help him understand what you are saying.

The parent as a final AUTHORITY for his child. During this phase it becomes important for your child to know that even though you love him some of his behaviors are not acceptable. It is helpful to start setting clear and definite rules for what is alright and what is not. When his behavior goes beyond the limits you have set, you must now begin to discipline him. Two methods of reasonable and effective discipline for a Phase V child are: (1) distract him from his unacceptable behavior by helping him to get involved in something else, and (2) change his surroundings by either moving him somewhere else or by removing the object causing the problem. By serving as a final authority for your child in this way now, you help him prepare for later real life situations.

What toys can make life more interesting?

Your Phase V baby is interested in, and can do, a lot of different things. At all times though it will be necessary for you to keep his safety in mind. Household objects or toys should not be so small or have small removable parts that baby might swallow. During baby's bath time or other water play, never leave him alone even for a second.

Toys that your Phase V baby might enjoy include:
• balls of different sizes
• stacking or hinged toys
• a surprise busy box
• a busy bath or other water toys
• books with hard pages
Spending time in a walker may also be entertaining to baby.

How will I know that my baby is nearing Phase VI?

Signs that your baby is approaching Phase VI are:

• your child's behavior will show "negativism," a normal and difficult development for parents. He begins to resist directions and requests. The word "no" becomes fascinating. He challenges and tests the rules you have set for his behavior.

• your child begins to be aware that he is a separate and independent person in his own right. He starts to use his name to mean himself and may become possessive about his toys and belongings.

• when it comes to something he wants, he persists in letting you know and is not easily distracted. He sometimes becomes angry if he does not get what he wants immediately.

• your baby is able to make himself understood by you and a few other people. He uses gestures that definitely mean something to him and that you begin to understand. He starts to talk by using simple words or sounds. You are able to understand what he is trying to tell you.

Language Development—Phase V

(8–14 months)

The greatest indication of a child's language development before age two is not what he says but what he understands.

Babies begin to understand the meaning of a few words as early as six or seven months of age. This is called receptive language. In order to understand the meaning of words, they must first listen—listen to people talking to them and people talking to each other.

By 11 or 12 months of age, children usually understand five words and a few simple instructions. By 14–15 months of age, children may understand as many as 40 words. These words are usually ones with meanings which are emotionally important or pleasurably exciting to them.

When you respond with words and actions to your child's grunts, gestures, and jargon (making a particular sound for a certain object, activity or person), you will be encouraging your child's efforts to communicate with you.

By giving your child lots of loving talk, he will learn the meaning of words. He needs to hear the words over and over again in different sentences with different tones and with different facial expressions and body language.

There are several guidelines to keep in mind when talking to your child during this phase:

- Talk to your child when you are nearby and looking directly at him.
- Use a level of speech that you think is slightly beyond your child. Keep the sentences and words simple.
- Talk to your child about what he is paying attention to. Explain to him what he is seeing, hearing, tasting, smelling, or feeling. Talk about what you think is interesting to him. Example: "Do you want your milk now?"
- Use key labeling words when you talk to him. If you are looking for his shoes, say, "Where are your shoes?" instead of, "Where are they?"
- When you talk about yourself, others, or your baby, use names or labels—what you would like him to call you, himself and others.

• Overreact and dramatize when you talk to him. Use big gestures and exaggerated expressions. Children usually learn exclamations first because of the exaggerated expressions and infectious excitement shown by the person using them.
• Try to understand what your child means when he makes a sound. Your reaction and understanding will inspire him to try to continue to talk to you. For example, when he makes a sound and looks at something, you can name all the things you see that he might be talking about. When you hit the correct one, his excitement will be immense.
• Help him use words in useful situations. For example, if you are playing with a ball with him and it rolls away, say to him: "Get the ball—Where's the ball?"
• Don't correct him or pretend not to understand what he says when he uses his own words for something. "Own words" will develop into proper language in their own time, not at your command. They are the best he has to offer at the time. Refusing to hand him his bottle until he says "bottle" or "milk" instead of "nana" will only discourage him. He will become frustrated and cross; you are likely to get tears from him instead of words.

• The words that your child will understand between 8–12 months of age will depend largely on what words you use frequently with him and around him in your everyday talk. Here is a list of some words that are frequently understood between 8 and 12 months of age:

mommy	ball
daddy	cookie
bye-bye	juice
baby	bottle
his name	no-no
shoe	wave bye-bye
names of other family members or pets	

• Ask the child questions. Asking the child questions is another way of helping develop better language skills. You might ask: "Where's your blue truck?" You don't expect an answer in words, but your child may find the object.

Curiosity—Phase V

(8–14 months)

This period of life is dominated by pure curiosity. To have a strong exploratory drive is vitally important for humans. Nothing is more fundamental to solid educational development.

At this same time most babies have developed some means of moving their bodies through space—first by scooting and crawling, and at the end of the phase, by cruising, climbing and walking. These achievements provide them with many new opportunities. Whereas a 6-month-old child is content to sit and stare at the attractive Christmas tree across the room, at 10 months he will crawl rapidly across the room, pull himself up on a nearby piece of furniture or possibly the tree itself, feel the pretty (sharp) needles, shiny (breakable) ornaments and the glowing (hot) lights. If he feels an urge, he may even put them in his mouth to explore them more completely.

It is obvious that there is a dual nature of curiosity. On one hand it is the motivational force underlying all learning, development and achievement and on the other hand it is the source of many childhood accidents and causes much normal anxiety on the part of parents. For the first time they are faced with two things:

- Setting reasonable limits to help the child feel secure and safe.
- Limiting the use of "no" so that it will have meaning for the child when needed.

Parents must also remember that the memory of a Phase V baby is still relatively short. He is likely to return to play on the hearth of the fireplace even though he cut his head on a sharp corner 10 minutes ago, if it is interesting to him and he is given the opportunity. The capacity of this baby to understand instructions is also very limited. "Don't pull on the cord because the lamp is about to fall off the table" has no meaning for him.

During Phase V parents assume the responsibility of designing an environment that is safe for baby's exploration. They must examine all rooms from the baby's point of view and look for:

- Access to cleaning materials and other poisonous substances
- Sharp utensils
- Breakable objects
- Electrical cords and outlets
- Sharp corners on furniture

- Poisonous plants
- Open stairways
- Unstable objects or furniture

Behaviors indicating emergence of curiosity are:

- Interest in the effects of his actions on objects—dropping, banging
- Interest in small particles
- Interest in voices
- Interest in sounds
- Interest in faces
- Interest in all behaviors of primary caretaker, but especially reactions to him
- Interest in exploring living area
- Interest in cause and effect of simple mechanisms
- Interest in consequences of his actions

Ways to Encourage Curiosity

Finding a Wrapped Toy

Wrap baby's favorite toy in a bag or piece of paper so it takes a little work for him to open it. Ask him to get the toy from inside the package. He may just rip the paper. Don't discourage this but try again and show him how he can use his fingers to open it without destroying the paper.

Hiding Object in Match Box

Place an object inside a match box and help baby learn to slide the box to get it out. Show and tell the baby what you're doing. Let him try.

Playing with Small Objects and Containers

Make available lots of containers and things to put into them:

- Drawer of his own
- Wicker basket
- Large coffee can
- Cardboard box about 10 inches deep—vary the things he can put into it
- Beads too large to put into his mouth
- Blocks
- Plastic cookie cutters with dull edges
- Spools
- Small cars and trucks
- Small plastic animals

Making a "Feely Box"

Assemble a box of these materials: fur piece, tissue paper, foam rubber sponge, elastic strip. While you and your child are sitting on the floor, take one piece out of the box at a time. Show him how to handle the piece (stroke, stretch, crumble, etc.) and talk to him about how it feels. Allow him to handle it and see what he does with it. Encourage your child to play freely with these materials from time to time. Occasionally, add new materials to his collection.

Covering and Uncovering Eyes with Hands

Sit across from your baby on the floor and say, "I have a new way to play peek-a-boo. Watch." Place your hands on the baby's wrists and cover his eyes with the palms of his hands. Wait a second. Then remove his hand and say, "Peek-a-boo!" Repeat several times, then show your baby how you can play the game with your hands and eyes. After playing the game several days, encourage him to cover and uncover his eyes without your help.

Playing in a Kitchen Cabinet

Select a lower kitchen cabinet and stock it with safe, unbreakable objects. When you are working in the kitchen, let your baby crawl on the kitchen floor. Partially open the cabinet door. If left alone, he will probably start examining the objects. He'll have a chance to touch them, bang them together, and listen to the sounds they make. Let him play as he wishes. But talk to him as he plays, and make sure he plays safely.

Social Development–Phase V

(8–14 months)

The most important aspect of social development is the attachment that forms between baby and primary caretaker. This is a gradual process which becomes established toward the end of Phase IV or early Phase V. A sign that attachment has taken place is when the baby responds differently to his primary caretaker than to other people. Babies who have formed a strong attachment are able to use the caretaker as a security base from which to explore their environment and satisfy their intense curiosity.

A child who feels good about himself will develop self-discipline and self-control. He will gradually learn to develop his abilities and wait a short while for attention. Learning to express feelings in an appropriate way is a necessary part of growing up. For example, the infant will cry when hungry. Later he will learn to point and make noises at food and still later learn to say, "I'm hungry," instead of crying for someone to satisfy his need. A baby who has been discouraged from displaying emotions or expressing himself may have trouble some time later in life relating to people.

Any activity that involves parent/baby interaction and focuses on an emerging skill or interest of the baby will promote social skills. The process of the interaction will show the baby that he is valued, that he is being helped to become successful at tasks, that the caretaker is genuinely interested in him, and that it is safe to develop his curiosity and try new things.

The baby's interest in the primary caretaker may very well overpower his interest in objects. He is beginning to learn the following:

- What he can and cannot play with in each room of the house
- How much he can get away with, with his primary caretaker
- Whether or not primary caretaker is a generally friendly person
- Subtle cues to identify mood of primary caretaker
- The same information about secondary caretaker
- Whether the primary caretaker will give him undivided or divided attention
- Watches actions of primary caretaker during many of his waking hours
- To use primary caretaker as haven when distressed
- To use primary caretaker for help when he needs it
- To try out new skill on primary caretaker by initiation of social game
- The feelings the primary caretaker has for him by response of the primary caretaker

Things to Do

SOCIAL SKILLS

The process that leads to the complicated and sophisticated two-year-old social person begins in Phase V.

Specific skills to be aware of:

- Preference shown for primary caretaker
- Endearing behavior
- Gradual narrowing of focus to nuclear family
- Appearance of stranger anxiety
- Establishment of social pact with primary caretaker
- Expressions of affection or annoyance
- Use of primary caretaker as resource when help is needed
- Shows pride in personal achievement

Behaviors demonstrating skill:

- Is more quickly soothed by primary caretaker
- Burrows into primary caretaker's neck—primitive hug
- Is more comfortable or smiles more with family members
- Turns away, cries or stares at unfamiliar person
- Initiates social games with primary caretaker
- Kisses, hugs, cries, throws
- Brings object to primary caretaker, points and/or makes noise indicating what he needs help with
- Turns and smiles at primary caretaker upon successfully completing task

Material based on the research of Dr. Burton L. White, author of *The First Three Years of Life*.

Appendix 26C:
Curriculum Outline

Phase VII: 25 to 36 Months

A. Purposes of work in Phase VII
  1. Keep the parents on track, and that includes avoiding mistaken program directions. For example, ideas such as Glenn Doman's on precocious development and the chronic problem of demands for specific, magical activities.
  2. Provide management training with respect to special needs, nursery schools, programs that promise precocity, toys, books, magazines, newsletters, Sesame Street and other television, etc.
  3. Provide support for parents with respect to difficult situations involving, for example, tantrums and sibling rivalry.

B. Likely special difficulties
  1. Sibling rivalry
  2. Overindulgence and tantrums

C. Curriculum
  The major point is that a shift in activities with respect to the group visits is necessary. There has got to be much more input from parents and correspondingly less from staff, given the slower rate of change in the children and the maturity of the parents.
  1. Three functions of the parents remain and have to be reinforced occasionally, i.e., providing interesting experiences, consulting and controlling.
  2. Language. Much speech now leads to conversation. Receptive vocabulary goes from 300 to 1,000 words, and expressive vocabulary is catching up.
  3. Intelligence. Thinking has surfaced, but it is egocentric thinking.

4. Social skills. We now see the development of true social skills with respect to agemates.

5. Interests. Major interests now are socializing with agemates, stories, television, puzzle play, imaginative play, language use in play, and gross motor activities involving tricycles, gyms, etc.

6. The nursery school topic. Explaining different kinds, such as Montessori vs. traditional, expectations vs. realities, etc.

7. Special needs. The field of testing—what can be done, and what is most important in this area at this stage.

D. Professional identity

All staff have to keep in mind the fact that, while parents have a lot of faith in us, we are primarily educators.

E. Group visit content

1. Phase VII video for the first group visit
2. Child Care: A Guide
3. Testing: Tests and What They Mean
4. Discipline, Overindulgence, and Tantrums
5. Toys: The Best, the Worst, and Homemade
6. Preparation for Playgroups and Nursery School

A reminder: all group visit material that is missed by parents who do not attend has to be incorporated into home visits. All home visits should focus on where the child is educationally, month by month, except for those home visits that involve screening.

F. Suggestions for home visits

Three of the home visits will be taken up by screening procedures. At 24 months, the Denver; at 25 and 36 months, language.

1. Details of the educational process: speech, conversation, vocabulary, language growth
2. Current issues: television, including Sesame Street, new books, magazines, and newsletters
3. Spacing and sibling rivalry
4. Peer relations

Regular features of all home visits should include suggested activities, soliciting the concerns of parents, and reassuring parents that they are receiving an educational check-up every time we visit.

G. Tips for maintaining educational focus during Phase VII

1. Group visits

   For the group visit just before two years, the video on Phase VII should be used, but first there should be 12 minutes of Tina in Phase VI for contrast purposes.

2. Home visits

   a. What will develop during Phase VII overview

      1) Social skills with peers
      2) Language (for details, see the Preschool Project Language Test and *A Parent's Guide to the First Three Years*)
      3) Intelligence (see egocentric thinking)
      4) Motor development: special skills, for example, riding tricycles, drawing, and many fine motor skills

   b. Evolution of interests

      1) Special: a shift in interest to peers—groups of two truly socializing, playgroups, nursery schools. End of the attachment process, hopefully.
      2) The sibling situation
      3) The end of negativism
      4) The ability to play alone well

   c. Motor development: new skills and action for the sheer pleasure of it, especially climbing

   d. Curiosity: everything new, including stories, scenes, people, places, records, letters, numbers, television, etc.

   e. Patterns of experience: the emergence of constructing products, conversing, gaining information from looking and listening, television, etc.

   f. Hazards to the best development

      1) Overindulgence
      2) Hearing losses
      3) Younger siblings
      4) Inadequate personal attention

Appendix 26D:
Sample NPAT
Group Meeting Agendas

NEW PARENTS AS TEACHERS

Group Meeting—Prenatal 1

Objectives

  I. Parents and Parent Educator will become acquainted with each other and others present.

  II. Parents will learn about the components of the program.

    A. Group meetings

    B. Personal visits

    C. Periodic educational and sensory assessment

  III. Parent Educator will describe the Resource Center facilities and materials.

    A. Parent meeting room

    B. Child care room

    C. Lending library

    D. Free materials

  IV. Parent will have a better understanding of labor and delivery.

Procedures

  I. Establish rapport.

    A. Allow each family to introduce themselves, supplying such information as:
    When are you due?
    What type of delivery do you anticipate?
    How do you think your life will change after baby arrives?

    B. Explain the components of the program as stated in Objective II.

    C. Discuss use of Resource Center.

  II. Labor and delivery presentation.

    A. Brief introduction to film on labor and delivery, such as "Labor and Delivery" or "A Baby Is Born."

    B. Show film.

    C. Discuss film.

    D. Allow time for questions and concerns regarding labor and delivery.

  III. Preview of next group meeting.

NEW PARENTS AS TEACHERS

Group Meeting #3—Age of Baby: 3½ Months

Objectives

I. Parents and Parent Educator will discuss and review Phase II characteristics based on their observations of the baby during the past few weeks.

II. Parent Educator will encourage discussion and sharing of new family experiences among parents.

III. Parents will learn more about Phase III characteristics.

    A. Infant uses hands together

    B. Infant reaches for objects

    C. Infant grasps objects accurately

    D. Infant becomes ticklish

    E. Infant enjoys affectionate play with people

    F. Infant associates caretaker's voice with presence

    G. Infant interested in sounds he can make with his own voice and saliva

    H. Infant locates the source of a sound consistently

    I. Infant brings objects to mouth and gums them

    J. Infant holds feet off surface of crib

    K. Infant supports weight briefly when held in standing position

    L. Infant's head does not lag when pulled to sit

    M. Infant begins to use methods (such as crying) to get caretaker's attention

    N. Infant rolls over—front to back and back to front

IV. Parent Educator will help parents develop observational skills through discussion of the videotape or film presentation.

V. Parents will learn about equipment and toys appropriate for the Phase III baby:

unbreakable mirror
safe crib toys
crib gym
kickboard (vinyl-covered toy fastened to ends of crib)

NEW PARENTS AS TEACHERS

Group Meeting #7—Age of Baby: 9 months
(Phase V-A: 8–11 months)

Objectives

I. Parents and Parent Educator will discuss and review Phase V-A characteristics (age 8–11 months) based on their observations of the baby during the past few weeks.

II. Parent Educator will encourage discussion and sharing of family experiences with the baby among parents.

III. Parents will learn about discipline and setting limits.

IV. Parents and Parent Educator will summarize information presented regarding discipline and setting limits.

Procedures

I. Establish rapport.

  A. Allow time for parents to talk informally.

  B. Begin meeting with brief discussion.

   1. How are things going?

   2. How has baby changed since last meeting?

  C. Review characteristics of Phase V-A, encouraging parents to discuss their observations of their baby.

II. Presentation and discussion about discipline and setting limits, using a child psychologist consultant.

  A. Discipline vs. punishment

  B. Issue of control—who is in charge—parent or baby

  C. Establishment of a new family unit—changes in relationship with family of origin and friends

  D. Issue of spanking

  E. Techniques of listening for and observing baby's cues

  F. Trial and error method of discovering what works for you and your baby

  G. Issue of parental disagreement

  H. Ways to structure daily routines so punishment is minimal

  I. Issue of overprotectiveness

III. Sharing by parents of family experiences and ways they set limits.

IV. Summarize presentation and discussion.

V. Preview of next group meeting.

NEW PARENTS AS TEACHERS

Group Meeting #13—Age of Child: 15 months
Phase VI (14–24 months)

Objectives

I. Parents and Parent Educator will discuss and review V-B characteristics based on their observations of the child during the past few weeks.

II. Parent Educator will encourage discussion and sharing of family experiences with the child among parents.

III. Parents will leave children in child care room with mothers from the program to supervise.

IV. Parents will learn about negativism, autonomy, and independence.

V. Parents and Parent Educator will summarize information presented regarding negativism, autonomy, and independence.

VI. Parents and Parent Educator will observe and interact with children in the child care room.

Procedures

I. Establish rapport.

  A. Allow time for parents to leave children in child care room and talk informally.

  B. Begin meeting with brief discussion.

    1. How are things going?

    2. How has baby changed since last meeting?

    3. What to expect next in terms of development.

  C. Review characteristics of Phase V-B.

  D. Discuss early Phase VI characteristics.

II. Presentation and discussion of negativism, autonomy, and independence.

  A. Emergence of negativism.

  B. Need for parents to set priorities regarding setting limits.

  C. Growth of child from total dependence towards becoming independent little person.

Appendix 26E:
Sample NPAT
Private Visit Agendas

NEW PARENTS AS TEACHERS

Personal Visit—Prenatal

Objectives

I. Parents will learn more about the components of the program than was explained in the initial contact.

  A. Group meetings

  B. Personal visits in the home or at the center

  C. Periodic educational and sensory assessment

  D. Resource Center

II. Parents will have a better understanding of labor and delivery.

III. Parents will begin to learn about Phase I characteristics.

  A. Infant is totally dependent on others.

  B. Infant is adjusting to life outside the womb.

  C. Infant is easily irritated when not asleep; mood changes suddenly from distress to comfort.

  D. Infant's major concern is being comfortable.

  E. Infant's movement through space is very comforting.

  F. Sucking on his fist or pacifier is very comforting.

  G. Behavior is fragmented; a small number of unfinished, isolated reflexes—rooting, sucking, and grasping.

  H. At one month, baby's common position is the tonic neck reflex.

  I. Infant is extremely sensitive to bright lights; he is more likely to open his eyes in a dimly lit room.

  J. Infant begins social smiling at end of Phase I; first sign of sociability is looking at the eyes of the person holding him.

  K. Infant begins to discover his hands when on his back in the fencer's position.

  L. Infant's head control gradually improves during Phase I, as does his ability to follow an object with his eyes and to bring his fist to his mouth.

Objectives—Continued

    M. Infant is given a feeling of being loved and cared for by the parents.

    N. Infant's distress is often relieved by the use of a rocking chair and a pacifier.

IV. Parent Educator will begin establishing rapport with the family.

Procedures

    I. Establish rapport.

  II. Explain components of the program as listed in Objective I.

III. Discuss developmental characteristics.

    A. Explain the phases of development through the first three years.

IV. Provide additional information as needed.

    A. Possible handouts:

        1. Notebook for families to keep program materials

        2. Phase I material

        3. *Parenting Insights*

        4. *Should You Stay Home With Your Baby?*

        5. *Don't Risk Your Child's Life*

    B. Discuss parents' questions or concerns about labor and delivery.

    C. Announce topic, time, place of next group meeting.

NEW PARENTS AS TEACHERS

Personal Visit #4—Age of Baby: 4½–5 Months

Objectives

I. Parent Educator will assess the development of the baby through the use of the Denver Developmental Screening Scale.

II. Parent Educator will help parent develop observational skills during the formal assessment.

III. Parent Educator will review Phase III characteristics with parent. See Objective II on Personal Visit #3.

IV. Parent Educator will provide information on providing a safe environment for the baby's exploration.

V. Parent Educator will continue establishing a relationship with the family.

Procedures

I. Establish rapport.

　A. Continue to relate to parents' feelings in adjusting to their new role as parents.

　B. Ask parents how things are going.

II. Review developmental characteristics using Phase III material.

III. Observe with parents the behavior of baby during the administration of the Denver Developmental Screening Scale.

IV. Walk through each room in the home.

　A. Look for possible safety hazards for a mobile baby.

　B. Discuss alternatives for correcting the safety hazards.

V. Provide follow-up activity for parents and baby.

　A. Activity to encourage skill development. Example: Put the baby on the floor several times a day to practice rolling, scooting, and sitting.

　B. Observe emerging skills. Example: Put pressure against the soles of the infant's feet. Watch if the baby delights in pushing powerfully against it.

NEW PARENTS AS TEACHERS

Personal Visit #13—Age of Baby: 14 Months

Objectives

I. Parent Educator will assess the receptive language development of the child through the use of the Stocking Language Screening device.

II. Parent Educator will help parents develop observational skills of the child's receptive language during the formal assessment.

III. Parents will learn about the characteristics which signal the onset of Phase VI.

Procedures

I. Observe parent–child interaction for approximately 10 minutes. Ask parents about changes they have observed in child since the last visit— new behaviors, favorite activities, preferred toys, etc.

II. Review with parents the characteristics which signal that the child is nearing Phase VI.

A. Child will show "negativism." He will challenge and test the parents.

B. Child begins to be aware that he is a separate and independent person.

C. Child becomes persistent and is not easily distracted when he wants something.

D. Child is able to make himself understood by parents.

III. Explain to parents the purpose and format of the Stocking Language Screening device.

A. Help the parents complete the inventory checklist on the language test.

B. Give the mother (or father) directions for eliciting responses from the child on the vocabulary and instructions subtests.

C. Observe with parents the behavior of the child during the administration of the test.

D. Explain and discuss the results with the parents.

NEW PARENTS AS TEACHERS

Personal Visit #23—Age of Baby: 24 Months

Objectives

I. Parent Educator will assess the development of the baby through the use of the Denver Developmental Screening Scale.

II. Parent will develop observational skills during the formal assessment.

III. Parents will learn about Phase VII characteristics:

A. True social interaction with peers.

   1. Leading and following peers.

   2. Expressing affection and mild annoyance with peers.

   3. Competing with peers.

B. Increasing interest in language, especially that directed toward him.

C. Practicing of simple skills on small objects.

D. Becomes more skillful at running and climbing.

E. Learns to ride a tricycle.

F. Makes first representational drawings.

G. Makes first "constructions" with blocks, boxes, etc.

H. Becomes more involved in imaginative and pretend activities, especially with primary caretaker.

I. Shows genuine interest in television viewing.

J. Understands the majority of simple words and sentences addressed to him.

K. Uses small sentences and carries on simple conversations.

L. Genuinely interested in new circumstances, new physical objects, new people, etc.

M. Is egocentric in his thinking, sees things exclusively from his own point of view.

N. Has more mature mental abilities.

   1. Anticipates consequences.

   2. Is able to reflect upon events and situations.

   3. Uses resources effectively.

27
Final Comments

The field of early education has come a long way since 1965, the first year of Project Head Start. Suddenly, the interest in learning in the first years of life expanded dramatically. That interest led to an unprecedented quantity of work, much of which has practical consequences of fundamental importance. We now know considerably more about how to help every child build the best possible foundations for lifelong learning than anyone ever knew prior to these advances. It is clear that there are still many subjects about which we know very little. This makes the work of the professional difficult. Because the subject of early learning is so important, and because much that is valuable is very new and much that is offered is not soundly based, the professional is faced with an epistemological challenge. That is why I spent so much time in this book on the subject of what we really know and what we just don't know yet.

I believe that it is important to point out that the dramatic breakthroughs we have seen in this field were created principally because of the growth of political power associated with the civil rights movement. I very much doubt that if the civil rights movement had not grown stronger in the late 1950s and early 1960s, we would ever have seen a Project Head Start. That project was a response by the federal government to substantial pressures brought to bear by self-appointed spokesmen for the civil rights movement. They pointed out that children from low-income black families especially were simply not doing well in the public educational system and, as a result, were not able to profit in general from the American society as much as they should have. They insisted on change. They focused attention on the public educational system in a most effective way. The creation of the Head Start project, with a first-year budget of $600 million, galvanized both professionals and large private foundations in this country. Their activities led to the creation of impressive activities, such as those of the Children's Television Workshop (most notably *Sesame Street*), and their impact spread to many foreign countries.

Especially now that we have the impressive results of Missouri's New Parents as Teachers pilot programs, we have what it takes to make a difference in the lives of future children. Having what it takes is clearly not enough, however, if all you mean is having the knowledge it takes. We also need advocates for more educational input to new parents, and we need decision makers with vision and courage. In Missouri, it took only two advocates and a state commissioner of education. That probably means it would not take a much larger group of people anywhere else, certainly in America. Fortunately, we have fifty states that generally act autonomously with respect to educational policy. It is my hope that as more and more information about the Missouri success is disseminated, such programs will become established in many places and ultimately will become a part of the national public educational system.

I have been engaged in research on the development of competent, decent people for a long time. Indeed, my interest in this subject goes back to the early 1950s, and that interest has never flagged. As those years have gone by, and today, I continue to believe that no work that anyone does—whether it be in space research, big business, art, or any other field—is more important than the work involved in helping a child off to the best start in life.

Appendix A:
Books on Early Development
and Child Care

M any books are available that promise to help parents raise their children. Over the past decade, more than 350 such books have been published in the United States alone. There is a tremendous demand for books on raising children—a demand that I believe is a direct consequence of the government's failure to meet a universal and deeply felt need for reliable information on this topic. Unfortunately, as is the case with toys for babies, books on parenting vary dramatically in quality, and most leave much to be desired. I review books as often as I can, but I do not have the resources to examine even half of them. Therefore, the following is an attempt at providing general guidelines for coping with the situation.

First of all, don't be deceived by appearances. For example, some of the best-designed books are those by Frank Caplan and the so-called Princeton Advisory Center on Infancy. These include *The First Twelve Months of Life* and *The Second Twelve Months of Life*, both of which have sold hundreds of thousands of copies. These books feature large print, double columns, great pictures, clear charts—and extensive publicity and marketing that imply an affiliation with Princeton University. There are at least three problems with these books. First, they are often seriously in error; that is, the authors are not adequately knowledgeable regarding early human development. Second, the group has no connection with Princeton University; it is simply located in Princeton, New Jersey. Third, many topics listed in the table of contents receive only a few dozen words of actual coverage in the text.

Next, note the credentials of the author. Authors in this subject area range from experienced M.D.'s, Ph.D.'s, and Ed.D.'s to various laypeople—some with interesting and valuable experience and others with not much more than chutzpah. If the primary focus of a book is physical health, then an M.D. (or an R.N.) is usually the most appropriate author (e.g., Drs. Spock and Gesell). If the subject is the development of personality or abilities, an author with a Ph.D. or an Ed.D. in child development, psychology, or education is usually a better bet than an M.D. If the subject is the feelings of parents, I would recommend a book that taps original sources, such as *The Mothers' Book* edited by Friedland and Kort. If the subject is traveling with small children, rainy day activities, or some other nitty-gritty topic, I would recommend a "based on experience" book, such as *Practical Parenting Tips* by Vicki Lansky.

The important point to note here is that although authors of childrearing books come from a variety of backgrounds and those backgrounds generally determine the value of the advice offered, authors sometimes roam from the area in which they are qualified. Even when an author concentrates on his or her appropriate subject matter, there is often a problem with regard to the knowledge base. The simple fact is that few authors are thoroughly familiar with what is known and what is *not known* about early human development.

The primary reason for this startling state of affairs is that the science of early human development is incomplete; there are large holes in what we'd like to know, and there are many misconceptions floating around. Witness an unusual suggestion by Fitzhugh Dodson, a very popular author (*How to Parent* and *How to Father*), that the reader turn to Gesell's work for the details of early behavior. If Gesell had done a comprehensive job on that subject, such a suggestion would not be unreasonable. However, what Gesell left out was enormous. The best introduction to the mind of the baby is the work of Piaget, and his ideas never entered the writings of Gesell.

Three important omissions typify the effects of the limited backgrounds of most authors of books about infants and toddlers. First, it is a rare book that covers the subject of sibling rivalry with any precision, despite the fact that in our research with average parents, hard feelings between closely spaced children were far and away their deepest concern. Most authors seem oblivious to this reality, and many continue to perpetuate the myth that siblings will naturally love each other and that "there's nothing to worry about." Second, child development research has focused more on early *speech* than on early *understanding* of language. As a result, even the most qualified authors have written very little on the important topic of receptive language learning; many others simply fail even to acknowledge its existence. Third, much of early development depends on normal hearing ability, a function very often at risk during the first years of life. However, the subject of mild or moderate hearing losses is rarely treated at all, let alone well.

Another important consideration in evaluating books for new parents is the scope of the book with regard to the age of the children being described. Many books that purport to deal with children "from birth to adolescence," for example, may contain a considerable amount of information about school-age children but relatively little that would be helpful to parents of infants and toddlers. An additional dimension to note is the scope of the subject matter. Many books, such as those by Spock and Lendon Smith, concentrate on the physical well-being and management of the child. Some, such as those by T. Berry Brazelton, deal directly with the emotional or stress-inducing aspects of parenting. Others, such as those by Burton White and Ira Gordon, focus on early learning. Several attempt to cover everything. Few succeed, although some, such as *Choosing Toys for Children* by Barbara Kaban or *Discipline Without Shouting or Spanking* by Wyckoff and Unell, manage to cover a large age span well by concentrating on one topic, and some, such as *The First Year of Life* from American Baby or *The First Wondrous Year* from Johnson & Johnson, manage to cover many topics well by concentrating on a narrow age span.

The major difficulty in selecting books on early development and parenting is determining the validity of the knowledge offered. Although I have suggested some guidelines, I recognize that the job of actually evaluating even a modest number of such books is beyond the time and energy limits of most professionals. Therefore, this appendix contains my opinions of those books that I have had a chance to review. Some reviews consist only of brief comments;

others are rather extensive. I hope they will be of assistance in selecting among the books that are currently available and that they will also be useful as models for evaluating new releases.

Author Index

Since the book reviews in this appendix are arranged in alphabetical order by book title, the following index is provided to help readers locate reviews of books by particular authors.

American Baby, *The First Year of Life*
Barber, L., and Williams, H., *Your Baby's First 30 Months*
Beck, J., *Best Beginnings*
Bell, T. H., *Your Child's Intellect*
Biller, H., and Meredith, D., *Father Power*
Braga, J. and L., *Children and Adults*
Brazelton, T. B., *Toddlers and Parents*
Burck, F. W., *Baby Sense*
Burtt, K., and Kalkstein, K., *Smart Toys for Babies*
Bush, R., *A Parent's Guide to Child Therapy*
Butler, D., *Babies Need Books*
Cahill, M. A., *The Heart Has Its Own Reasons*
Callahan, S. C., *Parenting*
Caplan, F. and T., *The Early Childhood Years*
Caplan, F. and T., *The Second Twelve Months of Life*
Chase, R. A., and Rubin, R. R. (eds.), *The First Wondrous Year*
Chess, S., Thomas, A., and Birch, H., *Your Child Is a Person*
Dodson, F., *How to Parent*
Doman, G., *How to Teach Your Baby to Read*
Dreskin, W. and W., *The Day Care Decision*
Fraiberg, S., *The Magic Years*
Friedland, R., and Kort, C. (eds.), *The Mothers' Book*
Galinsky, E., and Hooks, W., *The New Extended Family*
Gesell, A., and Ilg, F., *Infant and Child in the Culture of Today*
Glickman, B., and Springer, N., *Who Cares for the Baby?*
Gordon, I., *Child Learning Through Child Play*
Greenspan, S. and N. T., *First Feelings*

Gregg, E., and Knotts, J., *Growing Wisdom, Growing Wonder*
Hagstrom, J., and Morrill, J., *Games Babies Play*
Hanson, J., *Game Plans for Children*
Harmon, M., *A New Vaccine for Child Safety*
Harris, R., & Levy, E., *Before You Were Three*
Jones, S., *Crying Baby, Sleepless Nights*
Jones, S., *Good Things for Babies*
Jones, S., *To Love a Baby*
Kaban, B., *Choosing Toys for Children from Birth to Age Five*
Koch, J., *Total Baby Development*
Lansky, V., *Best Practical Parenting Tips*
Lapinski, S., and Hinds, M. D., *In a Family Way*
Leach, P., *Your Baby and Child from Birth to Age Five*
Lehane, S., *Help Your Baby Learn*
Lignon, E., et al., *Let Me Introduce Myself*
Loman, K., *Of Cradles and Careers*
Mason, D., Hensen, G., and Ryzewicz, C., *How to Grow a Parents Group*
Mayer, R., *Beginning Together*
Maynard, F., *The Child Care Crisis*
Miller, K., *Things to Do with Toddlers and Twos*
Murphy, L., *Personality in Young Children*
Pines, M., *Revolution in Learning*
Pomeranz, V., and Schultz, J., *The First Five Years*
Pulaski, M. A. S., *Your Baby's Mind and How It Grows*
Robertson, J. and J., *A Baby in the Family*
Salk, L., *Your Child's First Year*
Segal, M., *You Are Your Baby's First Teacher*
Shilcock, S., and Bergson, P., *Open Connections: The Other Basics*
Smith, H. W., *A Survival Handbook for Preschool Mothers*
Smith, L., *Improving Your Child's Behavior Chemistry*
Spock, B., *Baby and Child Care*
Stallibrass, A., *The Self-Respecting Child*
Stewart, A., *Childproofing Your Home*
U.S. Department of Health, Education and Welfare, *Infant Care*
Verny, T., *The Secret Life of the Unborn Child*
Warner, S. L., and Rosenberg, E. B., *Your Child Learns Naturally*
Wolf, A. D., *The World of the Child*
Wyckoff, J., and Unell, B., *Discipline Without Shouting or Spanking*
Zimbardo, P., and Radl, S., *The Shy Child*

Reviews

Babies Need Books: How to Share the Joy of Reading with Your Child
Dorothy Butler
Penguin Books, 1982

Get ready for a rave review. This is one of the finest works about the very young child that I have ever encountered. The author is described as a mother, grand-mother, teacher, and children's bookseller. Her position, magnificently presented in this little volume, is that books are more than just desirable and useful; they are mandatory for the very young child, starting during the first *months* of life. This book is extraordinarily well written by someone who not only is very intelligent and knowledgeable but is extremely passionate about the subject. Her grasp of the nature of the child, especially as it relates to the child's interest in sounds, words, themes, and stories—all placed within the parent–child relationship—is remarkable.

Butler advocates a long-term—indeed, a lifetime—process in which children begin to become acquainted with the wonders of language and the many benefits of the written word and associated illustrations in a manner that maximizes the joys and rewards of early childhood and parenting and leads to lifelong rewards. It would appear that she is familiar with thousands of books, some of which were published more than a hundred years ago. She has singled out those that she can recommend on a year-by-year basis, starting with the first year of life. In each instance, she carefully explains the reasons for her selection. She also provides an extremely detailed guide for the use of these materials from the time the baby is only a few months of age.

Butler is well aware that the language abilities of an infant are nil, at first, and only gradually emerge during the first two years of life. She has a conviction, how-ever, that by starting very early on, not only are there huge benefits but a lifelong habit is established, which she feels is much more difficult to establish if you were to wait until a child was three or four or more years old. Her arguments are con-vincing. In my view, she is somewhat less sensitive to the larger picture of early development than she might be. Her way of dealing with the desire of the one-year-old to reach for books and to handle them leaves a little to be desired, in that she seems to be only slightly aware of an infant's ordinary interest in hand-eye activities. Her focus on the emergence of the conventional use of books is under-standable, but parents may find a few problems surfacing as they attempt to use her ideas with a two-year-old child because of the modest neglect of the natural tendency of children under fourteen or fifteen months of age to rip pages from books and even attempt to eat them.

I don't mean to make too much of the few failings of this wonderful book. They pale in the light of its strengths. For professionals who are trying to cope with parents who have heard about programs (such as Glenn Doman's) to produce min-iature geniuses at age three, this book can serve an important function. In my opinion, the educational consequences of incorporating Butler's ideas into parenting education are likely to be far more beneficial than approaches that are motivated by too much concern with academic precocities.

In summary, I can't say enough to recommend this book. Its message is presented beautifully—and in my judgment, it is an extremely humanistic and important message. Although the author is British, I believe that most of the books she recommends are available in the United States and Canada. I simply have never run into anything else like this book, and I consider it a most valuable addition to the literature.

Baby and Child Care
Benjamin Spock, M.D.
Pocket Books, 1976

Spock's recommendations about how to cope with feeding and sleeping problems and other typical issues in childrearing have been more widely read and followed than those of any other single work over the past several decades. This book would not have been so popular if it were not such good, solid material. Spock performed an extremely valuable service to young families. The topic of management is a classic case of a topic that bridges two fields—medicine and educational psychology. Today, most pediatricians find themselves concerned not only with the physical welfare of the young baby but also with the parents' desire to raise that baby well.

Although whether the child eats or sleeps well is not an educational topic per se, understanding how to cope with such behavior problems requires knowledge not only of the child's physical makeup and health but also of the way his mind operates, the way he learns, what kind of discipline will work with him, and so forth. Therefore, when Spock gets into areas that are not exclusively within the medical realm, his advice is often skating on thin ice.

A Baby in the Family
James and Joyce Robertson
Penguin Books, 1982

The Robertsons have been involved in child care in Britain for many decades. They are a delightful, informed, and caring couple. In this little book, they describe with unusual impact and accuracy the growth of the love relationship between a baby and his nuclear family during the first year of life.

As a detailed guide to this core process, I have never found anything better. Although James Robertson is a psychoanalyst, there is little of the overemphasis on early psychoanalytic principles commonly found in books by authors of this ilk. Rather, there is an appropriate blending of some of those psychiatric notions with a good deal of common sense and first-hand experience.

The Roberstons are unabashed advocates of breastfeeding, and in their description of the early months, they present a convincing plea for close contact and breastfeeding if at all possible. The specific babies they focus on are their own grandchildren, so they have been able to supply dozens of outstanding photographs to illustrate the process in question.

In my view, the book does have weaknesses, and they are typical of what one would expect given the professional orientation of the authors. There is a tendency to give parents the impression that if they establish the love relationship, they have done 95 percent of the job. Unfortunately, in my judgment, that is not good enough. Also, I feel there should be some mention of the benefits of prolonged breastfeeding for boys with respect to mild to moderate hearing losses during the first year. In addition, they place the onset of stranger anxiety at six months, which is a bit early; seven to eight months is more common. Finally, in their remarks on what happens after the first year, although they do try to outline later emotional development, they say too little about negativism in the fifteen to twenty-one-month period and about sibling rivalry in situations where there are closely spaced children.

There are very useful sections on how to prepare for dealing with the hospital situation, particularly with the possibility that hospital policy and/or staff may not be sufficiently sympathetic to the parents' needs to be with the baby right from the beginning. The section on adoptive parents is also exceptional. Furthermore, along with the aforementioned illustrations, the writing is consistently beautiful. Therefore, all in all, I recommend this book highly.

Baby Sense
Frances Wells Burck
St. Martin's Press, 1979

This is an unusually clear, practical guide for the new parent. The treatment of crying and colic are extensive and reasonable and consist of known facts. The sections on toys are weak; otherwise, however, this is a good general treatment of the first stages of parenthood.

Before You Were Three
Robie Harris and Elizabeth Levy
Delacorte, 1977

This book is different from most treatments of the initial three years in that it is written with the child as its audience. It apparently is to be read by or to young children in an attempt to explain to them how they got to be the way they are.

The book features absolutely lovely photographs, large easy-to-read type, and very good writing. It focuses on the development of the walking and talking abilities, a baby's first explorations, and the evolution of feelings.

Overall, the book is an interesting mix of powerful and perceptive explanations, occasional errors of consequence, and a fair number of important omissions. It is strongest, perhaps, in describing the evolution of the ability to communicate. In looking closely at the first sounds and their link to meanings, the authors do a first-rate job. They also are quite good on the evolution of feelings of anger, pleasure, and affection. They are surprisingly inaccurate, however, in discussing the onset of various gross motor abilities, such as crawling, pulling to stand, and walking, in that they put each of these achievements considerably later in development than is actually the case. They also are weak with regard to the development of the ability to reach and also with regard to the emergence of memory.

One can put only a limited amount into such a short (136 pages) book. Nevertheless, the idea that this is a thorough treatment of the topics cited is implied by the authors, but their coverage leaves out several key elements. For example, in the development of feelings, it would have been of great practical value to address the issue of sibling rivalry. Few life experiences, especially during the first few years, are more likely to evoke stronger feelings than having either a slightly older or a slightly younger brother or sister in the family. The omission of this topic from the book is quite unfortunate.

In all, this is a considerably better than average book with a common degree of error with respect to the details of early development. With these shortcomings in mind, however, the book does fill a role that few other books do.

Beginning Together
Rochelle Mayer
St. Martin's Press, 1983

This is a rather unusual book. Basically, it is a journal for new parents, designed to be used during the period covering pregnancy and the first year. It contains sections in which to enter special events and emerging behaviors to help record the milestones of the infant's first year. The author interviewed many first-time parents to identify their range of interests and concerns so as to supplement the list she had compiled herself as she raised her first child. The result is a much more penetrating look at the early experiences of parenthood than is typically found in this kind of journal, which usually is characterized by brief, standard recordings of the course of early development.

Rochelle Mayer, who holds a doctorate from the Graduate School of Education at Harvard, is an unusually delightful person with a keen intelligence and a buoyant attitude. Her writing is of very high quality, and the book is strengthened by the inclusion of some superb photographs. I think this is an outstanding book, and I recommend it highly.

Best Beginnings: Giving Your Child a Head Start in Life
Joan Beck
Putnam's, 1983

Joan Beck has written for the *Chicago Tribune* for many years. During much of this time, she has written a syndicated column on raising children; more recently, she has concentrated on writing editorials for the paper. She has also written several books: *How to Raise a Brighter Child*, *Effective Parenting*, and *Is My Baby All Right?* (with Virginia Apgar, M.D.).

Over the years that I have been in the child development world, I have been interviewed by many journalists, but only a few stand out as having been extraordinarily capable. Ms. Beck is one of them, and this book reinforces her reputation in my mind. However, it also is an incredibly frustrating book.

I read the first 104 pages with mounting enthusiasm. Her analyses of genetic factors and other health issues during the prenatal stages are by far the best I have read anywhere. There simply is no substitute for a first-rate mind combined with dedication, energy, and years of work on a subject area. Add to that the fact that Ms. Beck writes extraordinarily clearly and this combination becomes even more impressive. One observation I made repeatedly as I read this first section of the book was how pleasant it was to be learning something as I read a book about raising children. Considering how many such books I have reviewed over the years, the process can get rather boring. It was refreshing to read one that contained documented information presented in an interesting manner.

Ms. Beck manages to boil a great deal of information down to specific recommendations, presented in understandable fashion. For example, after summarizing scientific research on the hazards of pregnancy, she then concisely lists particular considerations that prospective parents should pay most attention to. In my opinion, this section, entitled "Taking Care of Your Baby During Pregnancy," should be required reading for all expectant couples.

In the second section, where the focus shifts to learning during the first year, Ms. Beck gets off to a good start by dealing directly and well with the problem of the state of knowledge about early child development, as typified by her perception that "the research basis for child care theory is not very solid." Unfortunately, from this point on through the remainder of the second section, the flaws in the book surface and become rather substantial. Despite the author's expressions of skepticism and concern about what is and is not known, she repeatedly falls into the trap of accepting as fact claims that, though dramatic, are not supportable by research evidence. To complicate matters, these uncritical acceptances are interspersed with some very good information, and everything is written with equal style and clarity.

One of the several areas that concern me has to do with her interpretation of the effectiveness of Head Start—that is, center-based programs for three- and four-year-old children from low-income families. The author claims that most of the studies of the effects of Head Start show "not only immediate gains in learning, but long-term payoff." Later in the book, she points out that studies of the impact of infant care centers have been conducted, for the most part, by the people operating the centers. Her concern about resultant bias is not reflected in her discussion of the Head Start situation. In my opinion, the effectiveness of Head Start has been markedly less than what is claimed in this book (and elsewhere). Indeed, the best one can say about it is that the work of David Weikart at his Perry Preschool Project is the only such work that has demonstrated any lasting payoff (and limited payoff at that). As for short-term gains, only a handful of atypical, university-based programs have demonstrated significant short-term gains, and these gains were subsequently lost during the elementary school years.

A little further on, the author gets into trouble again when it comes to interpreting studies of temperament. Her claim is that "temperamental differences in children are likely to persist from infancy on." However, such is not the case, as follow-up studies of the only two substantial investigations of temperament have shown. The work of Brazelton and that of Birch, Chess, and Thomas have clearly demonstrated that temperamental characteristics present in the first weeks of life usually do not persist in any major way throughout infancy, let alone for longer periods.

Ms. Beck falls into another classic trap with respect to early tactile and kinesthetic stimulation. There is no question that babies profit from being held, moved through space, and stroked. But to follow the anatomical data and an occasional study of early handling with the statement that "your baby needs to be stroked and patted when you change his diapers, when you bathe him, and when you gentle him back to sleep" is to begin loading parents down with things to remember to do that really do not need to be remembered at all. In the ordinary course of events, babies will get all the tactile and kinesthetic stimulation they need, so long as their parents are routinely friendly, loving, and demonstrative.

On the same subject, the author claims that American infants develop a little more slowly during the first months of life because they have less physical contact with their mothers than infants in some other societies. This claim is clearly out of line. It is true that American infants develop a bit more slowly during this period than, for example, infants in some black African societies, but to claim that we understand exactly why and to link the differences directly to less physical contact is inappropriate. In my judgment, it seems far more likely that the differences are due to a genetic predisposition rather than to environmental factors.

In addition to these errors of commission, Ms. Beck makes some serious errors of omission in this section. Far too little attention is paid to the importance of early detection and treatment of mild to moderate hearing losses. (By the way, there is a common misconception that when a baby responds to his name at four or five months, it indicates he understands his name; in fact, he will respond to any name—or any fairly loud sound—addressed to him at this stage.)

There also is inadequate treatment of the need for safety-proofing the home in the period just prior to the onset of mobility. Moreover, the entire section on the first year of life says nothing whatsoever about social skill development. The acquisition of interpersonal abilities during the first year is at least as important as any other learning—even more important in the minds of some. The fact that children will begin to use adults as resources, to express emotions directly, and to expand their capacity to get attention during the first year should have been treated in this chapter.

Finally, another equally important omission of great practical significance is the failure to address the topic of sibling rivalry. Closely spaced siblings start to become very difficult to live with once the younger child reaches eight or nine months of age and starts to crawl. Unfortunately, for some reason, the author has neglected to alert parents to this fact.

The next section of the book deals with the period between one and three years of age. Considering how familiar Ms. Beck is with my work, it is surprising that, again, she has neglected to address adequately certain very important topics. For instance, there still is no mention of the common, typical problems that parents have with closely spaced children.

Also, and quite mysteriously, in talking about the twelve- to twenty-four-month period, she hardly touches on the fact that negativism becomes very clear and difficult to cope with before the second birthday. In fact, the author treats negativism as if it were strictly a phenomenon of the third year, thereby missing the opportunity to help parents avoid the development of tantrums. The "terrible twos" are not inevitable; only when the normal negativism of the second year is not handled well do children move into the third year engaging in troublesome tantrum behavior.

In dealing with the subject of toys for toddlers, Ms. Beck describes two toys that are notoriously *un*interesting to children—push toys and soft, fuzzy toys (such as stuffed animals and "security" blankets)—as just the opposite. It is true that these toys are of occasional interest to young children, but certainly not to the extent that the "Peanuts" cartoons would have us believe. It does not make sense to set parents up to think that there may be something wrong with their child if he does not have a security blanket, a favorite teddy bear, or whatever, when the fact is that few children actually do. Unfortunately, throughout the remainder of this section, the author continues to present a curious mixture of solid, helpful information combined with overstatements, misinformation, and neglect of some absolutely essential information.

After a section on the preschool years, the book turns around again in the fifth section, entitled "Combining Childcare and a Job." It is in this section that the book reaches its peak of excellence. Ms. Beck does a superb job on what is clearly the single most difficult problem facing young parents who are considering full-time work for both parents while their child is very young. On several occasions, I have attempted to express my concerns about this difficult situation, and of course I have had access to other writings on the subject. Nothing I have done or seen comes close to Joan Beck's effort. She handles this very sensitive subject brilliantly. Indeed, as I read this final section, I had the sense that the rest of the book was written only so that the author could have the opportunity to pour her heart into this particular issue. If that is the case, it was well worth it.

In summary, *Best Beginnings* is a remarkable book written by a person who probably is the finest syndicated columnist on the subject in the country, at least over the past two or three decades. I highly recommend the book for its sections on pregnancy and child care and on combining child care and a job. Unfortunately, I cannot recommend the sections dealing with learning during the first years of life.

Best Practical Parenting Tips
Vicki Lansky
Meadowbrook Press, 1980

This is perhaps the most useful book for parents ever published. It contains "over 1,000 parent-tested ideas" on everything from diapering and feeding through toilet training on to discipline and sibling rivalry.

Although she does not have a great deal of formal academic training in child development, the author of this book is a mother of two and has been publishing *Practical Parenting* newsletter for many years. Her ideas and suggestions are based on her own good judgment, common sense, and experience, as well as on the experience and consensus of thousands of parents around the country. As a result, she does not have much theoretical support or many research studies to back up what she says, but she has a great deal of evidence that this stuff "works."

Lansky also has a combination of wit and compassion that is unsurpassed by anyone else writing books for parents. Perhaps the following comment taken from this book's cover is most indicative of that: "Warning—this book can be hazardous to your mental health if you think you must try every idea listed. Trying them all may lead to a nervous breakdown. Thinking you should is guaranteed to produce an intense case of guilt."

Recently, through Bantam Books, Lansky has been publishing short, inexpensive paperbacks dealing with very specific subjects, including *Traveling with Your Baby*, *Getting Your Baby to Sleep*, *Welcoming Your Second Baby*, and *Toilet Training*. They are all full of down-to-earth, sane, useful suggestions, presented in the same easy-to-read, easy-to-follow style. I recommend them all very highly.

The Child Care Crisis
Fredelle Maynard
Viking, 1985

This is another superb book on this very important topic. The author is a most unusual person. She has a Ph.D. in Renaissance Literature from Harvard and she has had a long career as a self-taught professional in the field of child development. She has authored several books on the subject and has written hundreds of articles for various popular magazines. Dr. Maynard points out the rather unusual fact that she probably is the only person to have published simultaneously in *The New Republic, Reader's Digest*, and the *Journal of English and Germanic Philology*.

The book is distinguished by outstanding writing and clarity of thought as well as a great deal of warmth—indeed passion—about the issue. Some of the major headings in part 1 include "The Working Parents Dilemma," "Do You Really Want a Child?" "What Do You Want for Your Child?" and "Child Development and Child Care." In part 2, Dr. Maynard describes "The Options" and "The Kinds of Care Available," which include day care centers, nonprofit cooperatives, family day care, and nannies.

The author reveals that she has studied the day care issue upside down and backwards—and on an international basis. She talks about her judgments regarding the effects of day care on children's intellectual, linguistic, social, and moral development, concluding with a position that does not differ much from mine. That is, she expresses great concern about the poor prospects most families have when it comes to finding adequate services, and she strongly recommends that parents be very careful and make as little use of full-time day care as possible during the first two to three years of their child's life.

Dr. Maynard then moves on to the situation of the family that, for one reason or another, decides to use full-time child care, and she provides a very useful and high-quality collection of ideas regarding how to make the best decisions. There are appendix sections on sexual abuse in day care and suggestions for getting information and help.

I especially liked her response to the complaint that criticism of early day care lays a heavy guilt trip on working mothers: "But surely what is important here are the feelings, the *life* of children. If the best available evidence indicates that infants and toddlers need their parents, then it is irresponsible to pretend otherwise. To say that a substitute mother can be just the same as the real mother is at best double-think, at worst nonsense. Three decades of exciting, tumultuous social progress have established women's rights to move into the work world on a basis of full equality with men. Perhaps it is time to reaffirm their right as young mothers to stay home with children and to recognize child care as one of the most valuable kinds of work a man or woman can do." I agree wholeheartedly.

Anyone about to begin childrearing really ought to read this book. Anyone concerned with the quality of life of infants, toddlers, and preschoolers would profit immensely from considering this exhaustive, first-rate treatment of what is easily the most controversial topic in the field today.

Child Learning Through Child Play
Ira Gordon
St. Martin's Press, 1972

Dr. Gordon was one of the earliest members of the educational establishment to create training programs for young parents. His work concentrates on helping parents with very modest educational backgrounds and income levels to work effectively with their children. The curriculum itself does not come in any consistent way from a large body of relevant research information. Instead, it's eclectic, borrowing some things from Piaget, some things from various test items on standard achievement tests for infants, and some others from common sense. In my opinion, the curriculum does not seem to have any particular power.

Childproofing Your Home
Arlene Stewart
Addison-Wesley, 1984

This helpful, simple, and inexpensive book is a must for all new parents. The author does an extremely good job of pointing out common hazards and discusses how to avoid them in a clear, room-by-room approach.

Children and Adults
John and Laurie Braga
Prentice-Hall, 1976

The Bragas' work in this area is considerably more sophisticated than most popular books on this topic. They are extensively informed about much of the child development research that has been done over the years. Unfortunately, in my opinion, the majority of that work has to be interpreted very liberally for it to become directly applicable to the practical needs in educating young children. As a result, the book is not quite as useful as the talents of the authors might suggest.

Choosing Toys for Children from Birth to Age Five
Barbara Kaban
Schocken Books, 1979

The author of this book was the assistant director of the Harvard Preschool Project for many years, and she is as knowledgeable about the subject of toys as anyone. The book provides excellent general guidelines and cites many specific, well-chosen "recommended" and "nonrecommended" items. I recommend the book highly.

Crying Baby, Sleepless Nights
Sandy Jones
Warner Books, 1983

This book by Sandy Jones combines the strengths and weaknesses of her earlier writings—*Good Things for Babies*, which I thought was of outstanding value to parents, and *To Love a Baby*, of which I thought considerably less.

Now comes *Crying Baby, Sleepless Nights*. The first question is: Why write a book of this sort? Is it likely to meet a significant need? The answer is a definite *yes*. There is no doubt that crying babies produce stress in the lives of parents, especially first-time parents. In this book, you will learn everything you ever wanted to know about crying—and more. For the most part, the book concentrates on the distressful aspects of a baby's behavior in the first few months of life, although it does deal with stress-inducing developments throughout the first year of life. In particular, there are treatments of sleep problems, the evolving nature of the cry, working mothers, and the "perfect mother" myth.

The book is very well written. Its strongest treatments seem to be on the topics of breastfeeding—making extensive use of the wonderful work of the La Leche League; the development of personality—which is perhaps the most useful section of the book; describing a baby's symptoms to a physician—which includes a first-rate chart; and the "shut-down system"—a process whereby, among other things, when a baby is distressed and begins to suck vigorously, other sensations diminish in their impact.

Jones has scoured the American literature and many foreign studies for clues—sound and well-established clues as well as obscure and shaky ones. Her good treatments all deal with issues that are bound to be of concern to parents. Taken in proper doses, and with due caution regarding the less effective parts, they make the book potentially of great value.

I say "potentially" because the book does have weaknesses that prevent me from recommending it for parents. The most serious of the weaknesses began to be clear early in the book. In her zeal, Jones attempts to describe the full range of reasons for a baby's distress. After the discussions of birth complications, high blood pressure, drugs, milk reactions, and colic in chapter 2, I felt that any new parent reading this book would be on the verge of trauma. For instance: "Still another form of milk reaction is cow's milk allergy. The baby's immunity system—his defense against disease—goes awry, so that his body fights against protein found in milk as though it was a disease bearer rather than a harmless food substance. White blood cells mount a reaction by attacking milk particles directly, and others attach themselves to the offending protein, preparing to destroy it. Specialized cells, called mast cells, that line the baby's intestines on the inside, release chemical substances to enable the body's disease fighters to leave the blood vessels and enter the area where the body's battle is being waged." Although this is no doubt accurate, I think the author's choice of words is unfortunate.

This quality persists over several chapters. There is a chart in the same chapter, called "What May Be Causing Your Baby's Reaction to Formula," that consists of a list of fairly serious reactions to formula that occur rather rarely; when put into a lengthy chart these represent overkill. The next chapter is called "Urinary Tract Infections." When speaking of the diagnosis and treatment of such infections, the author writes: "The presence of pus is also noted, indicating infection. . . . He [the doctor] may also insert a tiny tube called a catheter up the baby's urinary tube (called the urethra) in order to get a clean urine sample." And later, in describing the tests used, the following are listed: "Blood Urea Nitrogen Test, Cystograms (called IVP Cystogram and Radioactive Cystogram), and Nuclear Medicine Scan." By the time parents get to page 36, my guess is that a lot of them will be shivering.

The next chapter, on colic and the digestive organs, involves more of the same. "The search for an understanding of a baby's digestion has been spurred on by Hirschprung's disease, a rare malfunctioning of the infant's colon, thought to be due to failure of the development of the network of nerves that oversee the smooth operation of the lower digestive tract. . . . If the baby's colon fails to go into action, even after medical practices such as drugs and stimulation have been used, then surgery may be necessary to remove the non-functioning part of the bowel, re-attaching the remaining colon to the rectum." This is just too much for parents. It is especially ironic when you realize that the purpose of the book is to make things easier for them. This is one of the reasons we think that the best use of this book is by professionals—professionals who are knowledgeable enough not to be alarmed by this book and tactful enough not to pass on needless alarm to their clients.

The second reason for my equivocal recommendation of the book has to do with the author's enormous capacity to explore, digest, and report on research studies. The time she invested in this book must have been very great, but she tends to be uncritical with respect to the research studies. Too many of them are single, small-sample studies that have not been replicated. A continuing problem in the field of child development is that readers of such studies tend to jump off the mark very quickly, as if every study produced valid results, when such is rarely the case—especially when dramatic claims are involved.

For example, the author points out that in the first weeks of life, babies will imitate facial expressions and tongue protrusions of parents. It is true that two or three studies within the past few years have reported behaviors of this sort and have claimed that Piaget's earlier notions about the inability of neonates to imitate were in error. Their claim is that within the first month, imitative behaviors are definitely there. If you ask these people whether you can expect to find the behaviors routinely, the answer is no. One problem with being able to elicit a behavior that some people interpret as "imitation" in a neonate is that you set up expectations for parents that, in nearly all cases, will not be fulfilled. What is going to happen when the nine out of ten parents who read this book try to get imitative behavior out of their infant and fail to get it? Is that going to soothe their anxieties? On the contrary. Moreover, other reports in the recent literature call to question the interpretation of these behaviors as examples of "imitation." I have mentioned this controversy in my work, but the idea of looking for other findings that would either support or contradict the kinds of claims that the author supports does not seem to be characteristic of her.

The same is true about the claim in the book that babies only a few days old recognize their own names. Such a claim may be true, but it certainly is inconsistent with hundreds of studies of the growth of understanding of language, which indicate that the recognition of one's own name does not ordinarily occur during the first six months of life. Again, the author either is unaware of the large body of literature on the subject or for some reason does not care to bring a balanced view into her mustering of evidence for her position.

On the matter of full-time day care, there is a section—albeit a very brief one—that addresses the issue of the mother who wants to return to work when her infant is very young. Good advice is given on how to select a caretaker—either one who will come into the parents' home or one to whom the child can be taken. I looked to see what would be said about other aspects of this highly inflammatory issue. Would the author talk about group care in centers? Would she talk about the clear conflict between her long-standing emphasis on the importance of loving relationships and prompt responses to the baby's distress, and the like, and the trend toward both parents working outside the home from the time their infants are only a few months old? The answer was no—she did not care to grapple with these questions. I believe that if you are going to introduce the topic of full-time child care, you have an obligation to air it thoroughly and to take a position, even if some people won't like what you write.

In dealing with sleep problems, the author recommends that parents take the baby into their beds routinely. In my opinion, she neglects the transition from the cries of a newborn to those of the five- to six-month-old who has learned to use the cry intentionally to bring the parents to him. The problem of late-night crying once the child gets to be over six months of age is a very common one for parents, and it relates to interesting and important issues in early learning and overindulgence. The treatment of it in this book, unfortunately, is inadequate.

In summary, I would urge that professionals make use of this book selectively. Certainly, it brings to our attention many studies, some of which unquestionably are sound and interrelate well with others, on the practical and significant issue of distress in normal babies during the first year of life. The treatment of distress during the first months of life is far more extensive than any I have read previously. The professional who uses this book will have to be careful about its weaknesses, however, most conspicuously its uncritical treatment of research reports and its problems in the treatment of sleep disturbances and day care. I do not believe it is an appropriate book for direct use by parents because of its unfortunate quality of intimidation and threat. I am sure the author did not intend this, but I think that in her zeal to produce an impressive book, she simply let things get out of hand.

The Day Care Decision: What's Best for You and Your Child
William and Wendy Dreskin
M. Evans, 1983

The single most inflammatory topic involving young children today is the issue of full-time day care for infants. I find it interesting that the topic appears to be more inflammatory among professionals than it is among parents. Parents are concerned, however. Indeed, many of them either are carrying a huge load of guilt because they are using full-time day care for babies as young as two or three months of age or are feeling a good deal of pressure because they are *not* using it and they are hearing messages to the effect that they are not doing enough with their lives. Ironically, these feelings run very high, even though all parties concerned are decent, caring people.

Five of six outstanding books on the subject have been published in recent years. In addition, the subject has been treated rather extensively in popular magazines, especially those addressed to mothers. This book by the Dreskins is unique. The Dreskins bring to this important topic a perspective of people who not only have been professionally involved in early childhood education for some time but also have participated in the recent evolutions leading to the popularity of full-time child care. They modified their nursery school to become a provider of day care as well as early education. After almost two years of such experience, however, they were so uncomfortable that they felt they could not continue to offer that kind of service. Furthermore, they became highly motivated to write about the issues involved. The result is this book—a book written by warm, thoughtful practitioners—a book that clearly is a product of passion and deep concern.

The book's primary messages are that full-time day care for children under three years of age is rarely advisable (except in cases of extreme hardship) and that the people who choose to be full-time caretakers of their own children deserve full support because they are involved in something that is at least as important as anything else they might be doing. In addition, the Dreskins make a very strong case for increased involvement of men in the parenting process.

Having run a day care operation, they are in a much better position than many commentators on this subject to talk about the nuts and bolts of such activities. The examples taken from their own journals are telling, though admittedly over-dramatic on occasion. The information presented about the health hazards due to the spread of contagious diseases and about policies of European countries is to the point and most valuable.

In all, their message is quite similar to my own, which has come from a very lengthy period of research on what's best for young children. Although some of their reasons for their recommendations are quite different from mine, the conclusions almost totally overlap. This book brings to the debate on whether to use full-time day care for infants considerable thoughtfulness about the impact on the child and helps correct the current imbalance of emphasis on the needs of the parents. Therefore, I strongly recommend it.

Discipline Without Shouting or Spanking
Jerry Wyckoff and Barbara Unell
Meadowbrook, 1984

This book claims to provide "practical solutions to the most common preschool behavior problems." The authors are a child psychologist and a mother of two who has been publishing literature for parents for many years. The book is well written, well organized, and fairly comprehensive. The strategies suggested are based, in part, on child development theory but more often on the actual experience of the authors and other parents.

Many of the recommendations involve verbal explanations, so they are largely applicable to children beyond our focus of birth to three years. However, some of them will be effective for infants and toddlers, and I think parents will be grateful to have such well-researched, well-tested ideas presented to them in such a clear, easy-to-follow (and easy-to-find) fashion. Therefore, I consider this an extremely valuable resource for new parents, particularly as their children approach two and three years of age.

The Early Childhood Years
Frank and Theresa Caplan
Bantam, 1984

In reviewing earlier works by these authors (e.g., *The Second Twelve Months of Life*), I have noted that they are very successful commercially but very weak when it comes to validity of content. I only concerned myself with part of this new book, since our focus is limited to the first three years of life. Nevertheless, I found repeated reasons for concern.

The book begins with a mini-course in child development, in which we learn that "a parent can manipulate the limbs of a newborn infant. . . . Even though they are not initiated by the infant, if repeated sufficiently, these induced movements will lead to that infant attaining these skills ahead of an infant who is not stimulated in this way." The authors are referring to head balancing, grasping, and sitting up. I am quite sure that such claims cannot be supported by evidence.

In their overview of the early childhood years, the authors explain that, by two years of age, preference for using one arm, hand, or foot over the other is not well established. Their reference for this and many other statements in their book is Gesell's *The First Five Years of Life*, published in 1940. Although Gesell made very important contributions to the field of child development, much of his work, the majority of which was done more than forty years ago, obviously cannot be considered reliable, accurate, or up-to-date. Therefore, extensive reference to his findings and claims are not good enough in this day and age.

In the area of language acquisition, the Caplans repeat the classic error found so often in books about young children—that is, equating "language" with "speech." As I have warned repeatedly, ignoring the development of receptive language, especially during the first three years, can lead to significant difficulties. The authors' advice on promoting language development starts with "let your child talk." Also, I could find no treatment of the important problem of widespread mild to moderate hearing losses during the first few years of life, which so commonly interfere with good language development.

In the section on intellectual development, the Caplans refer to Raymond and Dorothy Moore, who surfaced back in the mid-1960s to argue against calls for early schooling. In some ways, their position made sense, and I even supported parts of it. But to cite the Moores as experts on the course of learning is a bit farfetched, since their reputations as serious students of the developmental process are not much stronger than those of the Caplans.

Turning to play and toys, the Caplans say, "We cannot over-emphasize that building blocks are the finest home and school play materials for children from two up to seven years and even beyond." There is no basis for such a statement. In describing the twenty-five- to thirty-month-old child, the references cited are the aforementioned book by Gesell along with another one of their favorites, *Life and Ways of the Two Year Old*, by Louise Phinney-Woodcock. In the introduction, we learn that this author was a sensitive teacher in an experimental nursery school for two-year-olds in the 1930s and 1940s and that her book is no longer in print.

A little further on, we learn that "singing enhances language acquisition." There is not much wrong with making a statement of that sort if you don't pretend it is an authoritative one—but of course, this book purports to offer the most authoritative information available to help parents raise their children. Finally, the Caplans tell parents to expect negativism and resistant behavior during the third year of life—as if the negativism and resistant behavior of the second year didn't exist. As in pinpointing other developments, they are far enough wrong that parents who follow their advice can expect a lot of surprises.

If the Caplans were not so skillful in designing and marketing their books, and if the books weren't so successful in terms of sales, I wouldn't devote much time or effort to them. However, the fact is that they are on the shelves of large numbers of families. I think this is unfortunate. It is not that there is nothing good about them. It is not that they don't contain a fair amount of good information. They do. But they are loaded with misinformation, and that is not good enough for either professionals or parents. Once again, frustration at the inability of our educational system to help parents in this regard, to steer them to the good material and help them avoid the nonsense, is aggravated by the arrival of yet another product from an operation that, in my opinion, just isn't qualified to be doing this kind of work.

Father Power
Henry Biller, Ph.D., and Dennis Meredith
Anchor Press, 1975

Everything that we know reliably about the role of the father probably could be printed on a few pages. These authors have managed to produce almost four hundred pages on the subject, which is even more remarkable considering how much of our limited knowledge has been generated in the years since this book was published. Many of the thoughts and opinions expressed are interesting and potentially useful, but parents and professionals should be aware that much of what is being presented as authoritative information is at best, simply inappropriate extrapolations of the knowledge base and, at worst, wishful thinking or "what the reader wants to hear."

First Feelings: Milestones in the Emotional Development of Your Baby and Child
Stanley Greenspan and Nancy Thorndike Greenspan
Viking, 1985

The topic of this book is a much neglected and terribly valuable one. Stanley Greenspan, as founder of the National Center for Clinical Infant Programs, has done wonderful work in helping to advance infant mental health research and public awareness of the vital importance of good development in the early years. Unfortunately, however, I cannot give the book a rave review.

The authors use a six-stage framework to describe the progress of emotional development. They call the six stages emotional milestones. The first milestone begins in the early weeks of life, when babies are confronted with two simultaneous challenges—to feel regulated and calm and to use all their senses to take an interest in the world. The milestones move on through the fourth year of life, with the sixth stage consisting of an expansion of the child's world of ideas into the emotional realms of pleasure, dependency, curiosity, assertiveness, anger, self-discipline, and even empathy and love. Eventually, children learn to separate make-believe from reality and are able to work with ideas and to plan and anticipate. These six stages seem to be original with the authors.

They then proceed to go into detail about each of these stages. The subheadings "Observing Your Baby," "Creating a Supportive Environment," and "Reviewing Your Support" form the outline for the first three stages. They also are included in the next three stages, along with sections on "Emotions and Cognition," "Creating Ideas," "Appreciating How the World Works," "Your Child's Personality Functions," and "Emotional Memory and Repression." This is followed by a brief concluding section, and there is also an appendix in which the reader is helped to chart his or her own child's emotional milestones.

Traditionally, there has been a principal division in the field of child development research. On the one hand, there are people who are interested in the so-called hard topics—for example, the development of physical abilities, perceptual skills, language, intelligence, and the like. On the other hand, there are those who are interested in the so-called soft topics. This humanistic group orients toward the parent–child relationship, self-concept, creativity, emotional well-being, and other such topics.

The first group has achieved a deserved reputation for being more scientific and more reliable when it comes to research methodology and also for tending to have little or nothing to say about the subjects that are of concern to the second group. The second group generally is applauded because they investigate subjects that many people feel are the most important with respect to humanistic values. Research problems associated with investigating humanistic issues have always been considerably more complicated and resistant to solid findings than those associated with the topics favored by the other group of researchers.

Since I'm a humanist, I try to examine fairly all serious efforts of the second group and to apply considerably less rigorous standards to the evaluation of their research and their conclusions. In other words, I would rather have somebody investigate subjects that I value highly, using the best available methods, than remain safely in the work that can be done with greater validity but does not address what I consider to be the most important issues. It is from this background that I approach a book like this one.

One of the classic problems I keep running into when I read books by people from the second group is an almost routine tendency toward adult-amorphism—that is, the projection of some of one's own capacities as an adult into the mind of the baby. Much as I applaud and value the work of my colleague Berry Brazelton, I have often felt it necessary to complain about his style in that sense. Indeed, this is just about a tradition in the field of psychiatric writings.

In the introduction to *First Feelings*, I found myself writing "adult-amorphism" in the margin. This was after reading the following sentences: "In the early weeks of life, babies are confronted with two simultaneous challenges: to feel regulated and calm, and to use all their senses to take an interest in the world. . . . The ability to organize these sensations—to feel tranquil in spite of them and to reach out actively for them—is the first milestone." It may seem like nitpicking, but to talk about a newborn using all of his senses to take an interest in the world is to run the risk of subtly misleading parents about the capacity for initiative in the very young infant.

My standard for gauging the mental capacities of infants and toddlers is the work of Piaget. Not everybody would agree that Piaget was the outstanding authority in this area, but I cannot think of any substantial competition, including Freud. In Piaget's system, the first intentional behavior of babies surfaces at about six or seven months of age, when they simply push an object aside to get to one that they would like to reach. Before this, and especially in the first months of life, Piaget pictures babies as having no initiative but, rather, as being relatively mechanical responders to outside stimuli that mesh with their built-in reflex-like responses. In all the years I've studied babies, I have always found Piaget's position on this matter to be compatible with my own research and observations.

By the time I got to the end of the introduction to *First Feelings*, I simply wrote, "The writing is superb, but I don't know about the ideas. . . . I am skeptical." Later on, while discussing the newborn, the authors make the following statement. "His ability to look outward helps him to regulate his own internal reactions. . . . This ability to focus the senses on the external world in order to feel calm and relaxed is, perhaps, the newborn infant's greatest asset." Once again, this struck me as inappropriate.

In terms of providing advice to parents, I also wonder about the validity of the authors' position. On page 16 they state: "You can also help orient your baby toward a world that is rich and deep by helping him regulate his senses and by providing him with opportunities to experience a wide range of feelings." Although I have a lot of respect for Dr. Greenspan's competence and experience, I can't think of any research that supports this notion.

This is not the kind of book in which the authors are obliged to cite research to support their points of view, but I get very worried when recommendations do not relate to anything I've ever heard of in the literature. Farther down on the same page, the authors go on: "Good mastery of the first steps can strongly influence the climb to the next. But if for some reason this is not possible at first, there are always opportunities later on to go back a few steps and rebuild." Once again, I do not know any basis for these recommendations. Indeed, by the bottom of page 19, my commentary became stronger, and I wrote, "Where on earth do these ideas come from?"

The authors move on to talk about the interactions between parental personality and infant needs. This is a very interesting approach that has substantial promise. In talking about a relatively subdued parenting style, on page 33, they say: "When they talk to their baby or look at her, their faces lack expression or their vocal tone may be rather monotonous. Obviously this sort of behavior will give an infant a rather monotonous idea of what the world is like, but with active effort, such parents can nonetheless help their baby to see the world as an interesting place." First, I don't believe that there is evidence to support the claim of the impact of such parenting behavior. Second, I think it is unfortunate that the authors use the term "idea" when dealing with a baby who is less than twelve or thirteen weeks old. It is careless at best. In summary, I was very disappointed with the first segment of the book.

With regard to the two- to seven-month-old baby, the authors talk about parents who are sensitive to being rejected. "She expects wooing and comforting herself. Occasionally, the mother who is sensitive to rejection 'overwoos' her baby. In other words, instead of admitting her sensitivity, she says, 'Me, afraid of rejection? Never—I take what I want and I get what I take.' " At this point, I began feeling that the authors' lengthy experience in situations of emotional distress was impinging inappropriately on the topic at hand. Surely there are parents who have all sorts of emotional difficulty when dealing with new babies, but what this book is trying to do is address the entire literate population. As is so often the case with writings by people with one or another specialty, there is the risk of bringing indications of pathological or mildly pathological behavior into the description of the ordinary course of events.

I am reminded of *Crying Baby, Sleepless Nights* by Sandy Jones, in which the author describes the sources of discomfort for infants. In doing an exhaustive job, she ended up portraying the life of the young baby in often horrifying terms and, in the process, distorted what ordinarily takes place in a way that was not productive. The authors of *First Feelings*, in trying to deal comprehensively with parental fears, for example, devote a great deal of space to "Fear of Closeness," "Fear of Rejection," "Feelings of Envy," "Fear of Hurting Your Own Baby," and the like. I am afraid that represents overkill.

On page 68, I lost all control. My comments in the margin included "No, this isn't so!" "evidence?" "why?" "basis?" "how many?" At the bottom of the page, I wrote that it does not appear that these authors really know babies. Of course, if I make a statement like that, the authors and their supporters do not like to hear it. But for me, such a statement is a most serious indictment.

By the time the authors started dealing with children at ten months of age, I had added the comment that their treatment of sibling rivalry is inadequate. Further on in the book, I repeated this observation. It came as something of a surprise to me that sibling rivalry was not handled with any particular sensitivity, since this is the kind of issue on which the authors should be strong.

I don't want to belabor these points. Suffice it to say that this tone of skepticism, of concern about the depth of the authors' knowledge regarding the details of development, of concern about the tendency to see pathology or to talk in pathological terms when trying to educate the average adult continued to characterize my comments throughout the book, chapter after chapter. On the other hand, the book is always clear in what it is trying to say. There are occasional passages that are first-rate—and there are very few books that address this topic in any serious way at all.

In my opinion, this book makes for a good beginning on a very important subject. I would recommend it for professionals but, frankly, not for parents—especially not for first-time parents. Professionals who are knowledgeable about early development can take what is good from this book and will profit by adding it to their own backgrounds. However, I think parents would probably be misled too often and frightened too often, so that the book might actually hinder rather than help their efforts.

The First Five Years: A Relaxed Approach to Child Care
Virginia Pomeranz, M.D., and Jodie Schultz
Doubleday, 1984

This is the second edition of a book that was originally published in 1973 and apparently has sold very well. It covers both medical and educational issues; however, although it seems to do a good job with respect to the former, it does a rather weak job with respect to the latter. Recommendations concerning the day-to-day care of the child are quite impressive, but many recommendations concerning other aspects of the child's life reflect an inadequate understanding of the learning process during the first years of life.

As is the case with many other books for parents, much of the advice provided is appropriate only for children over two and a half years of age, even though the problem being addressed may surface well before that time. Typically, such advice prescribes relatively sophisticated verbal interchanges to manage the behavior of a child who, for a fair portion of the age range under discussion, may have a very limited command of language.

Furthermore, several important issues are addressed at inappropriate points in the developmental continuum, and others are not addressed at all. Safety-proofing a home is described too late, as is the concept of individuality. The discussion of discipline is quite vague, and nothing is said about television viewing. When sibling rivalry is finally treated, the treatment turns out to be quite poor. The section on pets is excellent, but the section dealing with toys leaves much to be desired.

The last portion of the book is devoted to "The 33 Most Asked Questions: A Checklist for Parents," which is pretty good. However, the few strengths of the book are outweighed by its shortcomings; therefore, I cannot recommend it.

The First Wondrous Year
Edited by R. A. Chase, M.D., and R. R. Rubin, Ph.D.
Johnson & Johnson Publications, 1979

No single book will meet all the informational needs of new parents. No single author knows enough to cover all the physical and emotional health issues, along with the topics of learning, discipline, and parental relations and anxieties. Even when a team is assembled to produce a book, the result cannot be expected to be fully comprehensive. This book appeared to be typically variable in accuracy in its early passages. However, I became increasingly impressed by it as I continued to read—so much so that I can add it to my modest list of valuable books for new parents.

The book's weaknesses are as follows. It often seems to be telling parents what they would like to hear rather than what is known, especially in regard to the role of the father (it's very important) and the impact of full-time day care on infants less than one year old (such infants profit from very early social experiences with peers; it's the quality not the quantity of parent–infant time that counts). The authors do a great deal of adult-amorphizing as well, a practice that seems appealing and harmless but that I think misleads the reader. For example, the entire treatment of what goes on in the mind of a neonate is contradicted by Piaget's work on the mental capacities of infants. In addition, the authors are not careful about the meaning of new research studies. They tend to accept as established findings conclusions that are based on single studies with very few subjects. They also seem to misinterpret others (e.g., the temperament studies of Birch et al.). Perhaps the most serious flaw is in the portrayal of sibling behavior as basically loving and helpful. Pity the poor parents of a two-year-old with a ten-month-old sibling who expect only sweetness from the older child toward the baby. Another major weakness is the failure to alert parents to the problem of moderate hearing losses during the first year of life.

Nevertheless, the book is worth having. The treatment of the emotional needs of parents and infants is the best I have seen anywhere. Colic, a most difficult phenomenon for many new parents, is dealt with beautifully, as are numerous other stressful conditions, such as the changes an infant produces in a marriage, the normal anxieties of parents in the first weeks, the "difficult" baby, and so on. The sections on physical development are very well done, especially as many photos are used to illustrate the points in the text. The sections on exploring, on moving, and on making the home safe and interesting for a baby are all first-rate.

In summary, I recommend this book as one of several that new parents would profit from. Its greatest strength lies in its treatment of the many important emotional aspects of the first year of parenting. It has other virtues as well, including its generally excellent treatment of physical development and its wonderful illustrations. However, the reader should be aware of its limitations in the area of educational development as well as its occasional significant errors.

The First Year of Life
Edited by the staff of American Baby Magazine
American Baby Magazine, 1981

American Baby magazine is one of the larger of several publications offered free of charge to new parents (income is derived exclusively from advertisers). I have had dealings with a number of such magazines over the years, and I have found that they vary widely in quality.

A few years ago, *American Baby* published a special edition, entitled "The First Year of Life," which they then made available in hardcover book form. This publication represented a switch from their previous reliance on the offerings of Frank Caplan (e.g., *The First Twelve Months of Life*) to a home-grown document with minor editorial assistance from outside consultants, including Burton White. (I mention my input because, in a sense, I am violating the principle of total impartiality here, and you should know it.)

I believe this publication is outstanding. It represents a comprehensive approach to child care, rather than a particular focus on physical, emotional, or educational needs. The writing, organization, and validity of information are all of unusually high quality. Much credit should go to the editor, Judy Nolte. I recommend this book for both parents and professionals.

Game Plans for Children
Jeanne Hanson
Penguin Books, 1981

The promotional material for this book says that it "shows busy parents how to set aside quality time each day . . . to improve a child's skills and creativity . . . [and] if the reader will invest ten minutes a day, substantial benefits will result."

The author, a journalist, and her husband both work outside the home and presumably share with other such couples a concern that they might neglect the learning needs of their children. Clearly, her goal is worthy, but to think that ten minutes a day can be a powerful preventive tool is simply fooling oneself.

Many of the suggested activities seem to reflect thoughtfulness, and some unquestionably would prove instructive. Yet the book as a whole has not roots that warrant confidence. There is no obvious reason why most of the activities are suggested, and there is no indication of likely effectiveness. It is difficult to understand why a major publishing company took a chance on this book.

Games Babies Play
Julie Hagstrom and Joan Morrill
A & W Visual Library, 1979

This handbook of games for babies from birth to one year of age was written by mother and daughter schoolteachers from California, and it is based on their experiences with their own daughter-granddaughter. The book reaches for numerous goals for infants, but the goals are not necessarily important or valid. For instance, some games recommended for the first six weeks of life are designed to "stimulate the newborn's perception," "help her recognize her own sense of rhythm," and "help her become aware of similarities between herself and others." The knowledge base upon which this book draws simply is too inadequate for me to recommend it.

Good Things for Babies
Sandy Jones
Houghton Mifflin, 1976

This is a clearly useful and unusual book for new parents. It is a practical guide to the selection and utilization of physical materials for children, such as car seats, walkers, toys, and the like. The author's judgment seems to be consistent with everything I know about young children, with only a few minor exceptions. Therefore, I recommend the book very highly.

Growing Wisdom, Growing Wonder
E. Gregg and J. Knotts
Macmillan, 1980

This book is intended to guide parents as they teach children from birth to five years of age. The authors are experienced and clearly talented early childhood educators, and the book is very well written. The writing reflects intelligence, warmth, and wit. Many of the recommended activities are compatible with what is known about early development, but many are not. The attempt to be thorough leads to shorter and less convincing chapters as the book progresses. Also, a conscientious parent would soon be overloaded by the number of "things to do." There are some significant errors and omissions on the subject of development. Overall, this is a much better than average treatment of early teaching, but it still leaves much to be desired.

The Heart Has Its Own Reasons
Mary Ann Cahill
La Leche League, 1983

This excellent book from the La Leche League deals with the subject of full-time day care for babies. Like its sister publication, *Of Cradles and Careers*, by Kay Loman, this book makes a sane and passionate case for parents to make every effort to retain primary responsibility for raising their own children. It presents case histories of parents who managed to do this, despite what seemed to be insurmountable career and financial obstacles.

Help Your Baby Learn
Stephen Lehane
Prentice-Hall, 1976

The author of this book is a member of the faculty of education at Kent State University, and he is very well informed about Piaget's views on the origins of intelligence. The book, suitable for parents and parent educators, describes 100 Piagetian-based activities for the first two years of life. Provided that these topics are approached in a low-key manner and that it is recognized that sensorimotor development ordinarily does not require special "teaching" or "exercise," parents and practitioners should find this book a valuable asset. Although the book does not represent a comprehensive or totally validated approach to raising children, it is basically quite sound.

How to Grow a Parents Group
D. Mason, G. Hensen, and C. Ryzewicz
International Childbirth Association, 1979

The Parent and Childbirth Education Society (PACES) is a remarkable parent support organization based in a suburb of Chicago. Many volunteer groups to help new parents have come into existence within the past ten to fifteen years. PACES is one of the oldest, largest, and best managed. In this well-written book, three of the key figures in the organization fill an important need by describing how to create and sustain a private parent support group without primary support from educational institutions or government or even substantial funds. I recommend it highly.

How to Parent
Fitzhugh Dodson
Signet, 1970

This book is very well written. The author speaks his mind clearly on a wide variety of topics. Unfortunately, his grasp of the knowledge base is very uneven, and it is particularly weak for the birth to three range. He refers the reader to Gesell for information on the first years, and he provides few details beyond that reference. Although I like Dodson's style, his content simply is not strong enough for me to recommend this book.

How to Teach Your Baby to Read
Glenn Doman
Random House, 1964

Glenn Doman is best known as the director of the Better Baby Institute in Philadelphia, where, for a fee, parents can spend a week learning how to be "superior parents"—capable of teaching their children to read, play the violin, do mathematics, and perform a host of other precocious activities while they are still infants and toddlers. Doman has never permitted an independent third-party evaluation of his work, and he has a long history of hostility toward those who seek to investigate what he is doing. Moreover, what he claims he can do goes contrary to hundreds of other studies throughout the history of child development research, which indicate that although amazing precocities can be achieved, they probably cannot be achieved without sacrificing something in the child's overall, well-balanced development.

This book outlines Doman's recommendations for teaching reading as well as some of his general philosophy. Some of it is quite insightful and interesting. However, most of what he says cannot be substantiated by any available evidence. Therefore, I feel that I must caution both professionals and parents about accepting his statements.

Improving Your Child's Behavior Chemistry
Lendon Smith
Pocket Books, 1976

This is one of several books by one of the more popular authors in the field. Dr. Smith is a clever and witty fellow who appears regularly on the Johnny Carson show, and he writes about "what you can do about the eating habits and vitamin imbalances that may be making your child unruly, unresponsive, and unhappy."

Since I am not a medical person, I am not qualified to comment on what is in this book. However, I have had contact with medical people all across the country who have warned me that Dr. Smith's ideas are not medically sound, and he has been taken to task by various medical credentialing bodies. Therefore, I hold this book up as another example of something that is commercially successful but not necessarily based on solid information.

In a Family Way
Susan Lapinski and Michael Decourcy Hinds
Little, Brown, 1982

In this charming book, the authors—both professional writers in their thirties—present the personal story of the pregnancy, delivery, and first year of their first child, Jessica. I found the book very easy to read. The authors write extremely well, and they write with enthusiasm, warmth, and sensitivity. The book could have been a highly egocentric and uninteresting product, but the authors' humor, sincerity, and talent seems to have prevented that from happening.

Although the authors are well-educated Northeasterners, thereby limiting the capacity of some readers to identify with them, we think their story is interesting enough that most people who are focused on the topic (especially first-time expectant parents) are likely to be touched and even informed in useful ways by this book. I recommend it highly.

Infant and Child in the Culture of Today
A. Gesell and F. Ilg
Harper, 1943

Gesell's work may strike readers as somewhat archaic. After all, most of it is more than forty years old. Gesell provided information of remarkable usefulness in the diagnosis of developmental difficulties in preschoolers. He was not very much impressed by the power of early experiences to influence development, however, and his views emphasized the role of genetics and maturation.

Infant Care
U.S. Department of Health, Education and Welfare
Children's Bureau Publication #8, U.S. Government Printing Office, 1967

For most of this century, editions of this book have been distributed broadly to the families of this country. Apparently, it is the single most popular document that the U.S. Government Printing Office has ever made available to the public. The fee for it always has been nominal, and within its pages are found a distillation of the conventional wisdom of each decade concerning the management of the child. Historical analyses of the contents of the many editions of *Infant Care* have shown that its recommendations to parents have shifted with whatever ideas were prevalent in child development research at any point in time. Furthermore, there are topics within the book wherein the directions to parents have taken a 180-degree turn in the space of only a few years. This vacillation on fundamental issues in childrearing is a reflection of the immaturity of the knowledge base in the field.

Let Me Introduce Myself
Ernest Lignon et al.
Union College Character Research Project, 1976

For many years, Dr. Lignon has directed the Character Research Project at Union College in Schenectady, New York. The project's goals, which have been laudable, have rarely been pursued by people in academic circles. Rather than concerning themselves with the child's intellectual development, the Union College Project people have been oriented toward the value systems and character formation of young children. Unfortunately, the project has been largely unsuccessful, and this book has had no adequate guidance from what we have learned from reliable research on young children. As a result, its claims for effectiveness seem to be quite unproven; therefore, I cannot recommend the book.

The Magic Years
Selma Fraiberg
Scribner, 1959

Although first published in 1959, this book maintains its youthful magic and delight for contemporary readers. It describes the young child from birth through six years of age, dealing largely with psychoanalytic concerns buttressed by Dr. Fraiberg's clinical experience. The author's fresh, creative style overcomes most shackles one might associate with the psychoanalytic tradition. The sections dealing with sex identity, however, do challenge the contemporary reader to rethink sex role assumptions. This is an excellent book for parents and professionals. It can enlighten and sensitize adults to the very special perspective of the young child.

The Mothers' Book
R. Friedland and C. Kort (eds.)
Houghton Mifflin, 1981

This is a superb, well-edited collection of essays by and interviews with sixty-four mothers, in which they frankly discuss their feelings about various aspects of motherhood. The range of topics is broad, covering both "popular" issues (e.g., breastfeeding, staying at home, etc.) and rather unusual ones (e.g., having triplets, dealing with the Oedipal triangle, etc.). The concerns shared also cover a wide range, from everyday hassles to political commitments, and the views expressed are equally varied and well-balanced.

Some of the essays and interviews are humorous, some are moving, and some are thought-provoking; some are all three (one by Maureen X. O'Brien, entitled "The First Six Months," is a particularly good example). The book has something for everyone, and I recommend it highly.

The New Extended Family
Ellen Galinsky and William Hooks
Houghton Mifflin, 1977

The authors of this book are specialists in early childhood at Bank Street College of Education in New York, a leading institution in early childhood education. The book provides an introduction to a variety of child care systems through a systematic analysis of fourteen programs that the authors consider "solid."

The book begins with a powerful statement to the effect that the idea that the American family is or can be independent is a myth. In the view of the authors, all families require help, especially those families in which the woman with children needs or wants to work. They are reinforced in this position by the report of the Carnegie Council on Children (*All Our Children*, by Kenneth Kenniston, 1977). Unlike the Carnegie Council, however, the authors choose to concentrate on the issue of full-time day care as a primary source of family support, rather than the host of other factors sometimes cited (e.g., low-income, the effects of television, etc.).

The second chapter presents a set of sixty-seven guidelines for evaluating child care systems. The authors cite "in what ways does the program respect and reflect the values and goals of the parents?" as the key criterion. The bulk of the book is then devoted to detailed descriptions of the fourteen types of child care systems, which range from after-school care for six- to twelve-year-olds in a Chinese neighborhood in New York, through public, private, and for-profit day care for infants and preschoolers, to an experimental attempt to identify and assist individual babysitters in several neighborhoods in Portland, Oregon.

The authors conclude with their views on the essential ingredients of high-quality programs. In particular, they underline the necessity for strong, totally dedicated leadership. They also provide recommendations for governmental actions that they and various program directors feel are needed for high-quality child care to survive and grow.

The identification and detailed descriptions of the programs constitute an important contribution to parents and professionals. Any parent seeking child care will gain a valuable perspective from reading this book. Also, the introduction, in warm tones, of the many devoted and talented program personnel makes for inspirational reading. The book is well organized and well written, and it is the only book of its kind that I have seen.

The book does have its weaknesses, primarily in the area of program evaluation. Although the programs are introduced as exemplary, the authors, as early childhood specialists, have a responsibility to provide assessments of the likely effects of these programs on children. However, the most reasonable assumption the reader can make is that whatever is promised by the program is delivered, whether it comes from a profit-oriented center director or a paraprofessional family day care worker. In fact, in describing the programs, the authors' routine comments suggest a rather thin background in evaluating child development research. For example, one program is described as having a particularly beautiful physical plant, designed by an architect so that each piece of equipment would encourage perceptual-motor and cognitive growth. The authors simply present such statements and then move on to the next topic, neglecting to point out that such promises are common in early education, but no one has yet shown how to design equipment with such beneficial effects.

Again, in describing a program for low-income families, a long list of goals is cited, including preparation for school and increases in self-image and self-respect. These are laudable goals, of course, but with no comment whatsoever by the authors, the reader is led to believe that the program does just what it says it aims for. Sadly, there is little reason to believe that many programs, including those described in this book, can deliver on such promises.

In a related area, a central concern that involved people have about full-time child care—the effects on the child's emotional tie to the parents—is treated altogether too briefly and too lightly. In fairness, however, the authors seem to be convinced that there is little threat to the child's emotional health, provided that the child care system in question is of high quality.

All told, I believe this is a valuable book for professionals in that it is a rich introductory survey of the many models of child care currently in existence around the country. It also can be of considerable value to parents as they begin to explore their options for child care services. Anyone who uses this book, however, should reserve judgment on the authors' evaluations of the effects of these programs on children, particularly children under three years of age.

A New Vaccine for Child Safety
Murl Harmon
Safety Now Company, 1976

The author of this book is a businessman who owns the Safety Now Company, which distributes literature, toys, and baby gear that he has screened for safety. The first chapter is devoted to safety in the first year. The greatest emphasis is placed on the use of a playpen whenever the baby is not eating or sleeping as the only safe place for the child to be. Ensuing chapters discuss safety issues up through adolescence. The scope of the book is cosmic—there is even a section on nuclear holocausts. Unfortunately, the general tone is amateurish, especially when dealing with developmental issues.

Of Cradles and Careers: A Guide to Reshaping Your Job to Include a Child in Your Life
Kaye Loman
La Leche League, 1984

As almost everyone interested in young children knows, the La Leche League has breast-feeding as its central focus. Closely allied to this concern is the league's apprehension about family situations in which there is a new child and both parents are working outside the home full-time. Rather than simply wringing their hands about it, however, the folks at the La Leche League are trying to offer constructive suggestions. This very special book is published in that spirit; in my opinion, it represents a wonderful contribution to the parent education literature.

The book is a serious attempt to encourage parents to "have it all" but in a realistic way. The book claims and documents the possibility of continuing a career *and* retaining primary responsibility for raising one's own children (and successfully breast-feeding as well, of course). Extensive, convincing case studies are presented of women who have managed to pull off this impressive achievement, along with extensive discussions of such concepts as flex-time, the reduced work week, shared jobs, self-employment, the role of the father, decision making in selecting child care, and so on. The book is very well organized and well written, and the appendix section contains an excellent and extensive listing of resources.

I believe this book is especially noteworthy because it goes beyond the polarized views of those who are either firmly for or firmly against full-time day care for young children. As I reviewed it, I looked for signs of extreme positions and strident statements, and I was pleased to find nothing of the sort. It is only fair to point out that I share many of the La Leche League's biases with regard to the topics covered in this book, so I may not be totally objective. Nevertheless, for any young couple trying to figure out what to do about the all-too-often conflicting demands of career and parenthood, this is by far the best book I have found, and I recommend it highly.

Open Connections: The Other Basics
Susan Shilcock and Peter Bergson
Open Connections, 1980

This is a pleasant and useful book, dealing with the creation of environments and materials for preschoolers that foster the development of "the other basics," such as decision-making ability and self-esteem. The authors have based their recommendations primarily on their own preschool and family experience, rather than on basic research and/or particular developmental theory.

Although much of this book deals with children older than three years, many ideas presented are relevant for younger children. Some of them, especially those dealing with the creation of safe but challenging learning environments, are remarkably on target, considering that the authors have had very little formal training in this area.

Although I am not qualified to comment on many of the topics covered in this book, I think that parents will find the Open Connections approach to early education interesting—and their infants and toddlers will find many products of this approach interesting as well.

Parenting: Principles and Politics of Parenthood
Sidney Cornelia Callahan
Penguin Books, 1974

This is an unusually valuable book. The author is a syndicated columnist and a mother of six children. She is a remarkably bright, well-read, and very skillful writer. This is not a "how-to" book, and it does not pretend to be a substitute for one. (In fact, the author recommends that parents read several "how-to" books, and there is an excellent chapter on how to read books by "experts.") Instead, this book is a guide to the general subject of parenting by an unusually thoughtful participant and observer of the process. Although the scope of this book is broader than the first years of life, a great deal of emphasis is placed on this important period. I recommend the book highly.

A Parent's Guide to Child Therapy
Richard Bush
Delacorte Press, 1980

For many years, I have been concerned with—and frustrated by—the problems surrounding emotional difficulties of young children. It is clear that sooner or later, some percentage of young children exhibit the kinds of behaviors that convince their parents or other adults that there is some sort of underlying problem. We do not typically call two- or three-year-olds "neurotic" or "psychotic." Instead, the term that has become popular is "behavior disordered." Children as young as three or four years of age can be considered to have problems significant enough to warrant this classification. Examples of behavior disorders are unusual aggression, withdrawal, and the like.

Until recently, I have been unable (with any degree of confidence) to suggest to parents what to do if their very young children begin to show such signs. Frankly, the reason for my reluctance to make recommendations has been a lack of confidence in the fields of child psychiatry and clinical child psychology. Nothing in my early training or subsequent experience had indicated to me that either field had dealt consistently well with children under five years of age. Of course, there must have been exceptions, but I did not know what or where they were and therefore felt unable to make positive recommendations. In fact, I have always had a sense that some forms of psychiatric treatment could do more damage than good to certain patients.

In any event, the book under review is, in my opinion, an extraordinarily valuable breakthrough. It is not that Dr. Bush points to methods of treatment that are likely to solve emotional problems in preschool children—he does not, except in very few situations. However, he does the next best thing—he provides a remarkably rational and comprehensive introduction to the whole subject of child therapy. For example, the title of part 1 is "When, Where, and How to Get Help." Bush then comes through on the promise in that title. Some of the chapter titles are "Does My Child Need Help?" "Emotional Problems of Childhood and Adolescence," "Learning Disabilities and Hyperactivity," "Places to Go for Help." Part 2, entitled "A Step by Step Guide for Getting Help," is every bit as sane and useful. Some of its chapter headings are "Obtaining Help from a Therapist in Private Practice," "Obtaining Help in a Clinic Setting," "Evaluating Therapy," "Psychiatric Emergencies," "National Organizations."

Bush provides a wealth of understandable, jargon-free information about the nature of the subject and how to cope with it; furthermore, this book is written in a realistic yet very reassuring tone. The author reveals a remarkable degree of common sense and a capacity for dealing with subjects in a concise and accurate way. Have you ever wanted to know more about the modern views on masturbation, enuresis, nail-biting, thumb-sucking, and rocking behavior? Well, it's all here, and it's presented in an altogether admirable manner.

By now, you may have sensed that this is a rave review. You also should know that I am generally considered a tough critic and not particularly in awe of people in child psychiatry. However, if you need a book to introduce parents to this subject, I urge you to get a copy of this one.

Personality in Young Children
Lois Murphy
Basic Books, 1956

Lois Murphy, working with four colleagues from related disciplines, studied the growth of personality in a group of nursery school children at Sarah Lawrence College in New York some thirty years ago. This entire book is devoted to a description of the ups and downs of one nicely put-together child from that study. It is a rich documentation of normal personality development.

Revolution in Learning
Maya Pines
Harper & Row, 1967

Ms. Pines is an unusually capable free-lance writer. She devoted a substantial period of time to the study of research in child development in the mid-1960s and then wrote this book. Her translation and interpretation of the research seems unusually accurate and fair.

The Secret Life of the Unborn Child
Thomas Verny, with J. Kelly
Summit Books, 1981

Thomas Verny, a Canadian psychiatrist, claims that when a fetus reaches the end of the sixth month of gestation, it becomes a sensing, thinking, decision-making being. He claims that the experience undergone during the birth process can be remembered in detail for many years. He cites one example of a six-year-old boy speaking Latin during regular nightmares, a language that he could only have learned when a priest administered the last rites at the boy's difficult birth.

Verny wants women to know that they have a wonderful opportunity (and presumably a nerve-wracking responsibility) to deliberately "shape" the minds of their unborn children. The book is well-written, and the author is no fool. However, his views are totally at odds with the most reliable information we have on the development of human abilities. The evidence supporting his position is far too slim to warrant serious attention.

The Second Twelve Months of Life
Frank and Theresa Caplan
Grosset & Dunlap, 1977

Few subjects are more written about than the care of children. Producing a child takes very little skill or specific knowledge, but when it comes to rearing a child, many parents feel that they need a good deal of both. Unfortunately, our educational system rarely provides any help for new parents. One can even hold a Ph.D. without ever having had any training for dealing with a baby. Small wonder that so many books and magazine articles on parenthood are written every year.

The Second Twelve Months of Life is a sequel to the Caplans' earlier book, *The First Twelve Months of Life*, which according to the publishers has sold more than 300,000 copies, making it one of the outstanding sellers on this subject. These books come from the Princeton Center for Infancy and Early Childhood—named for the town in which it is located, not the university, with which it has no affiliation. Mr. Caplan holds a master's degree in education, and both the Caplans have been involved for many years with the design, manufacture, and sale of children's toys and educational materials. The Princeton Center researches books on child care for parents and professionals and, according to this book's introduction, has surveyed some 1,500 volumes.

The book under review has several strengths. The sections on toys and equipment are impressive, which is understandable, given the authors' background. They also do very well in their treatment of language acquisition and temper tantrums. Furthermore, they cover just about every conceivable topic, including care of teeth, learning sex roles, the sense of smell, and helping children adjust to divorce.

Unfortunately, the amount of reliable knowledge we have about the second year is nowhere near adequate, and the weaknesses of the book are the result of this lack. The Caplans are strongest in areas in which they have had years of experience and in which child development research is fairly substantial (such as language acquisition). But their basic knowledge of children is borrowed from what is in those 1,500 books, and there are too many inaccuracies, too much uncritical acceptance of statements by "authorities" that either are outright nonsense or are not supported by any significant research.

For example, their description of the timing of motor development is way off the mark. The authors say that most children can sit up at eleven months, walk unaided at fourteen months, and climb chairs and tables at sixteen months; the more accurate ages would be eight, eleven, and eleven months. The errors in regard to sitting and walking unaided could cause some parents to think their children are precocious. Other parents might not expect their children to climb chairs, tables, and counters until they are sixteen months old—setting up the possibility of a serious accident.

Another problem with the book is its apparent endorsement of the psychoanalytic theory of infantile sexuality. For example, the Caplans write: "The child's discovery of the anatomical sex difference . . . takes place sometime during the 16th to 17th month or even earlier, but more often in the 20th or 21st month. The girl's discovery of the penis confronts her with something she is lacking. This usually brings on a range of behaviors that clearly demonstrate her anxiety, anger, and defiance. In girls, masturbation takes on a desperate and aggression-saturated quality more often than in boys and at an earlier age." The amount of scientific evidence for such views is negligible, and their inclusion in a book of this sort reinforces my skepticism about the book's general reliability.

The month-by-month treatment of the second year of life—the scheme the Caplans follow in this book—fails because children do not change that rapidly during this period. As a result, the authors are forced to be redundant, to insert topics in an arbitrary manner, and generally to confuse the reader. Indeed, the format is so inappropriate and the number of topics discussed so great (with as few as thirty-six words in one case) that confusion is inevitable. So, although this book contains some valuable information, its weaknesses are too substantial for me to recommend it.

The Self-Respecting Child
Allison Stallibrass
Pelican Books, 1977

This is a notable book. Ms. Stallibrass has had extensive experience with "free choice playgroups" for two- to five-year-old children in England. She also is an avid student of the child development literature, especially the works of Piaget, Robert White, Shinn, and Groos dealing with the subject of play. She makes a powerful case for the importance of play during the first few years of life, and she emphasizes the numerous physical activities that occupy so much of the time of the infant and toddler, particularly as they underlie mental and social development. In her view, the best conditions for the growth of self-respect in two- to five-year-olds involve many opportunities to choose activities for oneself while learning to interact with older children.

Her views are reminiscent of those of Peter-Pikler of Hungary in their emphasis on the central role of motor development in early education. However, her position seems more comprehensive and impressive than most of those who focus on early physical activities. Her analyses of the development of self-confidence and self-esteem go much further than most, and they deserve attention. Finally, the author shares my views regarding the universal needs of new parents for preparation and assistance in their role as their children's first teachers, as well as the significance of the task. I highly recommend this book.

The Shy Child
P. Zimbardo and S. Radl
McGraw-Hill, 1981

Shyness is an important and rarely addressed topic, and although most of this book deals with children over three, like many others, its principles of guidance presumably are applicable in a general way to children as young as one year of age or so. The primary question to raise about this book is the basis for its declarative statements and prescriptions. The authors certainly are able and well-trained. Zimbardo directs the Stanford University Shyness Clinic, and Radl is a published journalist. They have devoted much time and effort to the topic of shyness and probably know more about it than most anyone else.

Nevertheless, there are problems. There is no directly relevant research on shyness during the first years of life. What, then, should a professional look for in a book on the subject? I look for evidence of good judgment, knowledge, and logical thinking. For instance, the authors advise parents to teach their children "caring, sharing, daring, and swearing." Why? The answer is that that is the authors' "considered opinion." I don't dismiss the considered opinions of specialists, but such a basis for advice does not impress me as much as research-supported suggestions such as "Parents can help their shy children by inviting a younger child of the same sex over to play." This recommendation is based on a study at the University of Minnesota that showed clear beneficial effects from such experiences.

I have a tendency to be noncritical when advice seems sensible and attractive; for example, how could anyone argue against " 'I love you' was said and expressed physically with hugs and kisses every day from birth on"? The point is, however, that we would be much better off if we really knew how to avoid shyness, rather than having to rely on what is not much more than a good hunch that, in any event, is attractive to new parents.

Occasionally, the book makes statements that evoke somewhat harsher criticisms from me. For instance, there is a clear implication that parents must be loving and interested even when they are very tired, such as at the end of a work day, or they will be doing their child a disservice. This is likely to be a heavy cross for parents to bear. Also, the authors strongly endorse nursery school experiences to "help develop social skills early in life." Although preschool teachers will welcome this comment, it should be noted that existing evidence does *not* support the statement.

In summary, this is a good book on an important topic written by very able people. In its prescriptions for parental actions, however, it goes well beyond well-established knowledge and therefore does not warrant full confidence.

Smart Toys for Babies
Kent Burtt and Karen Kalkstein
Harper Books, 1981

This is a pleasant and useful book. The authors borrow extensively from *The First Three Years of Life*, and they are at their best when they stick to the subject at hand—how to make interesting and appropriate toys at home. They do not do so well when they talk about the educational implications of the toys—often extrapolating inappropriately from the knowledge base.

For instance, in talking about wrist bracelets for a three-and-a-half- to five-and-a-half-month-old, they say, "If your baby has not yet noticed her hand, these bracelets may capture her attention and lead her to focus on her hand." It is a very rare baby who has not been focusing on her hand by three and a half months of age, and if she hasn't been doing so by five and a half months, something more than bracelets may be called for. Another example is the statement that a homemade jack-in-the-box "will teach a baby that someone who disappears can re-appear." No small slice of experience alone can teach object permanence.

Although the authors cover most of the main points with regard to toys for children from birth to two, there are a few noteworthy omissions, such as the value of water (bath) play in the first year. Nevertheless, this book does contain a great deal of useful information and many good ideas.

A Survival Handbook for Preschool Mothers
Helen Wheeler Smith
Cambridge, 1982

The author of this book is a mother of five and a grandmother of eight who also holds a doctorate and has taught elementary and nursery school as well as parent education classes. The book represents an effort to combine the results of research studies with the experience of many years in order to provide parents with helpful suggestions regarding early learning, discipline, sibling rivalry, and a variety of other topics.

All in all, I would say that Smith has succeeded. She writes clearly and well, and most of her suggestions are sound. This book is not so comprehensive or clever as those by Vicki Lansky (e.g., *Best Practical Parenting Tips*), but I think it is a good addition to the parent education literature, and I recommend it.

Things to Do with Toddlers and Twos
Karen Miller
Telshare, 1984

This book offers more than four hundred activities, techniques, and designs for toys that are effective in working with very young children in home and group care settings. The author has a master's degree in human development and has attended appropriate workshops, including my own Institute on Educating the Infant and Toddler and Alice Honig's Quality Infant Caregiving Workshop at Syracuse University. She also is the mother of three and has been a child care professional for fifteen years.

Most of the recommendations in this book are sound and based fairly well on the knowledge base. Moreover, unlike many other such books, Miller also includes sections on "nonrecommended" toys and activities that are equally useful and reflect a good grasp of the literature and appropriate experience. Therefore, I recommend this book highly.

To Love a Baby
Sandy Jones
Houghton Mifflin, 1981

The body of this book is quite brief—119 pages, about half of which are glorious photos. It is a celebration of the emotional rewards of early parenthood. The balance of the book—37 pages—consists of brief explanations of selected research reports that deal with the emotional lives of infants and their parents.

The author holds a master's degree in psychology and has written a great deal on the subject of early human development, including the book *Good Things for Babies*, a valuable guide for new parents.

This book is (1) expensive, (2) pictorially splendid, (3) well-written, and (4) so effusive on the subjects of breast-feeding and the power of love that it almost defies criticism. Clearly, the author is very capable and has made an unusual effort to study much of the literature on the subject. However, the book does have significant weaknesses.

The directions to parents very often are based in small part on research and in large part on the author's passionately held private views. Many of the latter border on the extreme; for instance, "A birthing mother who speaks words of encouragement to her body will find that her womb and vagina respond with the same loving openness that she has given to her throat" or "energy gifts can come from worshippers in churches and audiences in theaters where energy circles and flows in the quiet." These ideas (and the book expresses many such ideas) put this book into a dramatically different category from the author's first work, which was strictly practical. My advice is to enjoy the beautiful pictures but beware of the text.

The reviews of research are of mixed value. Each is reasonably accurate, but important contrary findings are not cited. For example, subsequent failures to replicate the original findings of Kennell and Klaus on bonding are omitted. The result is an unbalanced, nonobjective presentation of the literature, which constitutes a disservice to the reader.

Toddlers and Parents
T. Berry Brazelton
Delacorte Press, 1974

Brazelton is one of the most experienced and influential pediatricians on the current national scene. He has had a long history of a very successful private practice in the Cambridge, Massachusetts, area, he has apprenticed to Harvard research programs directed by Jerome Bruner, and he has directed research programs of his own at Harvard Medical School. Finally, he is most interested in improvements in pediatric training.

I believe Brazelton's major strength lies in his compassion for the anxieties that new parents tend to have in regard to their infants, and his books are very useful with respect to that theme. They address individual characteristics of very young children and classic stresses with regard to childrearing in the first years of life. Brazelton is strong in the area of the child's physical development and well-being, but he should not be considered an ultimate authority with regard to the intellectual, social, and behavioral development of children during this time of life.

Total Baby Development
Jaroslav Koch
Wallaby, 1978

This book, by a child psychologist from Czechoslavakia, describes "over 300 exercises and games to stimulate your baby's intellectual, physical, and emotional development." However, the author's recommendations appear to have no solid roots in research, and his arguments for conducting over two hours of daily "exercise periods" for infants are very weak and unpersuasive. His views regarding the needs of babies, though presented in a strong, declarative manner, indicate an inadequate grasp of the literature. Therefore, I am unable to recommend this book.

Who Cares for the Baby?
B. Glickman and N. Springer
Schocken, 1978

This book promises a comprehensive analysis of all aspects of the problem of child care for children between birth and four years of age. One author is an early childhood specialist; the other is a professional writer with a master's degree in early education.

An introductory chapter spells out the design of the book and sets the tone for what follows by introducing a variety of challenging ideas. This is followed by an analysis of the many substantial pressures on young families that form the background of decisions about child care. Chapter 2 describes family responses to the pressures. Interview materials are presented, along with a wide variety of options that currently are chosen. Chapter 3 is a brief survey of day care centers. Chapters 4 and 5 report the authors' understanding of what research on other animal species as well as on young children seems to indicate about the advisability of child care systems. Chapter 6 presents an analysis of group care in other societies, most notably Russia and Israel. Chapter 7 consists of transcripts of interviews with two noted authorities, plus what the authors concluded from the discussions. The book ends with guidelines for those choosing alternative care for their children and a brief set of observations by the authors.

In my opinion, this is an outstanding book. What impressed me most was the talent of the authors. As I read, I repeatedly was impressed by the quality of their analyses of difficult topics, such as the nature of the infant's first attachment to another person and the origins and consequences of group child care in other countries. The authors think for themselves and they think clearly. These qualities are visible throughout the book, especially in the chapter where they grapple with two authorities in the field and come away clinging to their own point of view, not out of stubbornness (in my opinion) but on reasonable, independently constructed grounds.

Their guidelines for choosing a child care service overlap with the professionally oriented material suggested by Galinsky and Hooks (*The New Extended Family*), but they go further. They build a reasonable case for family day care as the least objectionable form of full-time child care, and their argument in favor of part-time work (if it can be obtained) coupled with part-time family day care makes excellent sense.

The book is not without aspects that merit criticism. Generally, the only weaknesses of consequence have to do with the authors' survey of the research literature. In light of the thousands of references in the literature on the effects of early experiences on the development of infants, the treatment given by the authors leaves much to be desired. It suggests a tendency to believe the results of research on the basis of the direction of the results rather than the quality and quantity of evidence. The same kind of bias seems to be present in their description of a seven-week-old in the care of babysitter: "The baby felt for a moment that it was going to get the breast it was after." No one yet knows how to determine the mental expectations for a seven-week-old child. Again, in the bestowal of success on a parent-child center, there is an absence of any objective evaluation, followed by a proper reticence about evaluating the effects on babies of communal living. The authors' preference for home care of children seems to reduce somewhat the objectivity of their analyses.

On the other hand, I must confess that although I found fault at times with their review process, I agree wholeheartedly with their conclusions. Based on over two decades of studying effects of experience on the development of infants and toddlers, I found that this book reflected a basically sound view of the needs of young families and the issues surrounding child care.

The authors conclude that children develop best when most of their experiences of the first years of life are shared by one person who cares for them more than anyone else in the world. They also emphasize that full-time care of babies is stressful at times for anyone and, therefore that part-time day care can have substantial value, even when a young parent is not seeking employment. This is an excellent book for those considering full-time child care and for prospective parents. I recommend it highly.

The World of the Child
Aline D. Wolf
Parent Child Press, 1982

This little paperback book is billed as "a fable for parents." It tells the story of a father who takes his family, including a two-year-old, to a carnival. In the beginning, he repeatedly has to deal with the annoying and frustrating capacity of his young child to do some things and the child's incapacity to do other things.

Eventually, the father wanders off by himself and enters one of the carnival tents. The next thing he knows, he finds himself in a giant world, where people speak strangely, walk very fast, and don't seem to be able to understand what he wants and what kinds of difficulties he's having. The furniture and utensils they use are too big for him to handle, and he continually has problems functioning, all the time receiving very little sympathy or assistance from the big people who inhabit the place.

At the end, the father returns to his family with a new sense of understanding and compassion for his two-year-old. The story and its "moral" are rather trite, but they are handled beautifully in this book; as a result, the message comes across clearly without being silly or "preachy." I highly recommend this sensitive and effective book.

You Are Your Baby's First Teacher
Marilyn Segal
Nova University, 1973

Marilyn Segal is a psychologist on the faculty of Nova University in Florida. Her curriculum for infant education, sponsored by the federal Office of Child Development, was created in connection with a proposed television series for new parents. I have reviewed the curriculum and some of the televised material, and I feel that neither is of outstanding quality.

Although Segal is reasonably well informed about the child development literature, her focus and the emphases are not impressive, and the result is an extremely lengthy list of recommendations, the majority of which are presented as important. Without a convincing evidential base on the one hand, and with a demand for an appreciation of far too many important things on the other, this manual is a classic example of what a good professional can do if she tries to include everything that seems to have any potential importance for new parents. Unfortunately, in our opinion, such an approach is neither feasible nor likely to be the best that can be done.

Your Baby and Child from Birth to Age Five
Penelope Leach
Knopf, 1977

This book is very helpful in providing information on general child care. There are more than 650 marvelous color pictures as well as many superb sketches to accompany the delightful text. The book covers many topics beyond education, including feeding, diapering, and toilet training. As the title indicates, it also covers a couple of years beyond age three. The book is extremely well organized, and there are excellent glossary and index sections.

Unfortunately, despite its comprehensive approach, the book lacks many specifics on educational development, particularly with respect to early receptive language (language is equivalent to speech in this treatment), social skills, and intelligence. The section on crib toys contains some weaknesses as well, in that many of the toys described are suspended over the crib by strings. However, so long as parents can be made aware of these few shortcomings, I recommend that they take advantage of the book's many strengths.

Your Baby's First 30 Months
Lucie Barber and Herman Williams
HP Books, 1981

The authors of this book come from the Union College Character Research Project, a group that has been studying the development of "healthy attitudes and values" for over thirty years—so far, without much success. The book is well organized and contains many gorgeous pictures and charts. Unfortunately, however, the content of the book is rather weak. Statements such as "When a baby is born, his five senses are usually in complete working order" indicate an inadequate grasp of the knowledge base; and references to the Moro and startle reflexes as "emotional responses" represent inappropriate extrapolations of the knowledge base. There is nothing in the book about negativism, sibling rivalry, receptive language, or hearing. In other words, coverage of key points regarding early development is simply too shaky for me to recommend this book.

Your Baby's Mind and How It Grows: Piaget's Theory for Parents
Mary Ann Spencer Pulaski
Harper & Row, 1978

This is a well-written guide to Piaget's theory by an experienced child psychologist. Although it contains occasional errors, it provides a first-rate service to parents and professionals in that it manages to distill the virtually unintelligible writings of Piaget into relatively simple form and accompanies this treatment with relevant suggestions for day-to-day activities. Unfortunately, even distilled and diluted, Piaget's theory comes across as quite complicated and sophisticated, so I would recommend this book only for parents with higher than average educational backgrounds. (It also makes an excellent text for college-level psychology courses!)

Your Child Is a Person
S. Chess, A. Thomas, and H. Birch
Penguin, 1965

Written by three professors of psychiatry, this book follows several children from birth through the first grade and emphasizes the importance of each child's innate characteristics in influencing his development. One major goal of the authors is to reduce parental guilt for their children's behavioral and emotional problems. Much of the material for the book was derived from a ten-year longitudinal study of the psychological development of 231 children. The research techniques employed are discussed in some detail and are of historic interest.

The authors give suggestions for dealing with sleeping, feeding, toilet training, limit setting, new situations, arrival of a new baby, and nursery school entrance in the light of a child's activity level, regularity, shyness, adaptability, intensity, distractability, and persistence. They discuss normal variations in styles of learning and in social development. There is a chapter dealing with handicapped children and one identifying childhood emotional problems requiring intervention. Both of these chapters are explicit and helpful.

This book helped start a trend away from extreme views that emphasized the influence and responsibility of the child's parents to the virtual exclusion of other possible factors. Although I do not consider it the "last word" on the subject, it was one of the first, it remains one of the few, and it is certainly worth reading.

Your Child Learns Naturally
Silas L. Warner, M.D., and Edward B. Rosenberg
Doubleday, 1976

Written for general consumption, this book discusses the intellectual and emotional development of children as the responsibility of parents. The major thrust is the effect of parental attitudes, pressures, and overindulgence on the child's psyche. Case studies illustrate how parental mistakes cause life-long problems for children, which psychiatric treatment may or may not be able to cure. A discussion of maternal deprivation might lead the reader to believe that the dire results of nonattachment are an ever-present danger in many homes. The teaching of morals is closely tied to toilet training. Chapters on discipline, fostering of curiosity, and need for psychiatric intervention emphasize the theme that "too much is as bad as too little." One wonders, however, how one would recognize the median point.

A chapter is devoted to the contributions of Montessori, Piaget, Burton White, Bruner, Kagan, and Skinner to the field of early development. Parents are reminded that each new piece of knowledge means more responsibility for them for incorporating that knowledge into their own childrearing practices. Then more case studies illustrate how parents may over- or underreact to their infants if they have read too many books on raising babies. Instead of concrete guidelines for the prevention of emotional and learning problems, platitudes are offered, which are guaranteed to stir up the free-floating anxieties that all new parents have. Therefore, professionals should be wary of this book and should be ready to ease the minds of parents who have read it.

Your Child's First Year
Dr. Lee Salk
Cornerstone Library, 1983

This is a rather short, handsomely put together, beautifully illustrated book by one of the country's more visible child psychologists. As usual, it pays to know something about the author's background. Salk currently is clinical professor of pediatrics and professor of psychology and psychiatry at the New York Hospital–Cornell Medical Center. Over the years, his work has featured private practice, teaching, and a modest quantity of research on the young child.

The book starts out well. Salk writes effectively and clearly, and he is passionately devoted to the health and welfare of parents and children. It is natural for him to emphasize the psychiatric aspects of parenting, and he does so in a very effective way. Given the kind of professional work in which he has been involved, one would expect that he would be particularly strong in the identification of typical concerns of young parents, as T. Berry Brazelton is.

One would not expect that he would necessarily be as sensitive as he seems to be to the importance of fathering. Perhaps this is a result of his personal experience, or perhaps it indicates a special sensitivity to the evolution of changing role models for young women. In any case, Salk repeatedly urges fathers to be involved as much as possible.

As many other writers on the subject do, he strongly encourages even inexperienced parents to place more faith in their own hunches and natural feelings than they might otherwise, especially in the face of contrary advice from friends, grandparents, and professionals.

Toward the end of the second chapter, I began to feel that Salk was imprecise about the details of early development. A certain vagueness was surfacing in connection with what an infant could see at different stages of the first months. The chapter on life with a newborn infant is especially strong, however, in its sensitivity to common concerns, such as postpartum depression and the feelings of anger that parents may have toward their new child.

Salk repeatedly underlines the special capacity of a child's parents to raise that child, although he doesn't explicitly argue against day care. In describing the young child, he places a good deal of emphasis on the sense of trust. This is not uncommon in books on the first years. The primary source of such ideas is the work of Erik Erikson, and not many people would quarrel with it. From this point forward, however, the book starts to reveal considerable weakness. Details about what the baby is like are either lacking, as in the importance of spotting mild to moderate hearing losses and monitoring the growth of receptive language; speculative, as in his interpretation of why babies cry; or imprecise, as in his statements about the abilities of babies at different stages of development.

In my own work with many families, I have routinely reported that for a family free from special needs, the biggest single source of stress in raising more than one child is when the children are closely spaced and the younger child begins to crawl about the home at seven months or so. This stress comes from normal sibling rivalry. Salk alludes to this problem in talking about the newborn infant but in a way that seemed to me to be inadequate. You can't talk about sibling rivalry without dealing with the question of the age of the older child. Salk, like so many who work in therapeutic situations, is strongest when it comes to verbal interchanges among people. If an older child in a sibling relationship is three, four, or more years old, then explanations are appropriate. But if you are dealing with an older child who is less than three years of age when the problems are likely to be most severe, such advice is not effective. That distinction isn't acknowledged at all in this part of the book.

The next chapter deals with breast-feeding versus bottle-feeding. Salk recommends breast-feeding and handles the emotional factors nicely. He recommends not using pacifiers, but his basis for this recommendation seems subjective, as do a number of other passages in the book where he reveals a willingness to advance opinions with great conviction but with not much else to support them.

The next chapter deals with a baby's emotional needs. Here, Salk's treatment of the issue of spoiling, which obviously surfaces in a clinical practice, seems to be oversimplified and vague. The statement that a baby's "strength comes more from having been satisfied than it does from constant frustration" leaves a parent with no notion of the limits that might be put upon a child's requests for satisfaction. Salk is against constant frustration—as most people are—but merely making this kind of statement simply doesn't provide enough for parents, especially inexperienced parents, to go by. If one doesn't use common sense in setting limits on what children can have and do starting at eight or nine months of age, one can easily end up with a two-year-old child who has learned that no one else's needs are nearly so important as hers.

On the other hand, Salk handles the problem of a baby who refuses to go to sleep at night with sensitivity and reasonableness. The treatment of stranger anxiety, a common phenomenon that surfaces at seven or eight months of age, is very short of details. On page 67, there is an illustration of a baby sitting up in her crib and playing with a crib gym. This is bad, since there have been several validated reports of children over six months becoming entangled in crib gyms. The wisest advice is to urge parents to remove crib gyms once the child can sit up.

Certainly one of the most dramatic emergents during the first year is the child's ability to move about on her own. Once crawling or scooting arrives, life with baby changes dramatically. There must be serious concern for accidents of various kinds, damage to the house, extra housework, aggravation of the slightly older child, and so forth. Salk's sensitivity to this dramatic change in circumstances seems inadequate. There is a very brief paragraph that suggests clearing poisons out from under the sink and putting away anything that is dangerous, but such brief remarks are, in my view, not nearly enough.

The next chapter deals with discipline, but it is a weak chapter. There is no question that discipline warrants special treatment. It is a nearly universal concern especially among new parents, but one simply has to do better than what is done in this book. This very brief chapter points out that the problems start when the baby gets to be about six months of age, which is fine. Salk suggests that the home be modified somewhat, but he provides few specifics. For example, there is no mention of how dangerous a bathroom is or of the fact that children spend a great deal of time in the kitchen.

Salk then goes on to describe what to do about situations that cannot be removed and yet constitute dangers, using the example of the electric outlet. He describes how to teach a child that you disapprove of exploration of electric outlets. He acknowledges that you have to stay with the child until the disapproval is firmly established in his mind; otherwise, the child will learn that it is all right to poke his finger in the outlet so long as you are not in the room. There is no question that the exploration of the home will start immediately upon the onset of mobility. That can happen at seven months, at nine or ten months, or as early as five or six months of age. However, this essential information isn't dealt with at all in the book. Next is the problem of how much a child can understand. If you leave a goodly number of dangerous situations intact in the home and follow Salk's advice, the child will come to associate your firm disapproval with his natural tendencies to explore. The point should be made to parents that as much as possible ought to be removed so that they don't have to say no too often to a baby.

Following this section, Salk turns to the topics of material rewards and spanking. The spanking section seems to vacillate from saying don't spank to saying that you should spank under certain circumstances. He finishes the chapter by declaring his opposition to mothers who threaten children with the statement "Wait 'til your father comes home. I am going to tell him what you did and he'll teach you how to behave." It would be a very rare baby under twelve months of age who would have the vaguest idea of the meaning of such a message.

In the next chapter, "Coping with Your Own Needs," there is a brief treatment of day care, sensitively and effectively done. However, it is followed by speculations about what is in the mind of a four-month-old child—speculations that seem inconsistent with the knowledge base: "As far as the baby is concerned, going to sleep has caused his parents to go away. The next time his father tries to put him to sleep by rocking and singing to him, he may understandably fight sleep out of fear that by giving in to his exhaustion, he'll cause his parents to disappear again." This sort of passage clearly is adult-amorphic, and other similar examples appear throughout the book. Salk returns to the subject of day care and takes essentially the same position I do—that it should be used sparingly during the first year of a child's life and with special precautions.

The next chapter is called "Handling Special Problems." Here we would expect Salk to be strong because of his clinical experience. The sections on hospitalization of the child are very well done, as are those on colic, sudden infant death syndrome, and teething. There is also an unusual section on how to deal with grandparents; it presents a balanced view of the benefits and the risks, and it presents it well. All in all, this is a good chapter.

The final chapter is called "Coping with Sibling Rivalry." Again, along with discipline, the topic of sibling rivalry is expected in a book like this because it is such a common concern for parents. This is an inadequate chapter. The primary problem I find with it is that it is not specific with respect to the age gap between children. Late in the chapter, it does address the desirability of spacing children three or more years apart, but this cannot undo the problems in the bulk of the chapter, which, in general, lead parents to believe that if you have done a good job with the first child, the first child will be secure enough that sibling rivalry won't be much of a problem, and that doing a good job involves a good deal of explanation before the baby arrives.

Parents are advised to explain to the older child that they are going to have a baby and to include him in planning and discussions before the new child is born. They should explain that the baby will be very little and won't be able to do much for a while, and so on. The bulk of the chapter thus focuses on what to do with children who are old enough to understand detailed explanations of a coming event and of the various limitations of living with the younger sibling. Therefore, it is appropriate only for a child who is old enough that sibling rivalry won't be much of a problem. What would be more useful for new parents would be some sort of help with respect to the child who is too young to understand detailed explanations. This kind of advice is not offered at all.

In summary, this book has sections that are useful, particularly those dealing with emotional concerns of new parents during the child's first years. Unfortunately, however, the strengths are counterbalanced by too much that is either missing, wrong, or inaccurate. The jacket of the book promises parents that they will learn what they can do to have a happier, healthier baby. There are a number of other books available that do that job much better. The book that most directly resembles this one is *Infants and Mothers* by T. Berry Brazelton. It, too, deals with the normal anxieties of new parents during the first year of a child's life, and it does a better job. Perhaps the best comprehensive book on the first year is *The First Year of Life* from American Baby; another book that should be considered is *The First Wondrous Year* from Johnson & Johnson.

Your Child's Intellect
T. H. Bell
Olympus, 1973

Considering the limits of the knowledge base at the time it was written, this is a reasonably competent guide to home-based preschool education. However the most noteworthy thing about this book is that the author makes a profound and passionate case for the importance of education during the first years of life and the importance of providing parents with the information and support they need to be effective first teachers of their children. Later, however, as secretary of education in the Reagan administration, Mr. Bell presided over the discontinuance of all federal programs addressing the goals he had so strongly advocated.

Appendix B:
Films on Early Development
and Child Care

I n working with the families of young children from various sectors of the U.S. population, I have found that films, filmstrips, and videotapes are useful in parent education programs. People at all levels of our society read considerably less than students in college or graduate school. This means that parent education activities must use other forms of communication. There are many films that deal with the educational development of the child in the first three years of life. As a service to professionals in education for parenthood, I have examined a large number of those films to find those best suited for use in parent education programs.

I have found that many films are custom built for use in introductory psychology courses in colleges. Another group of films has been designed for special-interest groups—for example, films that instruct in the use of a technical assessment scale or those that try to explain a highly specialized orientation to some topic in child psychiatry. It is a relatively rare film about educational development in the first three years of life that was specifically made for use with parents or for use with those who will work with parents.

The potential user of films, therefore, is faced with the need to sort out from the available films those films that are suited for parent or staff training. My experience has been that the yield is fairly small but that there are some excellent materials available.

The following evaluations present, first, factual information, such as the length of the film, whether it is in black and white or color, and so on. The descriptions of what is in the films and the statements on whether the information offered is solidly rooted in evidence or relevant experience and whether or not it is suited for use with parents or staff reflect my subjective judgments.

The evaluations are organized alphabetically by title. Next to each title (in parentheses) is an indication of where the film can be obtained. A key to these film sources follows this introduction. Most films can be either rented or purchased, and many distributors have special provisions for free previews by qualified groups.

Key to Film Sources

Badger   Earladeen Badger, USEP-Ohio, U/C College of Medicine, Dept. of Pediatrics, 231 Bethesda Ave., Cincinnati, OH 45267.

BU   Boston University, Krasker Film Library, School of Education, 765 Commonwealth Ave., Boston, MA 02215.

BWF   Bradley-Wright Films, 1 Oak Hill Drive, San Anselmo, CA 94960.

BYU: Brigham Young University, Education Media Service, 290 HRCB, Provo, UT 84601.

Campus   Campus Film Distributors Corp., 2 Overhill Rd., Scarsdale, NY 10583.

CM   Concept Media, P.O. Box 19542, Irvine, CA 92713.

CPE   Center for Parent Education, 55 Chapel St., Newton, MA 02160.

EDC   Education Development Center, 55 Chapel St., Newton, MA 02160.

Films   Films, Inc., 1144 Wilmette Ave., Wilmette, IL 60091.

GPN   GPN, University of Nebraska, Box 80669, Lincoln, NE 68501.

H&R   Harper & Row Media, 2350 Virginia Ave., Hagerstown, MD 21740.

HEW   HEW National Medical Audiovisual Center Annex, Station K, Atlanta, GA 30324.

H/S   High/Scope Educational Research Foundation, 600 North River St., Ypsilanti, MI 48197.

Kagan   Professor Jerome Kagan, Department of Psychology, Harvard University, Room 1510 William James Hall, Cambridge, MA 02138.

Ladoca   Ladoca Project and Publishing Foundation, Denver, CO 80216.

Lippincott   J.P. Lippincott Co., P.O. Box 4050, Princeton, NJ 08540.

McH   McGraw-Hill Films, 1221 Avenue of the Americas, New York, NY 10020.

NA-V   National Audiovisual Center, General Services Administration, Washington, D.C. 20409.

NCU   North Carolina State University, Infant Care Project, Greensboro, NC 27412.

Nova   Nova University, 3301 College Ave., Ft. Lauderdale, FL 33314.

NYU   New York University Film Library, 26 Washington Place, New York, NY 10003.

Olympus   Olympus Publishing Co., 1670 E. 13th S., Salt Lake City, UT 84105.

OSU   Ohio State University, Department of Photography and Cinema, Columbus, OH 43210.

P&G   Procter & Gamble Distributing Co., c/o Alert Letter Service, 718 Main St., Cincinnati, OH 45202.

ParMag   Parents Magazine Films, 52 Vanderbilt Ave., New York, NY 10017.

PELS   Parent Education Learning System, Sutherland Learning Associates, 8425 W. 3rd St., Los Angeles, CA 90038.

Perennial   Perennial Education, 930 Pitner Avenue, Evanston, IL 60202.

PIPS   Preschool and Infant Parenting Service, 8730 Alden Dr., Room E-105, Los Angeles, CA 90048.

Plainsong   Plainsong Productions, 47 Halifax St., Jamaica Plain, MA 02130.

Polymorph   Polymorph Films, 118 South St., Boston, MA 02111.

PrimeTime   Prime Time School Television, 40 East Huron St., Chicago, IL 60611.

Synchro   Synchro Films, 43 Bay Drive West, Huntington, NY 11743.

UCAL   University of California, Extension Media Service, Berkeley, CA 94720.

UILL   University of Illinois, Visual Aids Service, Champaign, IL 61820.

UTOR   University of Toronto, Media Center, School of Continuing Studies, Toronto, Ontario M5S1A1.

Reviews

Abby's First Two Years: A Backward Look (**NYU**)
Produced by Vassar College Department of Child Study, Dr. Joseph Stone, 1960.
16mm, Black and White, Sound, 30 Minutes.
Audience: Parents; Technical Rating: Good; Content Rating: Excellent

This film is organized in reverse sequence; that is, Abby gets younger rather than older as the film progresses. She is shown in routine situations, such as feeding, bathing, and play. The dropping away rather than accretion of new skills in loco-motion, posture, manipulation, and social relationships has more impact than the usual forward sequence. This is a good film, but very dated.

Adapting to Parenthood (**Polymorph**)
Produced by Polymorph Films, 1975. 16mm, Color, Sound, 20 Minutes.
Audience: Parents; Technical Rating: Excellent; Content Rating: Good

This film follows a young couple through the postpartum period. Feelings are openly expressed by the mother in the hospital and by both parents in the early days at home. Other young parents also discuss their initial problems. It is a real-istic presentation of the postpartum period of a very depressed young woman. Although I do not judge it to be representative of the experiences of most young parents, this film might be appropriate to stimulate discussion of postpartum prob-lems in a clinical setting.

The Amazing Newborn (**BYU**)
Produced by Case Western Reserve University Health Sciences Communications
Center, Drs. Maureen Hack and Marshall Klaus, Consultants, 1975. 16mm, Color, Sound, 25 Minutes.
Audience: Professionals and Paraprofessionals; Technical Rating: Excellent; Con-tent Rating: Good to Fair

The major objective of this film is to show that newborn infants have a wider range of sophisticated skills than is usually recognized. Three infants (described as being between one and seven days of age) are shown orienting to sounds, responding to social cues, visually following a small red ball, and attending to various geometric patterns. The work of Peter Wolff, Heinz Prechtl, and Robert Frantz is featured.

The film clearly demonstrates a range of impressive abilities of the newborn child. However, the film's producer goes some distance beyond what is supported by evidence, in my opinion, thereby reducing the product's overall value to a cer-tain extent. For example, a graph indicating the growth of wakefulness of the infant from the prenatal to the postnatal period indicates that newborns are awake eight hours a day. Also, the narrator states that about 10 percent of each day is spent in a state of quiet alertness. Both statements convey the impression that much of the newborn's day consists of active exploration. The only substantial data on the topic are from Wolff and Burton White, both indicating that alert activity averages less than 2 percent of each twenty-four-hour period.

The narrator states that infants illustrate visual "preferences" and "selections," implying mental capacities not generally agreed upon by students of the topic. The narrator also states that one can increase the newborn's alertness with visually stimulating objects. This, too, is unsubstantiated in the literature.

The behaviors illustrated are at times remarkable—for example, clear visual pursuit of a small ball by a baby less than a week old. This and some of the other behaviors seem atypical and precocious. At the end of the film, there is a disclaimer stating that the behaviors seen are not common and may not be elicited easily from newborns. In summary, there are some outstanding aspects to this film, but there is also a healthy portion of overstatement to convince the viewer that the newborn is indeed "amazing."

A Baby Is Born (**Perennial**)
Produced by Perennial Education, Henry Mayer, M.D., Consultant, 1974. 16mm, Color, Sound, 23 Minutes.
Audience: Parents; Technical Rating: Excellent; Content Rating: Good

This film follows a routine, modern hospital birth of a young couple's first child from the start of labor through a postnatal visit to the obstetrician. The film is thorough, with clear and explicit footage, carefully explained medical terms, and discussion that is primarily jargon-free.

In my opinion, this would be an excellent film for the prenatal part of any parent education program, although a medical person (e.g., an obstetric nurse) should be on hand to help elaborate on and/or update certain information.

Baby Meets His Parents (**NYU**)
Produced by Encyclopaedia Brittanica. 16mm, Black and White, Sound.
Audience: Parents; Technical Rating: Fair; Content Rating: Good

In this production, the infant's experiences with food, elimination, and loving care are discussed as the major factors in personality development. The major flaw in this film is a disparity between narration and footage (i.e., the infant frequently is not doing what the narrator describes him as doing). Several good points about baby care are made (e.g., the need for cuddling, the inability to spoil an infant). The theoretical basis is not discussed, though, clearly, the selection of personality factors results from some theoretical orientation. In general, I feel that this film is only of marginal value to new parents.

Bayley Scales of Infant Development (**NYU**)
Produced by the Psychological Corporation of New York. 16mm, Black and
White, Sound, 45 Minutes (first year), 60 Minutes (second year).
Audience: Parents and Professionals; Technical Rating: Fair; Content Rating:
Excellent

Although this film is worn in parts, the camera work and sound track are good.
The film shows how the Bayley Mental Scale is administered to children between
three and twenty-seven months. It demonstrates sample test items, explaining the
purpose behind most of them. The film illustrates the difficulties in testing infants
and in engaging and holding a subject's attention. It is not a step-by-step "how-to"
film; rather, it is a general education product.

The film shows a gifted examiner testing a variety of children with individual
behavior patterns. It explains how the examiner accommodates the test to each
child without sacrificing validity. In the first six months, it is not always clear what
constitutes passing of the test items; after that, however, age explanations are given
clearly. The debt to the Gesell Schedules is apparent in similarity of materials and
items.

This film would be a useful addition to a parent education program, especially
for parents with a high school or higher education. It is also appropriate for staff
training.

Bill and Suzi: New Parents (**EDC**)
Produced by the Education Development Center, 1975. 16mm, Black and White,
Sound.
Audience: Parents; Technical Rating: Good; Content Rating: Good

Parents of a five-week-old baby talk about their feelings of joy and their sense of
overwhelming responsibility. The father's statements about his feelings of closeness
and occasional jealousy are expressed naturally and openly. However, one must
recognize the natural inclination of parents to adult-amorphize their children, and
audiences may question such statements as "Mothers are more instinctively tied to
infants." In general, the parents are excellent models for new parents, and their
candor about their feelings should be very reassuring to other new parents.

Birth of the Red Kangaroo (**UCAL**)
Produced by the International Film Bureau, 1968. 16mm, Color, Sound, 21
Minutes.
Audience: Parents and Professionals; Technical Rating: Good; Content Rating:
Excellent

This film vividly documents the development of the Australian red kangaroo from
conception through the first year of life. Footage of the newborn making his way

from the birth canal to the mother's pouch is one of the most fascinating scenes of instinctive behavior I've seen, and it presents an excellent base for discussion of innate versus learned behaviors in young humans.

Call Me Mama (**Polymorph**)
Produced by Polymorph Films, 1977. 16mm, Color, Sound, 14 Minutes.
Audience: Parents and Paraprofessionals; Technical Rating: Good; Content Rating: Good

Miriam Weinstein, a thirty-year-old cinematologist, talks about her responsibilities, feelings, and perceptions of herself as a mother. We see her in various settings with Eli, her eighteen-month-old son. Although background noise from the child's play often drowns out the dialogue, this film should be useful for stimulating discussion about the demands of motherhood in parent education groups.

Care of the Infant: Animal and Human (**Perennial**)
An Ivan Tors Science Film, 1977. 16mm, Color, Sound, 22 Minutes.
Audience: Parents and Professionals; Technical Rating: Excellent; Content Rating: Excellent

This is a highly polished and very well put together production that compares childbirth, postnatal care, and early development among various animals (gazelles, baboons, giraffes, elephants) and humans. The footage is fantastic, and the voice-over is equally impressive and perfectly matched.

The result is a very moving and dramatic study of parenting across species. Although the amount of human parenting shown is negligible (a hospital birth and some "close contact" in African tribes), this film would be a delightful addition to any education for parenthood program. It has something for everybody and is suitable for high school students on up to the most well-educated parents and professionals.

Careers and Babies (**Polymorph**)
Produced by Polymorph Films, 1978. 16mm, Color, Sound, 20 Minutes.
Audience: Parents; Technical Rating: Excellent; Content Rating: Good

This film explores the lives, thoughts, and opinions of four women who have made different decisions about the title topic. The four women represent very different lifestyles and points of view, and their comments are interesting. My only reservation about this film is that the four types presented are rather extreme (e.g., one is a "classic" family woman totally devoted to home and motherhood, and another is a politician who has absolutely no time for or interest in having children). The typical parent-to-be or new parent is likely to have more mixed feelings and may have difficulty relating to the film's principals.

Causality (**UCAL**)
Produced as part of the AECOM Scales of Sensorimotor Development, S. Escalona and H. Corman, Consultants, 1965. 16mm, Black and White, Sound, 23 Minutes.
Audience: Those Interested in Assessment; Technical Rating: Fair; Content Rating: Excellent

This is an old film, and the technical quality is very uneven, ranging from adequate to very poor at times. The film demonstrates test procedures for determining Piagetian levels of sensorimotor development. The film begins with a lengthy introduction to Piagetian theory and then proceeds to show examiners testing babies, with explanations on the voice-over. The introduction is very good, as is the voice-over throughout the film. Escalona and Corman are leading proponents of Piagetian theory and are likely to get it right. Unfortunately, the footage, for the most part, does not support the text and is often inappropriate. The academic jargon and specialized focus of the film generally preclude its use in education for parenthood programs. Academically oriented parents, college students, and professionals—particularly those interested in assessment—may find it useful. However, the films on Piagetian testing done by Uzgiris and Hunt (*The Ordinal Scales of Psychological Development*) are superior to this film.

Child: Parts I, II, III (**NYU**)
Produced by the National Film Board of Canada and McGraw-Hill, Drs. Sam Rabinovitch and Jerome Kagan, Consultants, 1973. 16mm, Color, Sound, 30 Minutes (each).
Audience: Parents and Professionals; Technical Rating: Good; Content Rating: Good

These three films provide a general introduction to child development from birth to twenty-four months. Part I, "The First Two Months," illustrates a thorough medical examination of the newborn. Part II, "Two to 12 Months," and Part III, "12 to 24 Months," show different children in their own homes. The narrative is sensitive and thoughtful; however, some safety hazards are evident but not identified. For example, a child plays with a kitchen grater, and another child is seen with a pacifier tied on a string around his neck.

Child Development Videotapes: The Early Years (**H&R**)
Produced in Conjunction with the New York State Psychiatric Institute, Department of Educational Research, J. Ryan and C. Kestenbaum, Consultants, 1978. Videotapes, Color, Sound, 30 Minutes (each).

Audience: College Students and Professionals; Technical Rating: Excellent; Content Rating: Excellent

This is a very high quality production, and excellent "viewing notes" accompany the tape. Ten children ranging in age from four weeks to six years are used to demonstrate significant developmental stages of early childhood (about 75 percent of the tape deals with the first three years). The major themes included are attachment and separation, language development, and mastery. The tape presents early development from a strong psychiatric point of view, and there is a heavy emphasis on social and emotional development. However, the work of Piaget and others is brought in, giving the discussions a somewhat eclectic background.

The footage is excellent and appropriate to the voice-over. The information presented is reasonably accurate and valid, although the discussions do become a little sloppy at times. For example, it is implied that focused attention is not present until seven months of age (the more accurate age is about two-and-a-half months). However, the few weaknesses in this regard do not constitute a major threat to the overall integrity of the tape. A lot of academic and psychiatric jargon is used in the discussions, so the tape may be inappropriate for the majority of parent education programs. On the other hand, college students and professionals will find this production to be one of the better audiovisuals of this kind available.

Childhood—The Enchanted Years (**Films**) 16mm, Color, Sound, 51 Minutes.
Audience: Parents and Professionals; Technical Rating: Excellent; Content Rating: Good

This film, originally shown on commercial television, is a general discourse on child development. It begins with photographs of a fetus, continues with birth, and then presents shots (supposedly) from the infant's perspective, with distorted vision and sound. The work and theories of several child development researchers are presented, including Jerome Kagan, Grace Young, Nancy Bayley, Jean Piaget, T. Berry Brazelton, J.S. Bruner, and Burton White. There is some distortion of factual information for the sake of entertainment (e.g., animation sequences on cognitive stages and a child's understanding of idiomatic language), but this film can be useful as a supplement to staff training and for generating discussions among parents.

Children of Change (**NYU**)
Produced by the Mental Health Film Board, 1950. 16mm, Black and White, Sound, 31 Minutes.
Audience: Parents; Technical Rating: Fair; Content Rating: Poor

This is a dated discussion of working mothers. The material is obsolete, and the statistics quoted are inappropriate for use in today's society.

Children Growing Up (**UILL**)
A Series of Nine Films Produced by the British Broadcasting Co. and Distributed
   by Time-Life Films, 1971. 16mm, Color, Sound, 25 to 30 Minutes (each).
Audience: Parents; Technical Rating: Excellent; Content Rating: Fair

This is a series of nine technically proficient films that examine various aspects of
early childhood from physical growth to developing friendships and focus on children from birth to school age. The two films I viewed consist of lively and interesting scenes of children and parents in a variety of situations, accompanied by the
commentary of a BBC announcer.

   "Mother and Child" focuses on the mother–child relationship in the first three
years of life. Unfortunately, the film tries to cover too many subjects and, as a
result, gives a very brief treatment of each (the first year, overall, receives hardly
any attention). What is presented usually is quite good, but what is omitted is often
very significant. For instance, the narrator stresses the importance of language
teaching when the child is twenty-one months of age, but nothing is mentioned
about the importance of language in the earlier months. In the same vein, the
narrator warns mothers not to be too repressive when their children start to explore the world, but no advice is given regarding realistic limit setting. In some
cases, the footage is truly superb, such as the sibling rivalry scene and a section on
separation involving a hospitalized three-year-old. Unfortunately, the commentary
is not as good, and the subjects are dealt with inappropriately (as in the former
case) or incompletely (as in the latter).

   "All in the Game" focuses on the subject of play. Again, the footage is quite
good on occasion, and the commentary in this film is rather impressive. The narrator continually stresses that play is, indeed, "serious business" for the young
child. The section on imitation and aggression is particularly sensitive and well
done. Unfortunately, the film concentrates primarily on children in the two- to five-
year age range. Moreover, American audiences may find some of the references to
class and sex differences offensive.

   In general, I found these films pleasant and informative. However, their distinctly British perspective and their tendency to be arbitrary and incomplete in
terms of coverage will limit their utility to most parent education programs.

Development of the Child: A Cross-Cultural Approach to Cognition (**UILL**)
Produced by the Visual Aids Service, University of Illinois, Jerome Kagan, Consul-
   tant, 1975. 16mm, Color, Sound, 20 Minutes.
Audience: College Students; Technical Rating: Excellent; Content Rating: Fair

There is beautiful camera work and a clear sound track in this film directed by
Jerome Kagan. It shows children in three settings that differ in their economics,
access to education, and degree of isolation and modernization. These settings are

communities in Japan (modern industrial), Kenya (rural), and Guatemala (isolated rural). The film tries to make a point of the similarity of the children's cognitive development, despite their widely varying backgrounds.

During the sequences on infant development, distinctions are not made between very young infants and those many months older. In addition, statements that infants from eight to ten weeks of age are capable of memory and that children at the end of the first year are mature enough to "ask themselves questions" are of rather questionable validity. Although this film begins with sequences of infants, most of it focuses on older children and is therefore inappropriate for our focus.

Development of the Child (**Kagan**)
A Series of Three Films, Produced by Jerome Kagan. 16mm, Color, Sound, 20 Minutes (each).
Audience: Well-Educated Parents and Professionals; Technical Rating: Excellent; Content Rating: Good

"Cognition" is a film that a sophisticated audience might benefit from. It presents a very involved discussion on *thought*, defined as perception, memory, evaluation, and reasoning. It is a good film, but for the most part, the children depicted are beyond infancy and toddlerhood.

"Infancy" offers an excellent, comprehensive look at infant development, including object permanence, hypothesis testing, social attachment, and physiological maturations. However, as the film progresses, the emphasis shifts to Kagan's personal views of cognitive development. In particular, there is a good deal of discussion regarding his "discrepancy" hypothesis, a concept rooted in Piaget's work and of special interest to Kagan.

The narrative is overwhelming at points, demanding the audience's keen attention. In general, the information presented is commonly accepted by developmentalists as valid. However, the audience should be sensitized to the difference between generally accepted data and personal interpretations, as the film makes no distinction between them. Overall, this is a good film for professionals, staff, and parents with at least a college education.

"Language" examines early language acquisition through imitation, reinforcement, and modeling. Biological maturation is stressed as the "central factor" of language learning. The narration is easily understood, but the sound accompanying the natural setting is poor. Overall, the film content seems valid, but one fine point must be clarified. It is generally agreed that language learning *begins* when a specific level of maturation has been reached. On the other hand, a considerable body of data reveals that the *progress* of language learning is influenced by diverse environmental factors, not by maturation alone. I recommend this film for interested professionals, staff, and parents with a college background.

Early Words (**UCAL**)
Produced by the Harvard Center for Cognitive Studies, Jerome Bruner, Consultant,
    1972. 16mm, Color, Sound, 22 Minutes.
Audience: College Students and Interested Professionals; Technical Rating: Fair;
    Content Rating: Excellent

The camera motion in this film often is very jerky, the close-ups usually are too
close for clarity, and there is severe discoloration in many sections. The film consists of a close examination of language development in a single twenty-two-
month-old child, using samples of the child's language (mostly one-word utter-
ances) and gestures along with Bruner's analyses on the voice-over.

Bruner's narration is clear and literate, and his observations are unquestionably
outstanding. However, the scope of the film is too limited to constitute a substantial contribution to education for parenthood programs. It may be a modestly useful addition to college or graduate-level courses on child language, but the poor
technical quality diminishes its effectiveness.

Ego Development: The Core of a Healthy Personality (**UILL**)
Produced by Bettye Caldwell, 1974. 16mm, Color, Sound, 19 Minutes.
Audience: Parents and Professionals; Technical Rating: Excellent; Content Rating:
    Excellent

Bettye Caldwell traces the development of personality using the theories of Erik
Erikson. The approach is didactic, but it is lightened by scenes of babies in a center
and by the use of some high-quality animation. Caldwell's commentary is careful
and thoughtful, given the limited empirical research available in this subject area.
Although the narrative extends beyond the birth to three-year age range, I think
this film would be useful for most parent education programs.

Emotional Ties in Infancy (**NYU**)
Produced by Vassar College, Parent and Child Series, Dr. Joseph Stone, Director,
    1965. 16mm, Color, Sound, 12 Minutes.
Audience: Parents; Technical Rating: Good; Content Rating: Excellent

The attachment behaviors and distrust of strangers of nine- to twelve-month-old
infants are illustrated. Home-reared and institutionally reared children are shown.
The latter are contrasted in three experimental situations to illustrate degrees of
attachment and reactions to strangers. This film is very powerful. Parents can learn
some important material from it and usually are genuinely impressed by the
experience.

Families Alike and Different (**UILL**)
Produced by Churchill Films, 1976. 16mm, Color, Sound, 16 Minutes.
Audience: Parents; Technical Rating: Excellent; Content Rating: Good

This film illustrates the everyday lives of three six-year-olds living in Japan, America, and Mexico. The photography is beautiful and the content is appropriate for parents at the high school level on up.

The First Three Years (**CPE**)
Series of Eight 25-Minute Programs and One 55-Minute Summary Program Produced by the Westinghouse Broadcasting Co., Dr. Burton L. White, Consultant, 1977. Videocassette or 16mm Film, Color, Sound.
Audience: Parents and Professionals; Technical Rating: Excellent; Content Rating: Excellent

This unique television series about learning during the first three years of life was produced by Westinghouse and has been aired on commercial television stations throughout the United States. It is now available, through the Center for Parent Education, to schools, colleges, medical and social service agencies, parent education programs, and other appropriate groups for nonbroadcast purposes.

Each twenty-five-minute program focuses on one of the seven phases of early development I outlined in my book *The First Three Years of Life* (two programs are devoted to the fifth phase). The programs begin with a look at a typical child in her own home, while I describe the evolving interests and abilities of the child and point out what can be done to help children to the best possible start in life. These presentations are followed by question/answer sessions with me, the child's parents, and other parents of children at the same stage of development. I conclude the programs by providing guidance on safety-proofing a home, selecting toys, screening for hearing losses, and other topics of relevance to each phase. The fifty-five-minute summary program contains footage of children from all seven phases. I edited it to provide an overview of the entire learning process from birth to the third birthday.

In my (obviously biased) opinion, this is the best available introduction to early learning and the role of the parent as teacher. However, it is important to remember that the series was intended only to introduce these topics in an informative and entertaining manner. It should not be regarded as a substitute for a comprehensive course on child development or a comprehensive parent education program, although it would be an excellent adjunct to either one.

The First Two Weeks of Life (**P&G**)
Produced by Procter & Gamble, Pampers Division, 1980. 16mm, Color, Sound, 30 Minutes.
Audience: Parents; Technical Rating: Excellent; Content Rating: Good

This film addresses routine health care issues concerning the newborn—for example, changing diapers, feeding, bathing. The tone is very simplistic, and Procter & Gamble products are featured in most scenes. The film is targeted for viewers with very limited educational backgrounds.

The First Year of Life (**Nova**)
Produced by Nova University, Dr. Marilyn Segal, Consultant, and the U.S. Office of Child Development, 1975. 16mm, Color, Sound, 30 Minutes (each).
Audience: Parents; Technical Rating: Poor; Content Rating: Poor

This series of three films was adapted from videotapes, causing a loss in sound quality and picture rendition. Themes such as language development, attachment, and parental feelings are presented in a very loose, general, and basically incoherent fashion. Dr. Segal does not seem to be referring in any way to the research literature, and whatever she says is so general that there is little to quarrel with, except her failure to focus on anything of likely use to parents. Compared to other available films, this production is technically inadequate and does not seem to serve any particularly important function in regard to parent education.

Footsteps (**NA-V**)
A Series of 20 Programs, Produced by the U.S. Office of Education, 1978. 16mm or Videotape, Color, Sound, 30 Minutes (each).
Audience: Parents; Technical Rating: Excellent; Content Rating: Good

In response to the growing public interest in the educational development of very young children, the U.S. Office of Education has provided generous funds for the production of a television series on parenting. The prime mover for the series was Dr. T.H. Bell, former U.S. commissioner of education, then chief state education officer in Utah, and later U.S. secretary of education. The initial twenty programs of the series are now available for rental or purchase from the National Audiovisual Center; detailed discussion guides also are available for purchase.

Each program of the series begins with a five-minute introduction by a celebrity couple—either Rob Reiner and Penny Marshall or Mike and Judy Farrell. The next twenty minutes or so consist of a dramatization of some aspect of being a parent in today's society, using one of the five featured "families" (the episodes are fictional, and the characters are portrayed by professional actors). Each program concludes with a short commentary by a child development expert.

Remarkably, only four of the initial twenty programs focus on a family with a child under three years of age—and all four focus on the same family. That family consists of an only child, April, who is one year old in the first of the programs and two years old in the fourth. Her parents are young and divorced (both are featured). April lives with her mother, who works outside the home full-time, and she spends a great deal of time in day care.

I previewed three of these four programs. "The First Signs of April" focuses on the problem of infant understimulation. In "Love Me and Leave Me," conflicts over full-time child care are explored. The theme of "There Comes a Time" is the difficulty of obtaining day care services. The other program, "The Accident," which I did not see, deals with safety issues.

The technical quality of these programs is uniformly first-rate, and the acting is superb. Unfortunately, when it comes to providing solid information regarding the education of infants and toddlers, I find that the *Footsteps* series has taken relatively short strides. For the most part, the dramatizations concentrate on the adults involved, and the central themes often are ignored in favor of peripheral—if somewhat more dramatic—issues. For example, in "The First Signs of April," we see the child spending an inordinate amount of time in a playpen and in the care of a disinterested babysitter. However, the bulk of the program is devoted to various conflicts between the divorced mother and father, the father and his mother, and the father and the mother's new boyfriend. The concluding commentary, done by Ronald Lally, is sound but vague, and it provides little concrete guidance.

"Love Me and Leave Me" contains some excellent footage of mother–infant separation. However, the theme is developed only in general terms which results in a fairly weak picture of the child's development. For instance, it is noted that April is eighteen months old in this program, but there is no mention of the fact that this is a particularly sensitive period with regard to the attachment process. The closing commentary, featuring Bettye Caldwell, is excellent but too brief.

Educational development is completely absent from "There Comes a Time." Moreover, the program represents an endorsement of full-time day care for children under three. It is surprising that this program devotes itself solely to conflicts between parents and various public and private agencies and virtually ignores this important and timely issue as it relates to the educational development of the child.

All in all, I have to consider the Footsteps series somewhat disappointing. It is apparent that the first three years get comparatively little attention, and what little attention they get is predominantly in a day care setting, thereby leaving out parents caring for their children in their own homes. It is interesting to note that in conversations with professionals in education for parenthood around the country, I find that few have seen or even heard of the *Footsteps* program, despite the fact that they have been aired on public television in many cities. This is unfortunate, since even with its shortcomings, *Footsteps* could help focus more attention on the needs of parents and young children.

Four Families: Parts I and II (**BU**)
Produced by the Canadian Broadcasting Commission, Late 1950s. 16mm, Black and White, Sound, 30 Minutes (each).
Audience: Parents and Professionals; Technical Rating: Good; Content Rating: Excellent

This production features four approximately comparable rural families. Part I shows an Indian and a French family; Part II shows a Japanese and a Canadian family. Each family consists of a baby approximately ten months old, two older siblings, and two parents (the Japanese family also includes the child's paternal grandparents). Each family is filmed in similar settings, depicting food preparation, eating, bathing, division of labor, and layout of the home. Attitudes toward child-rearing, including punishment, roles of older children, and toys, are shown.

Margaret Mead discusses the relationship between childrearing and national characteristics. Unfortunately, in such a short film, the depth of discussion is limited. Parents may enjoy seeing other people in situations similar yet very different from their own, although this film is now somewhat dated.

From Cradle to Classroom: Part I and II (**BU**)
Produced by CBS. 16mm, Color, Sound, 50 Minutes (each).
Audience: Professionals; Technical Rating: Excellent; Content Rating: Excellent

These films were produced for airing on prime time television to examine the growing field of early childhood education. Walter Cronkite provides the narration. Part I gives an overview of several programs and research projects, including those of Merle Karnes, Ira Gordon, Earladeen Badger, O. K. Moore, the Pediatric Institute in Moscow, and Brown University. Part II examines in depth the programs of Bettye Caldwell at Syracuse and Engelmann in Wisconsin. Caldwell's segment deals with children under three years of age; Engelmann's program is directed at children over three. Both educators are interviewed, and extensive footage of their programs in progress is included.

Although these films provide a nice overview of the field, they would not be of much help in a parent education effort because they include neither child development information nor practical advice.

Gabriel Is Two Days Old (**EDC**)
Produced by the Education Development Center. 16mm, Black and White, Sound.
Audience: Parents; Technical Rating: Good; Content Rating: Good

This film presents a conversation between T. Berry Brazelton and the mother of a two-day-old boy. Brazelton examines the baby, discussing typical responses of newborns (i.e., reflexes) as well as the baby's individual character. The mother is encouraged to express her feelings.

For the most part, the information conveyed in the film is generally accepted as valid. However, a number of judgments are made and expressed with equal authority that do not merit unquestioned acceptance. For example, the naked baby's discomfort is attributed to "too much freedom for his own good," and swaddling is recommended. An explanation that is not considered is that the infant might be cold. Similarly, the infant's startle to a loud rattling noise is contrasted with his calm response to his mother's gentle voice with the suggestion of an innate preference for human voices. Such an illustration leaves open the uncontrolled difference in volume, which might easily explain the infant's responses. Finally, a remark like "[Gabriel is] so equal to taking care of himself" is hardly true, nor is it appropriate for an audience of new parents. In general, however, Brazelton's gentle pediatric manner and the information presented, with the noted exceptions, make the film acceptable for most programs.

Grasping/Mother Love/Smile of the Baby/Anxiety (**UCAL**)
Four Films Produced by Rene Spitz. 16mm, Black and White, Sound.
Audience: Professionals with Specialized Research Interests; Technical Rating: Poor; Content Rating: Fair

These films are highly technical, research-oriented presentations of the psychoanalytic work of Rene Spitz. They must be considered in the research context in which they are presented, as certain judgments raise serious questions. For example, in "Anxiety," an infant's fear of strangers is interpreted as a negative response to a human face and as evidence of a bad mother–child relationship. From my point of view, this is misinformation about a normal phenomenon in infants who discriminate between their parents and other people.

The narrator is often very difficult to understand. The age of the infants shown and discussed often is omitted, rendering the observations meaningless. I feel that these films are appropriate only for those with specialized interests strong enough to endure the poor technical quality.

Grief (**NYU**)
Produced by Rene Spitz. 16mm, Black and White, Silent, 12 Minutes.
Audience: Parents and Professionals; Technical Rating: Good; Content Rating: Excellent

This is an old film, and it is generally very well done, especially for a silent film. It is a classical work wherein Spitz describes, for all to see, the devastating consequences of rupturing or a failure to develop a strong maternal bond in the first three years of life. This film has had a profound impact on many people, both lay and professional, and it resulted in a huge amount of work on maternal deprivation and the mother–child relationship.

The only problem with this film is that its message is devastating and might be disheartening to new parents. Also, it might influence professionals to see pathology where none exists. But if these two unfortunate consequences can be guarded against, it is a powerful tool with which to show how important a good emotional relationship between infant and parent is during the child's early years.

Growing Up Safely (**NYU**)
Produced by the National Film Board of Canada and McGraw-Hill, 1965. 16mm,
    Color, Sound, 25 Minutes.
Audience: Parents; Technical Rating: Excellent; Content Rating: Excellent

This is an excellent, though now somewhat dated, presentation of the issue of
safety for children. The narrative gives a brief description of the child at a particular age, followed by suggestions for providing a safe environment. For example,
the helpless infant requires protection; the curious toddler needs supervised freedom. Unfortunately, nearly half of the film is devoted to children over three years
of age.

Growing Up Together (**NYU**)
Produced by the Children's Home Society of California, 1975. 16mm, Color,
    Sound, 60 Minutes.
Audience: Parents and Professionals; Technical Rating: Fair; Content Rating:
    Excellent

This film focuses on the problems of unwed teenage mothers, exploring their feelings as adolescents and their relationships with family and friends. The camera
angles are often awkward, and the dialogue is difficult to understand at times. As
no attention is given to the care of the baby, I feel that this film would be useful
only for people working with young unwed mothers.

Growth and Development Series (**Lippincott**)
A Series of 10 Films Produced by J. B. Lippincott Co., 1976. 16mm, Color, Sound,
    45 Minutes (each).
Audience: College Students; Technical Rating: Excellent; Content Rating: Fair

This is a series of ten films created for introductory courses in child development,
spanning the age period from three weeks to four years. A programmed text accompanies the films. Four children and their families are the subjects throughout
the series. The early films have a health orientation, with the focus on physical
care and development. Because the children are all filmed in a "homelike" setting
in a studio, the interactions have a staged and artificial quality. Presumably because
of the setting, all activity is adult-initiated, resulting in an appearance of a poor
balance in interactions.

The style of the narrative is to ask questions, which the viewer is to answer
through observation. Frequently, however, the answers are not obvious. In addition, this format allows for very little solid information to be transmitted. The
information is somewhat more substantial when the workbook is used in conjunction with the film. There also are some points of misinformation, such as the state-

ment that at three and a half months, vision is "flat" and "one-dimensional." Several inappropriate toys are given to the children without comment, including an unsafe plastic mobile for a six-month-old and a too-difficult lotto game for two-year-olds.

There is no solid information on educational development in these films. The question format, the artificial interaction sequences, and the misinformation seriously hamper the programs. Investment in this series and the workbooks was very large, and the work that went into the detailed plotting of the first four years of life for four children also had to be very substantial. It is unfortunate that the results were not more powerful.

Growth Failure and Maternal Deprivation (McH)
Produced by McGraw-Hill Text Films, 1967. 16mm, Black and White, Sound, 26
    Minutes.
Audience: Professionals; Technical Rating: Excellent; Content Rating: Good

This film follows the progress of an infant and a toddler (both of whom are black) who suffered neglect and consequent physical, mental, and emotional problems. It discusses the importance of "mothering" and shows the effects of deprivation and the results of intervention by medical and nursing personnel. The film follows not only the day-by-day progress that comes with good hygiene and nutrition but also the mental development and emotional stability gained through cuddling and stimulation. The interest remains high because of the curiosity of the viewer to see "before and after" results. Because of the hospital setting and the extreme deprivation of the children, this film is not a good one for illustrating normal development, but it beautifully illustrates the results of lack of mothering for a specialized audience.

Growth of the Infant: Behavior in the Early Stages (BU)
Produced by the Gesell Institute, 1940. 16mm, Black and White, Sound, 20
    Minutes.
Audience: Professionals; Technical Rating: Excellent; Content Rating: Excellent

Historically, this is an important film. Dr. Gesell explains his work, which has had an enormous influence in the past forty years. I believe that the commentary in this film is not as good as it could have been, but the film is still quite good.

Half a Year Apart (EDC)
Produced by the Education Development Center. 16mm, Color, Sound.
Audience: Parents and Professionals; Technical Rating: Good; Content Rating:
    Unknown

This slow-paced and tedious film shows Rachel, twenty-four months, and Josh, thirty months, engaging in water play. There is no narration, so the audience is left to its own observations and conclusions. The children are so close in age that contrast is weak, and the lack of direction through narration leaves the audience wondering what the film's point actually is.

Having Twins (**Polymorph**)
Produced by Polymorph Films in Conjunction with Harvard Medical School, 1978. 16mm, Color, Sound, 22 Minutes.
Audience: Parents; Technical Rating: Excellent; Content Rating: Excellent

This film presents the experiences of and discussions among parents who are about to give or have just given birth to twins. The tone of this film is very similar to that of the publications from the National Mothers of Twins Club—that is, very upbeat and informative. I strongly recommend this film for appropriate groups.

Home-Based Preschool Education (**Olympus**)
Produced by the Olympus Publishing Co., T. H. Bell, Author, 1975. Series of 10 Filmstrips and Audiocassettes, Color, 15 Minutes (each).
Audience: Parents and Professionals; Technical Rating: Excellent; Content Rating: Excellent

This series of ten filmstrips covers the period from infancy to age six. The majority of the pictures shown are of preschoolers, but the discussion is general enough to be applicable to any age. The materials present a simple discussion geared to the naive parent about the importance of the parents' role as their children's first teachers. Suggestions are given about how parents can enhance their children's educational development, with a strong sales pitch for the Olympus Toy Library. Ages at which various toys and toy-related activities are appropriate are not made clear.

The "teaching guides" included in each set are useful in helping educators plan discussions and activities around the filmstrips. There are suggestions for incorporating this parent education program into a public school curriculum. In general, this is a superior product, although the implication that one ought to purchase the Toy Library may be distasteful to some.

How Babies Learn (**NYU**)
Produced by New York University. 16mm, Color, Sound, 35 Minutes.
Audience: Parents and Professionals; Technical Rating: Excellent; Content Rating: Good

Bettye Caldwell narrates this film, which describes general development during the first years of life. The film stresses the infant's need for attachment to a "special person," using a ten-month-old with no special person to illustrate resulting social, physical, and intellectual retardation. There is some misinformation (e.g., hand preference evident at six months); on balance, however, the content is selected conservatively to present generally accepted developmental facts.

Human Development: A New Look at the Infant (**CM**)
Written and Produced by Hal and Lisa Smith, Concept Media. Series of Five Programs: Slide/Tape, Filmstrip/Audiocassette, or Videocassette.
Audience: Professionals; Technical Rating: Excellent; Content Rating: Excellent

The five programs in this series are entitled "The Development of Self: Three Views," "Social Cognition" (Parts I and II), "Infant Communication," and "Attachment." The list of consultants includes some of the outstanding people in the field of developmental psychology—Mary Ainsworth, Jay Belsky, Joseph Campos, Marshall Haith, Jerome Kagan, and others. The programs also come with a forty-four-page instruction manual.

The descriptive material accompanying the programs states that they will provide the best information generated by recent research on "the infant's highly sophisticated learning capabilities, their strong influence on adult caregivers, and the ways in which they establish their own identities." The works of Margaret Mahler, Michael Lewis, and many of the aforementioned consultants are emphasized, and the instruction manuals provide "suggested projects" to go along with the various topics.

In my opinion, these programs should be considered only for graduate-level training of future trainers of caregivers. The coverage of the literature, though necessarily selective and narrow, seems clearly superior in quality. However, much of the material covered simply is too esoteric to be of substantial value to anyone but the aforementioned audience—and even then, I am not sure it would be worth the rather substantial investment.

I'm a Parent Now (**NA-V**)
Produced by the National Institute for Mental Health, 1977. 16mm, Color, Sound, 17 Minutes.
Audience: Parents; Technical Rating: Excellent; Content Rating: Good

This film focuses on several different parents talking about their feelings and experiences with their babies and discussing what it is like to be a parent. Most of what is discussed is interesting and realistic. There is a somewhat heavy emphasis on the "quality versus quantity" of parental attention issue, apparently designed to help parents who work full-time outside the home feel less guilty.

The film deals with the feelings of parents, and little is presented directly regarding the educational needs of infants and toddlers. However, the film has a very practical orientation, and problems are discussed in jargon-free terms, making it a useful item for the prenatal or neonatal portion of a parent education program.

Infancy (BYU)

Produced by CRM Educational Films, Developmental Psychology Series, in Conjunction with Psychology Today, 1973. 16mm, Color, Sound, 20 Minutes.

Audience: College-Level Developmental Psychology Students; Technical Rating: Excellent; Content Rating: Excellent

This is a lavish production that demonstrates and explains various aspects of development during the first eighteen months of life, such as early visual contingent learning and attachment. Excellent live and animated footage of infants is interspersed with interviews with experts in the field. The film is basically conservative in its approach. The research people interviewed and quoted are outstanding, and no controversial subjects are discussed.

The film contains a great deal of academic jargon and was evidently put together with college-level developmental psychology students in mind. Therefore, it is not appropriate for most education for parenthood programs. The major strength of this film is its technical quality, which is definitely superior. Professionals may find it preferable to most of the films produced for the college market.

Infancy (NYU)

Produced by Harper & Row, Jerome Kagan and Howard Gardner, Consultants, 1970. 16mm, Color, Sound, 20 Minutes.

Audience: Professionals and College Students; Technical Rating: Excellent; Content Rating: Good

This film focuses on cognitive development in the birth to eighteen-month age range. There is a sound introduction to neonatal abilities. The narrative then moves to Kagan's theories of cognitive development. Viewers should be aware that the discussions of Kagan's speculations, which are not necessarily accepted by other researchers, are treated in the same manner as well-established information.

Infant Education Videotapes (H/S)

A Series of 9 Videotapes Produced by the High/Scope Education Research Foundation, Dr. David Weikart, Director. Videotapes, Black and White, Sound, 10 to 33 Minutes (each).

Audience: Parents and Professionals; Technical Rating: Fair; Content Rating: Poor

The camera work in these tapes is not outstanding; it is often difficult to judge what is happening because not enough of the scene is in view. The sound is easy to understand, however. The videotapes are arranged in three groups and there is also one other separate tape. The three groups are Child Development, with six programs, Parental Support of Early Learning, with seven programs, and Home Visitor Training, with five programs. The separate tape, which is the longest, contains a complete home visit.

In the descriptions of how a child learns, featured in the first series, the focus is almost exclusively on cognitive development according to Piaget's work on sensorimotor intelligence. No other content is addressed. In the materials entitled "What Parents Can Do" there are instructions regarding suitable toys for children, taking the baby's point of view, encouragement of learning, and the like. The impression one gets is that a great effort was made to be simple and understandable to people with very modest educational backgrounds.

The Home Visitor Training series is oriented toward professional training activities—describing how to build rapport, what kinds of problems might be encountered, and so forth. The home visit tape, of course, has the same sort of purpose. In much of the footage, the infant is on a tabletop between mother and visitor.

With the exception of the material that is based on Piaget's work on sensorimotor intelligence, the information underlying the observations and recommendations of the home visitor is extremely simple, unsophisticated, and general. The designers of the materials appear to base their advice primarily on what they have learned from a modest amount of experience in running their program, rather than from a thorough understanding of early human development. No sophistication is shown with regard to the steps of receptive language development or the growth of the child's social competencies. It is hard to tell that the people who created the tapes were professionals in child development, except for the references to Piaget. There are other materials available, for a good treatment of Piaget's work, most notably *The Ordinal Scales of Psychological Development* by Uzgiris and Hunt.

Considering Weikart's first-rate reputation in the administration of field-based compensatory education programs for preschoolers, these products are very disappointing. Where the content is strongest in connection with cognitive development, there is some reason to believe, from the research on the topic, that help is needed less in this area during the first two years of life than in other areas, such as language and social development. It is unlikely that any family or professional will be harmed by exposure to these materials; however, the prospective user should know that there are much stronger materials available (e.g., *Learning to Learn in Infancy*). In addition, the prices for these black and white videotapes are very high.

An Instant of Time (**Perennial**)
Produced by the National Film Board of Canada, 1984. 16mm, Film or Videocassette, Color, Sound, 13 Minutes.
Audience: Parents and Professionals; Technical Rating: Excellent; Content Rating: Poor

This film is about safety for infants. It features studio shots and narration by a pediatrician, Dr. William James; brief dramatizations of accidents involving babies; and studio shots of babies at play, with what is supposed to be the babies' voices superimposed on the soundtrack.

The narration and dramatizations are rather frightening, and the advice offered for avoiding dangerous situations is vague and disorganized. The ploy of having the babies "talk" is annoying, distracting, difficult to understand, and not well integrated with the subjects being discussed. All in all, this is a very disappointing film from producers that usually do much better work and a distributor that usually handles much higher quality products.

Is My Baby Okay?[a]
A Series of 6 Audiocassettes Produced by the Preschool and Infant Parenting Service (PIPS), Sponsored by the Thalians Community Mental Health Center.
Audience: Parents; Technical Rating: Excellent; Content Rating: Good

These audiocassettes, unusual with regard to their generally high quality as well as their availability, were produced by PIPS on the basis of their successful "Warmlines" program for parents. Such programs have come into existence over the last decade and do wonderful work in a variety of ways, consulting and consoling parents via the telephone.

This series features six titles: "Infant and Toddler Sleep Disruptions," "Toilet Training," "Temper Tantrums," "Problem Eaters," "The New Baby," and "Transitional Objects." The format usually involves an introduction by the director of the service—Helen Reid, M. S. W.—along with authoritative comments from professionals who work with her. The introduction is followed by excerpts from actual phone conversations received in the "Warmlines" program, expressing the concerns of several parents about each of these common problems of parenting. Finally, advice and explanations are provided.

In general, these products are extraordinarily good. The concept is a fine one, and the technical quality of the tapes is first-rate. Ms. Reid's style, which is warm, supportive, direct, and knowledgeable, is especially effective. Based on my own experience, I would agree with perhaps 80 percent to 90 percent of the advice given—and considering my stringent standards, this is an outstanding percentage.

My only consequential objections to the content of the cassettes relate to the utilization of the ideas of Freud and Erikson in the interpretation of baby behavior and in some of the resulting recommendations. For example, in dealing with sleep problems, the basis for some of the professional comments lies primarily in the concept of separation anxiety, a fundamental concept in infant mental health work. Certainly, separation anxiety during the first year of life is a reality, but to assume that a child only a few months of age is "in doubt that the mother will return" is

---

[a]This is not a film.

to perpetuate a classic weakness in the field. The problem is that it ascribes mental capacities to the very young infant that do not yet exist. I would prefer explanations that did not involve this kind of adult-amorphizing and that would take into account more conservative reasons for infant behaviors. Nevertheless, I feel that these cassettes will be helpful to many parents much of the time and that they would be a valuable addition to a parents resource library.

Jamie: The Story of a Sibling (**McH**)
Produced by the National Film Board of Canada, 1965. 16mm, Black and White, Sound, 22 Minutes.
Audience: Parents; Technical Rating: Fair; Content Rating: Good

This film focuses on the effects of sibling rivalry on an older child (approximately twelve years of age). Although it is a very powerful film it unfortunately does not focus on the birth to three age range (the young sibling appears to be at least four). If the topic is of interest, I recommend this film along with the other National Film Board of Canada film on this topic, *The World of Three.*

Labor of Love (**Perennial**)
Produced by Perennial Education, Dr. Art Ulene, Consultant, 1977. 16mm, Color, Sound, 27 Minutes.
Audience: Parents and Professionals; Technical Rating: Excellent; Content Rating: Fair

This is a very expensive and highly polished production, which demonstrates the procedures and techniques of the Le Boyer method of childbirth. Pro and con arguments from various medical personnel are interspersed throughout the film. Although the film purports to give an objective view of the method, it seems somewhat biased. The overwhelming majority of those interviewed favor the procedure, and many of their statements go unchallenged. For instance, comments such as "Babies have an awareness of what's going on long before birth," "The first cry is a cry of terror—not good health," and "The baby's face is contorted in agony" are presented without dispute. There also is an apparent endorsement of primal therapy. Psychologist Arthur Janov declares that the first minutes of life are fundamental to all development and that the baby "unquestionably" goes through various traumas during conventional childbirth.

A number of qualifying statements are made in the film, and some outright "con" arguments are presented. However, they consist primarily of repeated comments that there is "no scientific evidence" for many of the Le Boyer ideas. The commentary throughout the film is unobtrusive and intelligent, but such words as "primeval" are used in a rather casual manner. Thus, I would recommend this film primarily for interest professionals and for parents with a college background.

Ladoca-Denver Testing: Hearing (**Ladoca**)
Produced by the Ladoca Project and Publishing Foundation. 16mm, Color, Sound.
Audience: Those Who Test Hearing; Technical Rating: Good; Content Rating:
   Excellent

This film describes the anatomy of the ear, the physical causes of deafness, and the
use of the audiometer. This is an excellent training film for those who will test
hearing. It requires a manual or workbook as an accompaniment.

Language Development (**McH**)
Produced by McGraw-Hill Films. 16mm, Color, Sound, 20 Minutes.
Audience: Professionals; Technical Rating: Excellent; Content Rating: Excellent

This film outlines the process of expressive language acquisition. Dr. Menlee Oakes
narrates the film, citing the work of Dr. Roger Brown on the orderly and predict-
able sequence of language development, of Dr. Ursala Bellugi-Klima on how deaf
children learn American Sign Language, and of Dr. David Premack on teaching
chimps nonverbal language. The film provides a balanced view of the theoretical
field, suggesting the likelihood that both biological and learning-oriented view-
points are correct in some respects. It also provides an excellent overview of the
academic field of expressive language development.

Learning in Infancy (**BYU**)
Produced by Brown University. 16mm, Black and White, Sound, 28 Minutes.
Audience: College Students; Technical Rating: Good; Content Rating: Good

This is a highly technical presentation of research on infant learning from a specific
theoretical approach.

Learning in Joy (**Synchro**)
Produced by Synchro Films and Dr. Phyllis Levenstein. 16mm, Color, Sound, 17
   Minutes.
Audience: Parents and Professionals; Technical Rating: Excellent; Content Rating:
   Good

This is a first-rate, modern, professionally done film that essentially is a description
of Dr. Levenstein's Verbal Interaction Project procedures, with a focus on home
visits, the role of the toy demonstrator, and the training institutes that are run to
train personnel. I have no reason to doubt that this film describes the well-developed project properly. It is excellent for a quick introduction to the project, and

although it was created primarily as a training film, it could be used with parent groups.

Learning Through Play: Play Space (UTOR)

Produced by the Media Centre, University of Toronto, Dr. Sam Rabinovitch, Consultant, 1974. 16mm, Color, Sound, 28 Minutes.
Audience: Parents; Technical Rating: Excellent; Content Rating: Good

This film focuses on play and cognitive development in the young child. There are many effective scenes of children playing, and Dr. Rabinovitch and other experts provide a thoughtful and basically sound commentary. There is also an interesting discussion contrasting adults' view of "mess" and children's need for exploration and play.

Learning Through Play: Toying with Reality (UTOR)

Produced by the Media Centre, University of Toronto, Dr. Sam Rabinovitch, Consultant, 1974. 16mm, Color, Sound, 28 Minutes.
Audience: Parents; Technical Rating: Excellent; Content Rating: Fair

This film focuses on the meaning of "play" for young children. With regard to the birth to three-year age range, the narrative and interviews are consistently skimpy on details and not adequately based on knowledge of early development. The majority of the material is focused on children over three, and much time is devoted to interviews with experts rather than scenes of children playing.

Learning to Learn in Infancy (NYU)

Produced by Vassar College, Parent and Child Series, Dr. Joseph Stone, Director, 1964. 16mm, Black and White, Sound, 22 Minutes.
Audience: Parents and Professionals; Technical Rating: Excellent; Content Rating: Excellent

Technically, this film is an extremely well-done production, although it is now somewhat dated. It was originally created to train Head Start staff. The prime focus is on children in centers, demonstrating the intrinsic interest in learning shown by all healthy young babies. There is a description of the particular types of learning to be expected, and pointers are given regarding how learning can be encouraged as a child and a staff member go through their ordinary daily experiences.

Dr. Stone probably was the finest practitioner in the art of educational films for early childhood. There are few liberties taken with the knowledge base, and the commentary fits the pictures beautifully. This film is as good as anything else that is available and it is better than most of its competition.

Look at Me (**Perennial**)
Produced by WTTW Chicago for the PAR Leadership Training Foundation
    Through a Grant from the NIMH. Series of Six Films, 16mm, Color, Sound,
    30 Minutes (each).
Audience: Parents of Children from Three to Six Years of Age; Technical Rating:
    Excellent; Content Rating: Good

These programs show parents and children together in a variety of situations and
demonstrate how parents can teach their children using household materials and
everyday experiences. Most of the material is of very high quality and reflects the
evidently generous funds available for technical expertise. There does not appear
to be much that is controversial in the programs. The voice-over contains very little
jargon. But since most of the programs focus on children over three, there is little
that is relevant to the education of infants and toddlers.

Mother–Infant Classes (**Badger**)
Produced by Cincinnati General Hospital, Department of Pediatrics, Earladeen
    Badger, Consultant. 16mm, Color, Sound, 17 Minutes.
Audience: Parents and Professionals; Technical Rating: Good; Content Rating:
    Fair

This is a remarkably good production considering its low budget and its use of
many still pictures. The film describes Earladeen Badger's classes for low-income
mothers (most of whom are young and unwed), who are taught caretaking and
educational practices for their new babies.

There are problems, however. Ms. Badger is very ambitious with respect to the
scope and detail that she provides for the young women in her classes. Most of
what she says is perfectly justified, but she is prone to take more liberties with the
knowledge base than most people in the field and at times shows a less than ideal
correspondence to what is reliably known. She implies at one point in this film
that if you do not provide active stimulation of visual motor pursuit, the child
might not learn to follow objects smoothly with his eyes. This is not supported by
the literature. She also implies that nine-month-old babies are willing sharers. I do
not believe that this is a proper interpretation of the behavior of one child toward
another at this stage of life.

In these and other instances, there is an overly strong interpretation of the literature or of certain behaviors seen. Nevertheless, on balance, the effort is a laudable one, and it is a very good way to get to know a promising low-priced program
especially suited to young, low-income parents.

Mother–Infant Interaction Series: Forms of Feeding (**NYU**)
16mm, Black and White, Sound, 49 Minutes.
Audience: Graduate Students; Technical Rating: Poor; Content Rating: Fair

In this poor-quality production (the first in a series of six), mothers are observed feeding infants. Factors of feeding styles, such as empathy, control, and efficiency, are rated—though not clearly defined for the viewer. Emotions are attributed to mother and infants that are not substantiated. In general, the content is rather vague.

Motility in Parent–Child Relationships (**UCAL**)
Produced by the Public Health Service, Drs. Mittleman and Monroe, Consultants, 1959. 16 mm, Black and White, Silent, 40 Minutes.
Audience: Graduate Students and Specialists on the Topic; Technical Rating: Fair; Content Rating: Good

This film, which has a "home movie" quality much of the time, explains and demonstrates a theoretical position held by a specialized research team, proposing a theory of stages in the interaction between the development of motility and interpersonal relationships. The film deals with children from birth to one and a half years of age. It is difficult to judge the validity of this film, as the theory evidently never caught on, and corroborating research does not exist as far as I know. In any event, the film represents only the highly theoretical point of view of the research team, and it would have little interest for anyone except advanced graduate students and specialists in this particular field.

New Relations (**Plainsong**)
Produced by Ben Achtenberg, 1980. 16mm, Color, Sound, 34 Minutes.
Audience: Parents; Technical Rating: Excellent; Content Rating: Excellent

This is a beautifully put together film that explores the new relationship between filmmaker Ben Achtenberg and his son Jesse, the changes in Ben's relationship with his wife, and Ben's new perspective on his relationship with his own father. Still picture sequences are masterfully interspersed among interesting scenes of Ben interacting with Jesse during the one- to two-year period, discussing childrearing issues with his wife, and interviewing his father.

It is interesting that the Achtenbergs are involved in what I consider the ideal sharing situation with regard to child care. They each work part-time and take care of the baby part-time, and they use day care on a part-time basis as well. The opportunities for developing relationships and the problems of possessiveness and jealousy over the child experienced by the parents are presented in an especially sensitive and effective manner.

An Ounce of Prevention (**Campus**)
A Series of 12 Videotapes Produced by the American Academy of Pediatrics, 1976. Videotapes, Color, Sound, 30 Minutes (each).

Audience: Parents; Technical Rating: Excellent; Content Rating: Uneven, with
    Many Shaky Areas

This is a series of twelve technically first-rate programs consisting of interviews
with pediatrician Frederick Margolis by Nancy Mulnix, a journalist and mother
of four children. The interviews are accompanied by occasional scenes of children
and parents, and the topics covered range from prenatal nutrition to coping with
acne in teenagers. I viewed only two segments, "Building Love" and "Thinking
Ahead," which purported to deal with parenting concerns in the first years. In
general, Dr. Margolis appeared to be a warm, reassuring, and competent authority
on a variety of pediatric issues, although I am not qualified to judge the validity
of medically oriented statements.

For the most part, Dr. Margolis resisted the temptation to speak authoritatively
about subjects outside his realm of expertise—that is, the day-to-day experiences
of very young children and their parents in the home and the educational implications of those experiences. On the few occasions when his commentary did ex-
tend to such subjects, I found the treatment generally weak. His emphasis on the
importance of early experience for lifelong learning was fine, but he was often
inaccurate or misleading on the specifics. Although these videotapes may be useful
for orienting new parents to health-related topics, I caution anyone against using
them as a comprehensive introduction to parenthood.

Parentaid Series: Accident Prevention (**PELS**)
Produced by the Parent Education Learning System, Sutherland Learning Associ-
    ates. Videotape, Color, Sound, 8 Minutes.
Audience: Parents and Professionals; Technical Rating: Excellent; Content Rating:
    Excellent

This tape (and the accompanying manual) handles the topic of making the home
safe for an infant in a dramatic and effective fashion. It proceeds to cover accident
prevention for older children as well. This is one of a series of ten high-quality
tapes. I chose not to review the others because they all were exclusively oriented
toward medical issues, whereas this topic has relevance for education as well as
physical health.

Parenting Concerns: The First Two Years (**Perennial**)
Produced by Cine-Image Films, 1977. 16mm, Color, Sound, 21 Minutes.
Audience: Parents; Technical Rating: Good; Content Rating: Good to Poor

Generally, this is a highly polished product, but there are a few dark spots and a
sometimes obtrusive musical soundtrack. It is a very ambitious film that covers
just about every conceivable topic on raising a child during the first two years of

life. Topics ranging from feeding to stranger anxiety to self-exploration to sibling rivalry are touched upon—some well, others poorly. Also, some topics are included that involve the problems of parents beyond the education of the child (e.g., smoking, husband–wife relationships, etc.). There are discussions of a wide variety of child care activities, and the film provides advice and guidance for choices.

In general, the footage is excellent and appropriate, especially with regard to temper tantrums and the newly mobile child. The film does contain much good advice, for example, on baby-proofing a room. On the other hand, it is sometimes artificially precise ("respond promptly to cries during the first *four* months"), and much of the information supplied appears to be merely guesswork, particularly with regard to the second year of life. Discussions of stranger anxiety and working mothers, for example, provide "facts" that are not supported by research; the treatment of sibling rivalry is especially poor in this respect.

The film tries very hard to offer help on all important aspects of the first two years without going over anybody's head. Although it does succeed in some ways, it contains far too much arbitrary and ungrounded advice. The voice-over, which is directed toward parents (the second-person "you" is used throughout), is clear and jargon-free, although it often degenerates into a "lesson" tone and maintains a junior high school to high school level. Professionals and well-educated parents may find this approach sophomoric.

The Parenting Experience (**P&G**)
Produced by Procter & Gamble, Pampers Division, 1980. 16mm, Color, Sound, 30 Minutes.
Audience: Parents; Technical Rating: Excellent; Content Rating: Fair

This film presents "typical" pre-, peri-, and postnatal experience of parents in a very simplistic and condescending tone. Physical "closeness" is stressed repeatedly. The narrator has a tendency to adult-amorphize the thinking of the child, and the claim is made that virtually everything that happens from birth on is "vital" to the child's well-being. Thus, despite its technical attractiveness, I cannot recommend this film.

Parents Magazine Filmstrips (**ParMag**)
Produced by Parents Magazine Films, 1976, 1977 etc. Filmstrips with Audiocassettes, Color, Sound, 8 Minutes (each).
Audience: Parents; Technical Rating: Excellent; Content Rating: Excellent to Poor

This project, which is continually updated and expanded, represents one of the heaviest investments by a commercial operation in audiovisual materials for parents. In all, there are more than a hundred filmstrips, divided into several series.

Accompanying booklets contain the entire script. The authors range widely, from a newspaper columnist to a professor of child psychiatry. Their work was supervised by the editors of *Parents Magazine*. The materials seem to be geared toward inexperienced parents with a maximum of high school education.

Education is the major topic, but health and safety are also dealt with extensively. There is a strong emphasis on the birth to three period, although coverage extends to the sixth birthday. The validity of the educationally oriented material ranges broadly, from excellent in a few cases down to unacceptable in some. Of those that concentrate on infants and toddlers, I rate a few as very good and the remainder evenly divided between adequate and poor. Some of the strongest items were written by Diane K. Bert, who directs a parent education project in Detroit.

In my opinion, the best items for use with families with children less than three years of age are "The Parent as Teacher," and "Learning in the Home" from the "Effective Parent" series, and "How Careful is Safe" and "The Explorer" from the "Child Development and Health" series.

Pediatric Examination Videotapes: Examination of the Infant (**Lippincott**)
Produced in Conjunction with the Syracuse University Medical Center, 1978. Videotape, Color, Sound, 50 Minutes.
Audience: Medical School Students; Technical Rating: Excellent; Content Rating: Excellent

This tape is of outstanding quality, with a very clear sound track and magnificent close-ups. It consists of three pediatric examinations—a five-month-old, a two-and-a-half-month-old, and an eight-month-old. Since I am not a health specialist, the validity of the tape is difficult for me to determine. The examinations deal almost exclusively with the physical health of the children and do not cover educational topics to any significant degree.

The examinations shown are very long and very thorough, although attention to sensory processes, especially hearing, was surprisingly absent (at least with the five-month-old). The pediatrician performing the examinations appears to be very competent, but he tends to use a great deal of medical jargon, most of which he does not explain. Therefore, the tape would be inappropriate for most parents and even for most professionals and college students. However, the technical quality and the thoroughness of the production make it appropriate for medical students and for others with a strong background and interest in this area.

Person to Person in Infancy (**NYU**)
Produced by Vassar College, Parent and Child Series, Dr. Joseph Stone, Director, 1965. 16mm, Black and White, Sound, 22 Minutes.
Audience: Parents and Professionals; Technical Rating: Excellent; Content Rating: Excellent

This is a highly professional film with no technical flaws of any consequence. It was created by Dr. Stone for Head Start training purposes. The prime focus of the film is the emotional development of infants and toddlers. Emotional development is discussed in terms of caretaker–child interaction, primarily in a center where infants are being cared for. There is a good deal of emphasis on the need for lavishing attention on infants.

Dr. Stone knows how to use the knowledge base better than almost anyone else in the field, and rarely goes beyond what can be judged conservatively from that base. Therefore, the validity of the content is very high, except that there is a bit more emphasis on potential pathology than is warranted for average families and for general parent education purposes. All in all, this is another superb, though now somewhat dated, film from Joseph Stone.

Principles of Development (**McH**)
Produced by McGraw-Hill Text Films. 16mm, Black and White, Sound.
Audience: College Students; Technical Rating: Good; Content Rating: Good

This film presents general principles of development in a very didactic, textbook style. The major theme is that "development follows a pattern."

Psychological Hazards in Infancy (**NYU**)
Produced by Vassar College, Parent and Child Series, Dr. Joseph Stone, Director, 1965. 16mm, Black and White, Sound.
Audience: Professionals; Technical Rating: Excellent; Content Rating: Excellent

Technically, this is a first-rate product. The film focuses on the possibilities of emotional injury to humans in the first years of life. It borrows a great deal of footage from Dr. Rene Spitz's original work on the effects on young infants of institutionalization and prolonged separation from mother. Those pieces have a shocking quality to them, and the overall impression is that of danger. It clearly is possible to devastate a child's future in the first years of life, and Dr. Stone seems to be much more heavy-handed in underlining this possibility than in other films he's done.

There is no question about the validity of the content. The relationship to the knowledge base is carefully considered, as it is in virtually every Stone production. Because of the strong emphasis on the hazards of the first years, however, I believe this film is less appropriate for parents than for staff. The impression given the average parent would be somewhat inappropriate, to the extent that one would be implying that it was likely that they could do such damage to their own children. It is a rare family that treats its children with the kind of emotional abuse pictured in many of the scenes in this film.

Rainbow Road (**GPN**)
Produced by KAID-TV, Boise, Idaho, in Cooperation with the Association for the
    Humanities in Idaho, 1980. Four Videotapes, Color, Sound, 30 Minutes (each).
Audience: Parents; Technical Rating: Excellent; Content Rating: Good

This series of videotapes was designed to assist parents in teaching their preschool
children "reading readiness" skills. A workbook accompanies the videotapes. I
liked the general philosophy—that is, "You are your child's first and most important teacher,"—and some of the skills addressed are on my list of those that characterize all-around well-developed children (e.g., dual-focusing ability and discrim-
inative abilities). Unfortunately, the programs spend hardly any time on the first
three years and therefore are largely inappropriate for our focus.

Rearing Kibbutz Babies (**NYU**)
Produced by Vassar College, Dr. Joseph Stone, Director, 1965. 16mm, Color,
    Sound, 25 Minutes.
Audience: Parents and Professionals; Technical Rating: Excellent; Content Rating:
    Excellent

This superb educational production provides extraordinary examples of babies
being photographed in their natural environment. The film describes how the children are reared, with great professional skill and warmth, in one of Israel's outstanding kibbutzim. It is clear that the subject is very carefully dealt with and that
what we are seeing actually does exist. This is a truly outstanding product. It is a
pleasure to look at, and it is instructional for anyone interested in group care of
young children.

Right from the Start (**PrimeTime**)
Produced by Scott Craig Productions, 1981. 16mm Film or Videocassette, Color,
    Sound, 55 Minutes.
Audience: Parents; Technical Rating: Excellent; Content Rating: Good

Technically, this is a superb production. Substantial funding was provided by the
Harris Foundation, the MacArthur Foundation, and the National Science Foundation—and the quality of the sound, camera work, and so on, reflects every
penny. This film has been shown by the Public Broadcasting System, and it apparently has been designed for commercial television broadcasting as well.
    In terms of content, also, the film is very impressive, reflecting the input of an
advisory council that includes many of the top people in the fields of pediatrics
and pediatric psychology, such as T. Berry Brazelton, Selma Fraiberg, and Sally
Provence. The script is well written and organized, and Sada Thompson does an
excellent job with the narration.
    The message of the movie is that it is very important to have a good, loving,

active parent–child relationship from the very beginning of life. Topics such as alternative birth methods, bonding, attachment, and the work of Harry Harlow, Rene Spitz, and others are covered. In all cases, the coverage is thorough and well balanced.

I have only three major criticisms. First, although the coverage is balanced, there is a tendency to highlight dramatic findings in a way that gives them more validity than they deserve. For instance, although the narrator points out that there has been failure to replicate the original Kennell and Klaus findings on bonding, she then goes on to say, "Still, they are striking."

The second criticism has to do with the tendency of many of the experts interviewed to adult-amorphize the behavior of very young infants. For example, a two-month-old child is described as "trying to get the mother to respond," and a newborn is described as "knowing that he brings joy to his mother." Unfortunately, this practice of ascribing sophisticated mental abilities and motives to infants is a relatively common practice among people in pediatrics and pediatric psychology.

The third criticism is that the subject of full-time day care is never dealt with. Considering the film's subject, the prevalence of the practice, and the importance of its consequences, day care should not have been overlooked. I can only assume that the producers did not want to arouse the harsh feelings that almost always accompany a discussion of this topic.

Nevertheless, despite these criticisms, I feel that with proper commentary by the professional in charge, this film would be an excellent addition to most parent education programs.

Rock-a-Bye Baby (**UCAL**)
Produced by Time-Life Films. 16mm, Color, Sound.
Audience: College Students; Technical Rating: Good; Content Rating: Excellent

In a highly academic fashion, this film examines the phenomenon of maternal deprivation. The work of Rene Spitz and the work of Harry Harlow are highlighted and are accurately portrayed.

Routines Can Be Fun (**NCU**)
Produced by the University of North Carolina Infant Care Project and Training
　　Center for Infant and Toddler Care. 16mm, Black and White, Sound.
Audience: Professional Day Care Staff; Technical Rating: Good; Content Rating:
　　Excellent

This film gives the viewer a chance to observe, without commentary, a highly competent woman caring for five toddlers (twenty-one to twenty-eight months). The film focuses on the routines of daily living in a day care center. No free play is shown. This film might be useful as a springboard for a discussion in a training session for members of a day care or nursery school staff.

The Sensational Baby: Parts I and II (**Polymorph**)
Produced by Polymorph Films, 1984. Slide/Tape, 16mm Film, or Videocassette,
    Color, Sound, 22 Minutes (each part).
Audience: Parents; Technical Rating: Excellent; Content Rating: Poor

This two-part program originally was produced as a slide/tape show, but it is also
available in film or videocassette format. Part I, entitled "From the Beginning to
Birth," focuses on fetal development. Part II, entitled "From Birth On," focuses on
the first few weeks of life. The still pictures used are beautiful, and the narration
is clear and well integrated. A printed study guide accompanies the audiovisual
material.

The program was inspired by the Infant Stimulation Education Association,
based at UCLA, and the consultants used include an impressive array of R.N.'s,
M.D.'s, and Ph.D.'s from some fairly prestigious institutions, including Children's
Hospital in Boston. The purpose of the program evidently is to impress parents-
to-be and new parents with the notion that the fetus and newborn is capable of
sensing, understanding, and reacting to all sorts of stimuli more extensively and in
a more sophisticated manner than was previously believed. It claims to represent
the latest research on fetal and neonatal development, and there is a very strong
message regarding fetal and neonatal life, along with accompanying parental
responsibilities.

In my opinion, the message is overstated and distorts the knowledge base in a
way that is not beneficial for the intended audience. I would put the program in
the category that includes such films as *The Amazing Newborn* and such books as
The Secret Life of the Unborn Child by Thomas Verny. What is presented is misleading at best and simply inaccurate at worst.

For instance, changes in fetal activity in response to different stimuli, such as
music by Chopin versus music by Mozart, are repeatedly referred to as the fetus
showing a "preference" for one type over the other. Similarly, in talking about the
activity of the fetus, terms such as "swimming through the amniotic fluid" are
used, implying that the fetus is making controlled, skillful movements.

The program focuses on the senses of the fetus and newborn, and these senses
routinely are depicted as functioning in all "all or nothing" manner. For example,
it is claimed that hearing is "fully developed" at six months gestation and that at
birth, the newborn is capable of "seeing your eyes and face clearly." In fact, the
claim is that the newborn has "keen senses" in every regard and is intensely aware
and interested in everything going on about him. Unfortunately, this simply does
not fit with a more conservative interpretation of the many studies that have been
done over the years on the development of vision, hearing, and so on, in babies.

When the program attempts to describe what is going on in the mind of the
fetus and newborn, there is a constant tendency to adult-amorphize. For instance,
the viewer is told that just prior to birth, the fetus "shares" the mother's emotions
of "excitement," "joy," and "anxiety" and that right after birth, the newborn feels
"secure" and is "eager to explore." The claim is made that the newborn is "as
curious about his parents as they are about him." Again, none of this fits with

more generally accepted notions about how the mind develops, and one wonders what the producers of this program are basing such ideas on.

In my judgment, such programs give parents a set of false expectations and therefore set them up for disappointment when they discover that their babies do not appear to be particularly interested in or adept at various activities and do not seem to be particularly interested in or adept in interpersonal relationship during the first days of life. I realize that a number of people in the field may disagree with me regarding the physical and mental functionings of the fetus and newborn, and I might simply chalk this program up as another instance of such disagreement. However, there are occasions when the producers of this program show a lack of knowledge about the details of early development and/or a serious lack of experience in working with babies, the result being that they provide information that is not only wrong but potentially dangerous as well.

For instance, in talking about vision, the somewhat inaccurate statement is made that "whatever babies can reach they can see clearly." As if that weren't bad enough, the program goes on to suggest that mobiles should therefore be placed close enough to the baby in the crib so that he can reach the suspended objects. Mobiles are designed to be looked at, not touched. To avoid harm to the baby, mobiles should always be kept out of reach. Once the baby becomes adept at batting objects (at about two months), mobiles should be supplemented with sturdy crib gyms.

Another even more unfortunate example occurs when the senses of taste and smell are being discussed. The claim is made that these senses are fully developed at birth and that they guide infants toward substances that are good for them and away from those that are not good for them. This is extraordinarily naive, and if parents believe it, they and their babies could be headed for real trouble. Studies have shown—and anyone who has worked extensively with babies will tell you— that infants and toddlers will eat *anything* when they're hungry enough and will drink *anything* when they're thirsty enough, no matter what those things smell, taste, look, or feel like. That is why it is imperative for parents to remove all harmful substances from their child's access during the first years of life.

In summary, the general tone and direction of this program are such that I feel it would probably add to the anxieties of parents-to-be and new parents inappropriately, rather than helping them. Furthermore, certain specific statements that are made constitute not only a disservice but actually a danger to the viewers. I recommend avoiding this program.

Social Development (**NYU**)
Produced by Elizabeth Hurlock, 1950. 16mm, Black and White, Sound, 16 Minutes.
Audience: Parents; Technical Rating: Fair; Content Rating: Good

This film provides a reasonable introduction to social development. It includes discussions about negativism, parallel play, and cooperative play. However, not enough detail is given, and the narrative moves quickly out of the birth to three-year age range. The film has many good scenes of children playing, but it is now very dated, and it suffers from stilted dialogue and a somewhat faulty soundtrack.

A Special Time for Parents and Children (**Perennial**)
Produced by Warren Johnson, Ed.D., 1979. 16mm, Color, Sound, 15 Minutes.
Audience: Parents; Technical Rating: Excellent; Content Rating: Excellent

The message of this film is that parents should set aside some time every day for play with their children. However, the age range of the children discussed is too broad and the treatment of the topic too general for this product to be of more than marginal use for parent education groups focusing on the first three years.

The Springs of Learning (**UILL**)
Produced by the British Broadcasting Company. Series of 6 Films, 16mm, Black and White, Sound, 30 Minutes (each).
Audience: Parents; Technical Rating: Good; Content Rating: Poor

This series of six films deals with the development of the child from birth to age five. The one film I viewed, "Babyhood," consists of a very stiff BBC interviewer talking with a "doctor" about some brief scenes of children and their environments. The "doctor" is obviously well-meaning, but his comments often lack precision. Moreover, the coverage is extremely arbitrary and skimpy. In general, the perspective of this production simply is too British (and too dry) to be of much interest to American audiences.

Teaching Infants and Toddlers (**GPN**)
Produced by Bowling Green State University, Professor Doris Williams, Advisor, 1978. Series of 7 Videocassettes, Color, Sound, 9 to 13 Minutes (each).
Audience: Parents; Technical Rating: Fair; Content Rating: Fair to Poor

This series of programs was designed to show parents how to help their children develop various skills during the first one and a half years of life. The seven programs are divided into one to three months, four to five months, six to eight months, nine to eleven months, twelve to fourteen months, fifteen to twenty months, and twenty-one to twenty-nine months.

Each program is divided into several segments that address different aspects of development, such as "seeing," "hearing," "feeling," and "general development" in the first program. The picture and sound track are clear, but the camera work leaves something to be desired, and the footage often fails to support the narration. The script is directed toward parents with a modest educational background.

I viewed the first (one to three months) and fifth (twelve to fourteen months) programs. Although they occasionally made good points and demonstrated acceptable practices (the section on imitation in the twelve- to fourteen-month period, for example, was very good), most of what I saw reflected an inadequate grasp of the knowledge base and little experience in observing the day-to-day activities of young children. For example, the first program claimed that a parent could "stimulate" the development of vision using a mobile and could "increase development" by placing a rattle in the baby's hand. There is no evidence for either of these statements. Moreover, rattles and the kind of mobile shown are notoriously uninteresting to babies. There were similar ungrounded claims about auditory and tactile stimulation. Much of the equipment shown was inappropriate, such as a crib toy that had objects suspended by strings. In the fifth program, "problem solving" was said to "begin" at twelve to fourteen months, whereas six to eight months is more accurate. Also, too little attention was paid to the development of receptive ability in the discussion of language development.

In general, these programs contain many overstatements, many inaccuracies, and many poor examples of materials. Therefore, I cannot recommend this series.

Terrible Twos and Trusting Threes (**NYU**)
Produced by Cawley Films of Ottawa, Canada. 16mm, Black and White, Sound, 27 Minutes.
Audience: Parents and Professionals; Technical Rating: Excellent; Content Rating: Excellent

This is a first-rate product, with engaging outdoor scenes in sharp, clear, photography. It describes the typical behaviors and interests of the two- and three-year-old child, speaking of personality as well as general behavior. This film is not oriented toward childrearing practices but merely toward explaining what such children are like. Although there was a potential for gross distortion of the knowledge base, this film skillfully avoids such distortion and seems to be very consistent with well established evidence. It is a particularly delightful film with a good deal of wisdom and humor.

Testing Hearing in Preschool Children, Six Months to Six Years (**HEW**)
Produced by HEW National Medical Audiovisual Center. 16mm, Color, Sound, 20 Minutes.
Audience: Professionals; Technical Rating: Good; Content Rating: Good

This film shows and describes relatively simple hearing testing in younger infants, using sounds, such as bells, with localization by the infant as a test of hearing. For older infants, there is some description of more sophisticated tests using localization. Since there is no other good "quick and easy" screening test for hearing at this age, this approach is acceptable. The film describes some of the pitfalls in the procedure (e.g., mother holding infant, visual attention, etc.). However, it does not deal well with levels of hearing intensity in the younger subjects or with testing of voice. Nevertheless, this approach is worth knowing about and perhaps incorporating, so long as its weaknesses are recognized.

The Ties That Bind (**Polymorph**)
Produced by Case Western Reserve University, Drs. M. Hack, M. Klaus, and J. Kennell, Consultants, 1980. 16mm, Color, Sound, 27 Minutes.
Audience: Parents; Technical Rating: Good; Content Rating: Poor

This film addresses the subject of attachment, but more from the perspective of the bonding proponents (note the consultants) than from longstanding established research. As a result, many claims are made that cannot be substantiated—for example, "Emotional ties develop during pregnancy," "The husband/father's presence during labor is needed," "Bringing an older sibling to the [lying-in] hospital will alleviate rivalry problems," and the like.

In addition, there is inappropriate use of the literature on nonhuman subjects, and several conflicting and confusing statements are made during the course of the film. For example, at one point, the narrator says that "attachment has taken place" a few hours after birth, then later says that "attachment takes place over the next two years." The technical quality of the film is okay, although the sound track is muddled at times. All in all, I cannot recommend this film.

Tim: His Sensorimotor Development (**H&R**)
Produced in Conjunction with the UCLA Medical Center, Arthur Parmalee and Clair Kopp, Consultants, 1974. 16mm, Color, Sound, 31 Minutes.
Audience: College Students; Technical Rating: Excellent; Content Rating: Excellent

This film demonstrates Piagetian ideas about sensorimotor development through the use of two test procedures—one involving a mirror and the other involving a hidden object in a matchbox. Discussions of exploratory behavior begin with a seven-month-old child, and discussions of object permanence begin with a nine-month-old. The voice-over in this film is very literate and scholarly. Unfortunately, there is too much of it. The problem is compounded by the fact that the footage is not effective in demonstrating the growth and development that is being talked about.

Although the technical quality of this production is superior, the films on Piagetian ideas by Uzgiris and Hunt (e.g., *The Ordinal Scales of Psychological Development*) are superior in terms of getting the basic message across. Also, the academic jargon used throughout the film makes it appropriate primarily for college students, rather than for most parent education groups.

250,000 Ways to Destroy a Child's Life Without Leaving Home (**UILL**)
Produced by the Children's Hospital of Wayne State University, with Support from
    the Junior League of Detroit, 1975. 16mm, Color, Sound, 16 Minutes.
Audience: Parents; Technical Rating: Excellent; Content Rating: Excellent

This is a superb production on the subject of accidental poisonings in the first years
of life. Three stages of early childhood are dramatized—the crawler, the toddler,
and the climber—and the film shows how such accidents can happen and what
can be done to prevent them. The only significant error I could detect was that
climbing counters and such is said to begin after fifteen months of age, when, in
fact, children will start doing so several months earlier. In general, however, the
admonitions and advice presented are quite sound.

The tone of the film is a bit heavy-handed (e.g., there are some very scary accounts of what happened to various poisoning victims), and it does concentrate on
accidental poisonings to the exclusion of other safety-proofing considerations. A
few of the terms used are inappropriate for audiences with limited vocabularies.
Nevertheless, I feel that this film would be a valuable addition to any parent education program.

What a Child Is (**NCU**)
Produced by the Appalachian North Carolina Child Care Program, 1975. 16mm,
    Color, Sound, 15 Minutes.
Audience: Parents and Professionals; Technical Ratings: Excellent; Content Rat-
    ing: Unknown

This is a carefully produced film with excellent photography and good natural
sound. It is designed for those who want to run preschools for children two and a
half to five years of age. However, much of the commentary describes an academically oriented preschool experience with no particular distinguishing
characteristics.

With Care and Respect (**BWF**)
Produced by the National Commission on Resources for Youth, 1978. Series of 3
    Films, 16mm, Color, Sound, 14 to 17 Minutes (each).
Audience: Parents and Professionals; Technical Rating: Excellent; Content Rating:
    Poor

This series of three films depicts the philosophy and teachings of Resources for
Infant Educators, a group of professionals highly influenced by the work of the
Hungarian infant specialist, Dr. Emmi Peter-Pikler. The two films I viewed were
superb technically, but extremely weak in terms of content.

"On Their Own with Our Help" features Magda Gerber, a child therapist who has developed a following in California. There is some good footage of eight- to eleven-month-old children in a group setting, and Mrs. Gerber is shown "selectively interacting" with the children in a variety of situations. In the voice-over, she explains her special criteria for intervening in the children's activities and her special style of doing so. She implies that children in this age range are capable of having knowledge and sensitivities that are very powerful and important. Although I agree that the matter in which adults "selectively intervene" in the activities of children may have significant consequences, in my opinion, Mrs. Gerber's approach involves far too much adult-amorphizing. Her statements about what the infants are thinking and feeling lack validity, and they can be very misleading to new parents.

"The Way We See Them" features Dr. Thomas Forrest, a pediatrician from the Stanford University School of Medicine. Again, the footage is excellent, this time showing a newborn, some ten- to eleven-month-olds, and a five-month-old, accompanied by Dr. Forrest's comments about how to observe them and what they are up to. In my opinion, although Dr. Forrest is very sensitive in pointing out individual differences (a la Brazelton), his inferences about the children's behavior are often hard to believe. For example, he says that the newborn is "very resourceful" and that "she wants to quiet herself" when he observes her sucking her thumb.

In general, I feel that there is not much in these films that would be helpful to parents or professionals. Parent educators seeking audiovisual assistance in dealing with these topics would be well advised to use the Joseph Stone film, *Learning to Learn in Infancy*, instead. Although that film is rather dated (produced in 1965) and may not be as technically proficient as these films, Dr. Stone's commentary on how to pick up on the cues of infants and how caretakers can either help or hinder development by their responses is far superior in my opinion.

The World of Three (**NYU**)

Produced by the National Film Board of Canada, 1965. 16mm, Black and White, Sound, 28 Minutes.

Audience: Parents; Technical Ratings: Good; Content Rating: Excellent

This is a very sensitive and authentic presentation of the sibling rivalry issue. The camera acts as a third-person observer in the home of a three-year-old boy with his parents and new sibling. The perspective of the three-year-old boy is assumed in several sequences, heightening the viewer's empathy. The boy is followed through his day—at home, largely restricted to his bedroom; at the park; in his father's office; and at the dinner table. His behaviors range from curiosity about the baby to a variety of attention-getting tactics and a tantrum. The viewer is particularly struck by the parents' often insensitive responses to the child's behavior.

This film is an excellent springboard for discussion of sibling rivalry, parental responses, and the feelings of a three-year-old child.

Your Baby's Day: A Time for Learning (**H/S**)
Produced by the High/Scope Educational Foundation, 1980. Filmstrip with Audio-
    cassette, 15 Minutes.
Audience: Parents; Technical Rating: Excellent; Content Rating: Fair

This short filmstrip with audiocassette uses attractive pictures and a clear, simple
narrative to explain how parents can foster the development of their child during
routine, day-to-day activities. The filmstrip is divided into three major sections—
birth to four months, four to eight months, and eight to twelve months—and the
primary focus is on feeding, bathing, and changing.

Several good points are made by the narrator, such as the importance of talking
to the baby and allowing the child to explore. However, many points are oversimplified and overstated—for example, "By teasing, tickling, and blowing on the
infant's tummy you will help the infant learn about her own body and encourage
her to respond" or "A game like peek-a-boo also helps children learn that things
exist when they can't see them—an important concept."

Despite the ease and relatively low cost of using filmstrips, I feel that most
parent education groups would be better off using a more accurate and enlight-
ening product, such as the film *Learning to Learn in Infancy* for the purposes of
introducing new parents to their role as facilitators of early development.

Your Baby's First Days (**Polymorph**)
Produced by Polymorph Films, 1980. 16mm, Color, Sound, 21 Minutes.
Audience: Parents; Technical Rating: Excellent; Content Rating: Good

This film shows a class for new mothers at a Seattle Hospital. The woman conducting the classes presents information and demonstrates practices related primarily to the physical care of the child in a straightforward and apparently competent manner. However, on several occasions, she strays from health areas into
educational issues, for which her comments sometimes lack validity (e.g., there is
a tendency to adult-amorphize the infant's thoughts). Therefore, although I would
recommend this film for its primary function, I suggest that the viewer be cau-
tioned about its extramedical coverage.

Appendix C:
Other Resources for Parents
and Professionals

Magazines for Parents

American Baby Magazine
575 Lexington Ave., New York, NY 10022

Twice-monthly publication, free to new parents (income derived solely from advertisers). In my opinion, it's tops in its field, featuring well-researched and well-edited articles on a variety of topics. The special edition entitled "The First Year of Life" is the best comprehensive treatment of the subject I've seen anywhere, and it is now available in hardcover and softcover book form as well.

Baby Talk
185 Madison Ave., New York, NY 10016

Monthly publication available by subscription. Good articles on a variety of topics of interest to new and expectant parents.

Mothering
P.O. Box 2208, Albuquerque, NM 87103

Quarterly publication available by subscription. Beautifully designed and illustrated, with a very warm, loving approach. Good articles stress that mothering is a marvelous and vital role, and an extensive letters section provides much practical information and many interesting opinions.

Mothers Today
Box 243, Franklin Lakes, NJ 07417

Formerly *Mother's Manual*. Bi-monthly publication available by subscription. Variable in quality, but often contains useful articles.

The Pre-Parent Advisor/The New Parent Advisor/The Parent Advisor
13-30 Corporation, 505 Market St., Knoxville, TN 37902

Series of three magazines published annually, available free to expectant and new parents. Sponsored by Johnson & Johnson, the sole advertiser. The first focuses on the prenatal period, the second on early infancy, and the third on later infancy and toddlerhood. All are high-quality, well-written, and well-organized publications, containing brief treatments of many topics of concern to the target audiences.

Twins Magazine
P.O. Box 12045, Overland Park, KS 66212

Bi-monthly publication available by subscription. High-quality, helpful articles for parents of multiples.

Newsletters for Parents

Baby Bulletin
Johnson & Johnson Baby Products, 6 Commercial St., Hicksville, NY 11801

A series of eight newsletters provided free by Johnson & Johnson. The first issue focuses on the newborn, the eighth on late toddlerhood. The advisory board is very impressive, but the quality of the articles is highly variable.

Doubletalk
P.O. Box 412, Amelia, OH 45102

Quarterly publication available by subscription. Contains interesting and helpful articles for parents of multiples.

Gifted Children Newsletter
P.O. Box 115, Sewell, NJ 08080

Monthly publication, available by subscription. Features articles and announcements of interest to parents of precocious children.

Growing Parent/Growing Child
22 North Second St., Lafayette, IN 47902

Monthly publication available by subscription. Subscribers are asked to give the expected or actual birth date of their child, and they subsequently receive issues containing well-written and informative articles specifically addressed to the child's current stage of development.

Imprints
Birth & Life Bookstore, 7001 Alonzo Ave. NW, Seattle, WA 98107

Monthly publication available free to customers of the bookstore (each issue is a store catalog as well). Contains excellent and extensive reviews of books for parents and books for young children.

MOTC Notebook
5402 Amberwood Lane, Rockville, MD 20853

Quarterly publication of the National Organization of Mothers of Twins clubs ("Where God Chooses the Members"), available by subscription. Provides a wealth of information and ideas for parents, teachers, and others who have responsibility for or interest in the development of multiple gestation children.

The Newsletter of Parenting
2300 W. Fifth Ave., P.O. Box 2505, Columbus, OH 43216

Monthly publication from Highlights for Children, available by subscription. Scope is very broad—that is, issues contain articles on infancy and the teenage years and everything in between. Although attractive and well-written, the quality of information provided is quite variable.

Pediatrics for Parents
176 Mt. Hope Ave., Bangor, ME 04401

Monthly publication available by subscription. I am not qualified to comment on the validity of the articles, but they appear to be helpful, informative, straightforward, and well written.

Practical Parenting
18318 Minnetonka Blvd., Deephaven, MN 55391

Bi-monthly publication available by subscription. Produced by Vicki Lansky, a very capable free-lance writer who specializes in parent-oriented articles. Contains a wide variety of interesting and helpful announcements, reviews, and advice for parents of children of all ages, much of it coming from the readers themselves.

Pro Parent Resources
614 Walmer Road, Saskatoon, Saskatchewan S7L OE2

Bi-monthly publication available by subscription. Strictly a "seat of the pants" affair, but what it lacks in style and polish it more than makes up for in a variety of useful reviews and suggestions for parents of young children.

Salk Letter
941 Park Ave., New York, NY 10028

Monthly publication available by subscription. Written by noted clinical psychologist Dr. Lee Salk, its scope goes beyond the birth to three-year age range, but new parents may find his advice about parent–child relationships useful.

Note: The following newsletters are oriented toward specific geographic areas and/or program members. However, they are interesting and well-done publications that may serve as useful models. Sample copies usually are available upon request.

Austin's Child
P.O. Box 33370, Austin, TX 78764

Monthly publication featuring articles, announcements, and advertisements of interest to parents in central Texas.

Avance Newsletter
132 Torres, San Antonio, TX 78237

Bi-weekly publication of the Avance Parent–Child Education Program. An excellent example of a bilingual newsletter for parents.

Baby Briefs
MELD, 123 East Grant St., Minneapolis, MN 55403

Bi-monthly publication featuring items of specific interest to those in the Minnesota Early Learning Design Program.

Beginning Family
14260 Lake Hills Blvd., Bellevue, WA 98007

Informative bi-monthly publication for parents in a high-quality program in the Seattle area.

Birth to Three Newsletter
2374 Onyx St., Eugene, OR 97403

Unusually high-quality monthly publication providing advice and announcements of interest to new parents in central Oregon.

Bridges
14-153 Richmond St., Thorold, Ontario L2V 3H3

High-quality monthly publication providing information and ideas to new parents in the Niagara region.

Chatterbox
Lodge Continuing Education Center, W3410 Ft. Wright Dr., Spokane, WA 99204

Informative monthly publication produced by a parent education program operating out of a community college.

The Chronicler
CER, Fayette Bldg., 5 E. Second Ave., Conshohocken, PA 19428

Very impressive bi-monthly publication of the Childbirth Education Association of Greater Philadelphia. Contains articles by "guest" experts as well as announcements and advertisements.

The Early Edition
Ladue Early Childhood Center, 9137 Old Bonhomme Rd., St. Louis, MO 63132

Simple but very useful and fun publication from the Parents and Children Together (PACT) program.

The Family Newsletter
Box 225, Hardwick, MA 01037

High-quality bi-monthly publication provides a forum for Massachusetts parents to exchange information and express opinions about a variety of issues concerning children of all ages.

Leaves from the Family Tree
P.O. Box 51394, Lafayette, LA 70505

Small but informative bi-monthly publication from a high-quality program. Contains advice, announcements, and the like.

Listening Booth
City Line and Overbrook Aves., Philadelphia, PA 19131

Monthly publication of the Booth Maternity Center. Provides articles and announcements of interest to member families and to the greater Philadelphia community in general.

The Pacesetter
P.O. Box 213, Western Springs, IL 60558

Very high quality monthly publication of the Parent and Childbirth Education Society (PACES). Provides members with a variety of interesting and informative articles, reviews, and announcements.

Parent Education Newsletter/Directory
Family Health Association, 3737 Lander Rd., Cleveland, OH 44124

Information-packed bi-annual publication of the Family Health Association. Focuses on childbirth and parent education services in the greater Cleveland area.

Parenting Center News
200 Henry Clay Ave., New Orleans, LA 70118

Monthly publication from a first-rate parent education program. Contains superb articles on child development topics as well as local announcements.

Parenting Press
P.O. Box 24, Peoria, IL 61650

Monthly publication of the Peoria Parent Education Association. Although not as flashy as some other newsletters, in my opinion, it's one of the best. In addition to its many announcements and bits of advice, it features regular listing of useful resources, ranging from national organizations providing help to hearing impaired children to the names and phone numbers of local parents who—through first-hand experience—have become "experts" in dealing with various problems, such as excessive colic, accidental poisoning, teething-difficulties, corrective shoes.

The Parent's Press
P.O. Box 3826, Littleton, CO 80161

Monthly publication featuring articles, announcements, and advertisements of interest to parents in the Denver metropolitan area.

Magazines and Journals for Professionals

Childbirth Educator
575 Lexington Ave., New York, NY 10022

High-quality quarterly publication from *American Baby Magazine*, available free to qualified professionals. Contains articles on current issues, book reviews, information on products and services.

Child Care Information Exchange
P.O. Box 2890, Redmond, WA 98052

Bi-monthly publication available by subscription. Designed specifically for directors of child care facilities.

Child Development
University of Chicago Press, 11030 Langley Ave., Chicago, IL 60628

Quarterly journal published by the Society for Research in Child Development, which also publishes *Child Development Abstracts* three times a year and *Monographs of The SRCD* at irregular intervals. All three publications are available by subscription. Most major libraries subscribe to these publications.

In my opinion, *Child Development* is the best journal available for professionals in this field. Being one of the most prestigious, it receives many new reports of research on young children, and the editors do an excellent job of selecting the cream of the crop. In recent years, articles on children in the birth to three age range have been running at about 25 to 30 percent. *Abstracts* provides what is probably the most thorough regular overview of new research, and *Monographs* presents longer reports and commentaries.

Children Today
U.S. Government Printing Office, Washington, DC 20402

Bi-monthly publication of the Administration for Children, Youth, and Families, available by subscription. The scope is rather broad, but certain special issues, such as "The Family" and "The Earliest Years," contain excellent articles of interest to those focusing on infant and toddler development and parent education.

Developmental Psychology
American Psychological Association, 1200 7th St. N.W., Washington, DC 20036

Bi-monthly publication of the APA, available by subscription to nonmembers. Also available at most university libraries. More esoteric than *Child Development*, but does contain many high-quality and useful research reports.

Early Childhood Education (Annual Editions)
Dushkin Publishing, Sluice Dock, Guilford, CT 06437

Annual collection of more than fifty articles on a variety of topics of interest to professionals in the field.

Early Childhood Education: The Year in Review
Hacienda Press, P.O. Box 222415, Carmel, CA 93922

Small annual publication, edited by Dr. James L. Hymes, provides extensive insights from one of the field's very experienced and highly respected citizens.

Journal of Applied Developmental Psychology
Ablex Publishing Co., 355 Chestnut St., Norwood, NJ 07648

Relatively new quarterly journal, supported in part by the Educational Testing Service (ETS), available by subscription. The scope is broad, but it contains a fair number of interesting reports of research on the development of infants and toddlers.

Young Children
National Association for the Education of Young Children, 1834 Connecticut
  Ave., N.W., Washington, DC 20009

Bi-monthly journal of the NAEYC, available by subscription to nonmembers. The
scope extends beyond the birth to three age range, and it covers a lot of NAEYC
business matters, but it often contains useful and informative articles of interest to
those working with infants and toddlers and their parents.

Newsletters for Professionals

Center for Parent Education Newsletter
55 Chapel St., Newton, MA 02160

Bi-monthly publication available by subscription. Features articles on important
topics and issues, reviews of books, films, and toys, and announcements of events
and opportunities—all specifically of interest to professionals concerned with the
educational development of infants and toddlers and with education for
parenthood.

Childbirth Alternatives
15 Brewster Lane, East Setauket, NY 11733

Quarterly publication available by subscription. Devoted to the promotion of
home birth and other safe alternatives in childbirth.

Day Care U.S.A. Newsletter
8701 Georgia Ave., Suite 800, Silver Spring, MD 20910

Bi-weekly publication available by subscription. Despite its high price, I feel that
the detailed, up-to-date information it provides regarding federal government policies and programs for young children makes it worth the investment.

ECE Options
255 North Road, #110, Chelmsford, MA 01824

Edited by Dr. Bettye Lewis, published five times a year, and available by subscription. Provides a wealth of information about ideas, programs, opportunities, and
issues of interest to early childhood education teachers at the postsecondary level.

First Teacher
P.O. Box 29, Bridgeport, CT 06602

Monthly publication available by subscription. Contains items of interest to day care, preschool, and kindergarten personnel.

Growing Child Research Review
22 North Second St., Lafayette, IN 47902

Published nine times a year by the editor of Growing Parent/Growing Child, available by subscription. Provides summaries of research reports on current topics of interest. Well-written and well-organized but often uncritical of some of the research that is reported.

Human Intelligence Newsletter
P.O. Box 1163, Birmingham, MI 48012

Bi-monthly publication available by subscription. Internationally oriented, focusing on research and programs concerned with increasing cognitive growth in young children.

Parent Educator's Exchange
P.O. Box 1635, Columbia, MO 65205

Bi-monthly publication of Practical Publications, available by subscription. Contains news, resource listings, and reviews of interest to early educators working through the family.

Pediatric Mental Health
P.O. Box 1880, Santa Monica, CA 90406

Bi-monthly publication available by subscription. Provides information and advice on dealing with very young children and their families from a medical perspective.

Six Months to Six Years
Box 448, Eureka Springs, AR 72632

Published ten times a year, available by subscription. Contains lists of government agencies, notices of conferences, and other items of interest primarily to those who market and distribute educational materials.

Totline
1004 Harborview Lane, Everett, WA 98203

Bi-monthly publication available by subscription. Claims to be "full of creative and challenging ideas for working with preschool children," but contains mostly advertising and a few rather unimpressive articles.

Zero to Three
815 15th St. N.W., Suite 600, Washington, DC 20005

Published four to six times a year by the National Center for Clinical Infant Programs, available by subscription. Features articles and announcements of interest to those working with very young children and their families from a pediatric/psychiatric perspective.

Note: The following newsletters are oriented toward specific geographic areas, organization members, and/or program affiliates. However, they are interesting and well-done publications that may serve as useful models. Sample copies usually are available upon request.

Early Childhood Newsletter
School of Education, Oakland University, Rochester, MI 48063

Quarterly publication. An excellent example of a simple but very useful newsletter for students in an early childhood education program.

Family Resource Coalition Report
230 N. Michigan Ave., Suite 1625, Chicago,IL 60601

Excellent, information-packed, bi-monthly publication of this extensive network of family resource programs throughout North America.

High/Scope Bulletin
600 North River St., Ypsilanti, MI 48197

Quarterly publication. Reports the activities of David Weikart's research and training center. Relatively few items relate to infants and toddlers, and those items are of variable quality. However, as is the case with most of Weikart's work, this publication is a model of excellent writing and organization.

Oaks and Acorns
1006 11th St., Box 94, Denver, CO 80204

Monthly publication. Provides up-to-date information to professionals affiliated with the Metropolitan State College Parent Education Resource Center.

Parenthood Education Report
Box 81, Peabody College, Nashville, TN 37203

Regular publication of the Betty Phillips Center for Parent Education. Provides articles and announcements to those focusing primarily on teenage parents.

Teaching Young Children with Special Needs Newsletter
Wheelock College Graduate School, 200 The Riverway, Boston, MA 02215

Quarterly publication. Provides articles, announcements, and resource reviews for professionals affiliated with a high-quality academic training program.

Resource Centers for Professionals

Center for Parent Education
55 Chapel St., Newton, MA 02160

Publications, training, consulting, and a variety of resource materials designed specifically to assist those concerned with the educational development of infants and toddlers and with education for parenthood.

American Red Cross
17th and D Streets, Washington, DC 20006

Various publications and other resource materials, including parent education curricula.

American Guidance Service
Publishers Bldg., Circle Pines, MN 55014

Various publications, including the Systematic Training for Effective Parenting (STEP) curriculum and the "Small Wonders" curriculum (neither recommendable, in my opinion).

Betty Phillips Center for Parenthood Education
Box 81, Peabody College, Nashville, TN 37203

Summer training institutes, information on exemplary programs, reviews of materials, newsletter. Focuses on teenage parents.

Children's Health Council
700 Willow Rd., Palo Alto, CA 94304

Dr. Annye Rothenberg and her colleagues hold professional workshops, and they have produced an excellent parent education curriculum, "Parentmaking."

Child Welfare League of America
Center for Governmental Affairs, 1346 Connecticut Ave., N.W., Washington, DC
    20036

Several publications, including a twenty-five page directory, *Foundations Supporting Child and Family Serving Organizations.*

Education Development Center
55 Chapel St., Newton, MA 02160

Information, publications, curricula ("Exploring Childhood"), primarily for high school parent education programs.

ERIC Clearinghouse on Early Childhood Education
College of Education, University of Illinois, 1310 S. 6th St., Champaign, IL 61820

Numerous articles and several excellent bibliographies, such as *Family Day Care* and *Infant Care.*

Family Focus
2300 Green Bay Rd., Evanston, IL 60201

Successful family support service, also provides publications and training for professionals.

Family Resource Coalition
230 N. Michigan Ave., Suite 1625, Chicago, IL 60601

Organization providing information and support network for family resource programs serving communities throughout the United States and Canada.

First Moments
55 Northern Blvd., Greenvale, NY 11548

Provides free samples of top-quality products and literature (including "The First Year of Life" issue of *American Baby*) for new parents through qualified professionals.

Frank Porter Graham Child Development Center
University of North Carolina, Chapel Hill, NC 27514

Several publications and a bibliography entitled *Planning Programs and Activities for Infants and Toddlers.*

High/Scope Foundation
600 North River St., Ypsilanti, MI 48197

David Weikart's group, offers training, consulting, publications, audiovisuals for professionals in preschool education. Stronger in the three to five age range than in infancy and toddlerhood.

Infant Care Center
School of Home Economics, University of North Carolina, Greensboro, NC 27412

Various publications, including *Easy to Do Toys and Activities for Infants and Toddlers* and *Designing a Day Care Center.*

Kansas Parent Education Resource Center
State Department of Education, 120 E. 10th St., Topeka, KS 66612

Low-budget, state-funded office, provides information on parent education relating to children of all ages.

Lekotek
613 Dempster St., Evanston, IL 60201

Provides excellent information and advice for setting up toy lending libraries, including *Guide to Good Toys*.

March of Dimes
Public Health Education, 1275 Mamaroneck Ave., White Plains, NY 10605

Provides curricula and education for parenthood materials, designed primarily for pregnant teenagers.

National Association for the Education of Young Children (NAEYC)
1834 Connecticut Ave., N.W., Washington, DC 20009

Conferences, publications (send for *Books, Etc*), information for those working in early childhood education. More oriented toward children over three, but has several interesting items for those dealing with infants and toddlers.

National Center for Clinical Infant Programs
815 15th St. N.W., Suite 600, Washington, DC 20005

Large-budget group, offers publications, training, conferences for those working with young children and their families from a pediatric/psychiatric perspective.

National Resource Center on Family-Based Services
University of Iowa, School of Social Work, Oakdale, IA 52319

Many publications, including *Planning and Supervising the Home-Based Family-Centered Program.*

The Parent Center
5422 Maryland, Little Rock, AR 72204

Junior League–sponsored, has library and provides other information services covering parent education relating to children of all ages.

New York City Public Library
Early Childhood Resource and Information Center, 66 Leroy St., New York, NY 10012

Extensive resource collection of materials covering all aspects of child development and parenting.

New York State Center for Parent Education
State Department of Education, Albany, NY 12234

Small-budget, state-funded office, has annotated parent education bibliographies and "state of the art" papers relating to children of all ages.

Parenting Materials Information Center
Southwest Educational Development Laboratory, 211 E. 7th St., Austin, TX 78701

Large catalog of publications, audiovisuals, and the like, for parent education relating to children of all ages.

Pediatric Projects
P.O. Box 1880, Santa Monica, CA 90406

Books, articles, and toys to help professionals and parents deal with medical problems in early childhood.

South Carolina Parent Education Center
State Department of Education, 706 Rutledge Bldg., Columbia, SC 29201

Substantial-budget, state-funded office, provides audiovisuals, publications, curricula, workshops oriented toward home-based programs.

Syracuse University
Department of Child and Family Studies, Syracuse University, Syracuse, NY 13210

Dr. Alice Honig conducts annual workshops, "Quality Infant Caregiving," and provides publications, research reports, and other resources for day care personnel.

Utah State Board of Education
250 East Fifth South St., Salt Lake City, UT 84111

State-funded operation, provides curricula and information for high school parent education programs.

U.S. Office of Education
Parent/Early Childhood Education (Attention: Dr. Frances Yvonne Hicks), 400
    Maryland Ave., S.W., Washington, DC 20202

Free computer searches and printouts for research, publications, audiovisuals relating to education for parenthood and child development.

Bibliography

Abravanel, E., and Sigafoos, A.D. Exploring the Presence of Imitation during Early Infancy. *Child Development* 55 (1984): 381–92.

Ainsworth, M.D., Bell, S.M., and Stayton, D.J. Individual Differences in the Development of Some Attachment Behaviors. *Merrill-Palmer Quarterly* 18, no. 2 (1972): 123–43.

Anderson, S., and Messick, S. Social Competency in Young Children. *Developmental Psychology* 10 (1974): 282–93.

Bowlby, J. The Nature of the Child's Tie to His Mother, *International Journal of Psychoanalysis* 39 (1958): 350–73.

Brazelton, T.B. *Infants and Mothers.* New York: Delacorte Press, 1969.

———. *Neonatal Behavioral Assessment Scale.* Philadelphia: Lippincott, 1973.

Broad, F.E. The Effects of Infant Feeding on Speech Quality. *Child & Family* 12, no. 3 (1973): 211–25.

———. Further Studies on the Effects of Infant Feeding on Speech Quality. *Child & Family* 15, no. 3 (1976): 231–41.

Bronfenbrenner, U. *Is Early Intervention Effective?* HEW Publication No. OHD–74–25, Vol. II. Washington, D.C.: U.S. Department of Health, Education and Welfare, 1974.

Cahill, M.A. *The Heart Has Its Own Reasons.* Franklin Park, Ill.: La Leche League International, 1983.

Chess, T.A., and Birch, H. *Your Child Is a Person.* New York: Viking Press, 1965.

Clarke-Stewart, A. And Daddy Makes Three: The Father's Impact on Mother and Young Child. *Child Development* 49 (1978): 466–78.

Downs, M.P. That a Child May Hear. *Receiver: Deafness Research Foundation Newsletter,* Fall 1978, pp. 1–3.

Escalona, S.K., and Heider, G.M. *Prediction and Outcome.* New York: Basic Books, 1959.

Fantz, R.L. Pattern Vision in Newborn Infants. *Science* 140 (1963): 296–97.

Field, T.M., Cohen, D., Garcia, R., and Greenberg, R. Discrimination and Imitation of Facial Expressions by Term and Preterm Neonates. *Infant Behavior and Development* 6 (1983): 485–89.

Fraiberg, S. *Every Child's Birthright: In Defense of Mothering.* New York: Basic Books, 1977.

Fries, M.E., and Woolf, P.J. Some Hypotheses on the Role of the Congenital Activity Type in Personality Development. *Psychoanalytic Study of the Child* 8 (1953): 48–62.

Gesell, A., and Amatruda, C.S. *Developmental Diagnosis.* New York: Hoeber, 1941.

Gesell, A., and Ilg, F.L. *Infant and Child in the Culture of Today.* New York: Harper & Row, 1943.

Goodson, D.B., and Bronson, M.B. *Guidelines for Relating Children's Ages to Toy Characteristics.* Washington, D.C.: U.S. Consumer Product Safety Commission, Contract No. CPSC–85–1089, 1985.

Hayes, L.A., and Watson, J.S. Neonatal Imitation: Fact or Artifact? *Developmental Psychology* 17 (1981): 655–60.

Hunt, J.M. *Intelligence and Experience.* New York: Ronald Press, 1961.

Kennell, J.H., Jerauld, R., Wolfe, H., Chesler, D., Kreger, N.C., McAlpine, W., Steffa, M., and Klaus, M.H. Maternal Behavior One Year After Early and Extended Postpartum Contact. *Developmental Medicine and Child Neurology* 16 (1974): 172–79.

Kenniston, K. *All Our Children.* New York: Harcourt Brace Jovanovich, 1977.

Klaus, M.H., and Kennell, J.H. Mothers Separated from Their Newborn Infants. *Pediatric Clinics of North America* 17 (1970): 1015–37.

Loman, K. *Of Cradles and Careers: A Guide to Reshaping Your Job to Include a Child in Your Life.* Franklin Park, Ill.: La Leche League International, 1984.

Lorenz, K. *King Solomon's Ring.* New York: Crowell Collier and Macmillan, 1952.

Maslow, A.H. *Motivation and Personality* (2d ed.). New York: Harper & Row, 1970.

Maynard, F. *The Child Care Crisis.* New York: Viking Press, 1985.

Mediax Associates. *Head Start Profiles of Program Effects on Children.* Newsletter, Issue III. Westport, Conn.: Mediax Associates, January 1980.

Meltzoff, A.N., and Moore, M.K. Imitation of Facial and Manual Gestures by Human Neonates. *Science* 198 (1977): 75–78.

Muir, D., and Field, J. Newborn Infants Orient to Sounds. *Child Development* 50 (1979): 431–36.

Pfannenstiel, J.C., and Seltzer, D.A. *Evaluation Report: New Parents as Teachers Project*. Jefferson City: Missouri Department of Elementary and Secondary Education, 1985.

Pierson, D.E., and Sperber, R.I. *The Brookline Early Education Project: An Issue for National Educational Policy*. Brookline, Mass.: The Brookline Early Education Project, 1974.

Pulaski, M.S. *Your Child's Mind and How It Grows: Piaget's Theory for Parents*. New York: Harper & Row, 1978.

Reynell, J., and Huntley, R. New Scales for the Assessment of Language Development in Young Children. *Journal of Learning Disabilities* 10 (1981): 10–18.

Saarinen, U.M. Prolonged Breastfeeding as Prophylaxis for Recurrent Otitis Media. *Acta Paediatrica Scandinavica* 71 (1982): 567–71.

Sameroff, A.J. (ed.). *Organization and Stability of Newborn Behavior: A Commentary on the Brazelton Neonatal Behavior Assessment Scale*. Monographs of the Society for Research in Child Development, no. 177. 1978.

Schacter, F.F., Cooper, A., and Gordet, R. A Method for Assessing Personality Development for Follow-up Evaluations of the Preschool Child. *Society for Research in Child Development* 33, no. 119.

Schaefer, O., and Spady, D.W. *Changing Trends in Infant Feeding Patterns in the Northwest Territories 1973–1979*. Edmonton, Alberta: Northern Medical Research Unit, 1980.

Spock, B. *Baby and Child Care* (Rev. ed.). New York: Pocketbooks, 1976.

Svedja, M., Campos, J., and Emde, R. Mother-Infant Bonding: Failure to Generalize. *Child Development* 51 (1980): 775–79.

Swift, J.W. Effects of Early Group Experience: The Nursery School and Day Nursery. In M.L. Hoffman and L.W. Hoffman (eds.), *Research on the Development of the Young Child*, Vol. I. New York: Russell Sage Foundation, 1964.

Thomas, A., Chess, S., and Birch, H.G. *Behavioral Individuality in Early Childhood*. New York: New York University Press, 1963.

Ulich, R. *Three Thousand Years of Educational Wisdom*. Cambridge: Harvard University Press, 1961.

UNESCO. *Meeting on Preschool Education as the First Phase of Lifelong Education: Final Report*. Paris: UNESCO, January 1976.

Uzgiris, I.C., and Hunt, J.M. *Assessment in Infancy: Ordinal Scales of Psychological Development*. Urbana: University of Illinois Press, 1975.

Verny, T., with Kelly, J. *The Secret Life of the Unborn Child*. New York: Summit Books, 1981.

Weikart, D. *Young Children Grow Up: The Effects of the Perry Preschool Program on Youths through Age Fifteen.* Ypsilanti, Mich.: High/Scope Educational Research Foundation, 1980.

White, B.L. *Human Infants: Experience and Psychological Development.* Englewood Cliffs, N.J.: Prentice-Hall, 1971.

————. Education for Parenthood. *Journal of Education* (Summer 1981): 205–18.

————. *The First Three Years of Life* (Rev. ed.). Englewood Cliffs, N.J.: Prentice-Hall, 1985.

White, B.L., Kaban, B.T., and Attanucci, J.S. *The Origins of Human Competence: The Final Report of the Harvard Preschool Project.* Lexington, Mass.: Lexington Books, 1979.

White, B.L., and Watts, J.C. *Experience and Environment: Major Influences on the Development of the Young Child,* Vol. I. Englewood Cliffs, N.J.: Prentice-Hall, 1973.

White, B.L., Kaban, B.T., Attanucci, J., and Shapiro, B.B. *Experience and Environment: Major Influences on the Development of the Young Child,* Vol. II. Englewood Cliffs, N.J.: Prentice-Hall, 1978.

Zajonc, R.B. Family Configuration and Intelligence. *Science* 192 (1976): 43–47.

Zigler, E. Project Head Start: Success or Failure? *Learning* 1 (1973): 43–47.

Photograph Credits

Index

About the Author

Burton L. White is the founder and director of the Center for Parent Education in Newton, Massachusetts. He also founded the Harvard Preschool Project and served as its director during the thirteen years of its existence. Dr. White was also the first director of the Brookline Early Education Project and the senior consultant to Missouri's New Parents as Teachers project. He has taught at Harvard University, Brandeis University, and Tufts University.

Dr. White is the author of *The First Three Years of Life* as well as four major textbooks and numerous scholarly articles. He was also host of a television series, *The First Three Years*.